ADVANCE PRAISE FOR

Global China and the Global Game in Africa: China–Africa Engagement through the Lens of Football

"No matter if political sciences, international relations, economics, or global studies, the subject of China–African relations has become an essential subject to properly understand the dynamics that shape our world. But until now, the role of sport in this connection was often merely a footnote. With this book, Jonathan Sullivan, Tobias Ross, and Angela Lewis have put together an excellent collection of case studies that puts the shared enthusiasm for football in the centre of this politically, economically, and culturally loaded relationship. This makes not only for an enticing read, but also for an outstanding and much-needed resource across many disciplines."

—Dr. Tobias Zuser, Assistant Professor, Chinese University of Hong Kong

"This book provides a comprehensive examination of the multifaceted interactions between China and Africa through football. Edited by Jonathan Sullivan, Tobias Ross and Angela Lewis, the book explores a wide range of topics, including stadium diplomacy, labor migration and sports diplomacy, and shows how football serves as an important conduit for political, economic and cultural exchange. The book offers a nuanced perspective on the intersection of sport, politics and international relations in the bilateral character of this engagement, moving beyond simplistic accounts to highlight the wider geopolitical and economic implications of China's presence in African football."

—Dr. Ilker Gündoğan, Researcher, Ruhr University Bochum, Germany

Global China and the Global Game in Africa

Sport in East and Southeast Asian Societies

Geopolitical, Political, Cultural and Social Perspectives

J. A. Mangan
Series Editor

Vol. 6

Global China and the Global Game in Africa

China–Africa Engagement through the Lens of Football

Edited by
Jonathan Sullivan, Tobias Ross, and Angela Lewis

PETER LANG
New York - Berlin - Bruxelles - Chennai - Lausanne - Oxford

A CIP catalog record for this book has been applied for at the Library of Congress.

Bibliographic information published by the Deutsche Nationalbibliothek.
The German National Library lists this publication in the German National Bibliography; detailed bibliographic data is available on the Internet at http://dnb.d-nb.de.

Cover design by Peter Lang Group AG

ISSN 2689-3460 (print)
ISSN 2689-3479 (online)
ISBN 9781636676494 (hardback)
ISBN 9781636676500 (ebook)
ISBN 9781636676517 (epub)
DOI 10.3726/b21200

Published by Peter Lang Publishing Inc., New York, USA
info@peterlang.com - www.peterlang.com

This publication has been peer reviewed.

Contents

List of Figures

List of Tables

1

China–Africa Relations through Football

Jonathan Sullivan[1]

Two-way exchange between China and Africa is multifaceted and long-standing (Large 2021). Since 2000, diplomatic, economic, cultural, and educational engagements have been consolidated and institutionalized through the Forum on China–Africa Cooperation (FOCAC). Trade relations are intense, and African countries constitute a significant cohort of partners involved in the Belt and Road Initiative (BRI). Reliable data are scarce, but there are likely several hundred thousand Chinese citizens residing in Africa and around 200,000 Africans living in China. Over the past two decades, China's presence and purported ambitions in Africa have attracted significant attention, skepticism, and criticism, especially in western nations (Mawdsley 2008). In China's relations with many African countries there are real inequalities and serious substantive and normative issues to consider. These issues are sometimes captured by the amorphous term "neocolonialism" (Negi 2008), a combination of economic and political influence that leverages China's power differential to the detriment of African partners. There is, however, no evidence that China is "seeking colonies, using prisoners as cheap labor or any of the other lurid accusations made against

1 Jonathan Sullivan, Associate Professor, University of Nottingham, jonathan.sullivan@nottingham.ac.uk.

'the Chinese' in Africa" (Taylor 2014, 121), and Hirono and Suzuki (2014) argue that the tenor of related debates "reflect deeply rooted western anxieties that their traditional dominance in Africa is about to be overthrown by a non-western power" (455).

The observation that China–Africa engagement goes beyond the repertoire of stylized "myths" that Hirono and Suzuki (2014) identify is not to dismiss Chinese government support for illiberal regimes, Chinese companies' pursuit of African natural resources, the lending practices of state financiers or a host of other issues. However, it is a reminder that moving beyond the "myths" there is a multiplicity of exchanges occurring in both sites, with influences traveling in both directions. The chapters in this book show how football is one site where these multi-directional processes play out. Indeed, football is an illuminating case study in China–Africa exchange and a useful vehicle for exploring the complexities of the transcontinental relationship at different levels: from nation-states, corporations, and institutions, to clubs, players and fans. China–Africa and Africa-China exchanges in football are germane to numerous highly salient research areas, including soft power, international media, commercialization, South-South relations, geopolitics, international sports governance, diplomacy, labor migration and transnational fandoms. These issues are explored in the book by a multidisciplinary cast of scholarly experts on China, Africa, and football.

Since 1969–1970, China has constructed, financed or gifted dozens of football stadiums across the African continent (Xue et al. 2019). To date, China has contributed sports infrastructure in 36 different African countries. Known by the (generally) negatively valanced descriptor "stadium diplomacy," the practice has been viewed with skepticism by western observers (Dubinsky 2021). Put charitably, such interpretations of stadium financing and construction reflect a focus on contrasting motivations and interests, and differential power and exchange relations that are also associated with China's exploitation of African natural resources, corruption and "debt traps" (Brautigam 2020). Chapters 2 and 12 of this volume explore an alternative perspective on African countries' continuing willingness to accept Chinese-funded stadiums, but neither denies the negative externalities observed in cases where stadiums go unused or scarce resources have been wasted. More broadly, it is undeniable that some African countries' engagement with China has produced observably negative outcomes for those societies, including the enrichment and entrenchment of repressive and self-interested regimes and the failure of African resource wealth to benefit local people through re-investment in industrial capacity, healthcare, or education. Local society-led resistance to the presence and practices of Chinese actors has been observed in several African countries (Leslie 2016). These issues deserve appropriate scrutiny and criticism. Equally, however, the mono-dimensionality and normative basis for some depictions of "China in Africa" require redressing, and African perspectives brought back in (Sautman and Yan 2009). This is arguably the case in football exchange too, where stadium diplomacy is just one among many forms of connection between China and African countries. The desire to contribute a more holistic and balanced understanding of engagement through football underpins the motivation for this book. Moving beyond stadium diplomacy as a manifestation of China's instrumental use of sport to gain influence and advantage in Africa, the chapters in this book use the diversity of exchanges in football to explore a range of political, economic, social, and cultural issues. The resulting collection provides an original treatment of China–Africa and Africa-China relations that accounts for African agency, speaks to the diversity of practitioners and stakeholders, and leverages perspectives from individual African nations and China.

Engagement in football represents a conceptual and empirical challenge to conventional western "China–Africa" narratives, not least by undermining the implied unidirectionality of influence. In football, "Africa-China" engagement is as salient as "China–Africa." One need only consider some of the many African players to have contributed to the development of the Chinese Super League (CSL)—Cameroon's Stéphane Mbia, Ivorian Didier Drogba, the D. R. Congo's Cédric Bakambu, Ghanaian Asamoah Gyan, Mali's Frédéric Kanouté, Nigeria's Yakubu Ayegbeni, and Senegal's Demba Ba. And let us not forget the contribution of African talent to the Chinese Women's Super League, including Zambian superstar Barbra Banda (who moved to Orlando Pride in spring 2024 for a near world record transfer fee). Football labor migration is only the tip of the iceberg. China and African countries are relevant to global governance of football, where placing officials in executive roles and securing voting blocs that determine hosting rights in multilateral bodies can be highly consequential economically (Chadwick et al. 2022). Football possesses abundant "soft power" potential (Grix and Houlihan 2014), as well as the perils of "sport washing" (Skey 2023). Chinese investors and sponsors play an important role in the development of football in Africa, exemplified by Chinese involvement in the continent's crown jewel international competition, the African Cup of Nations (AFCON) (Cockayne et al. 2022).

Bilateral partnerships are manifest in relations between the Chinese Football Association (CFA) and numerous African Football Associations (FA). The deal agreed with the Ghanaian FA in 2012 and formally commencing in 2017 was typical. China, a global power in women's football, opened its facilities to the Ghanaian women's team and arranged friendly matches in advance of Ghana hosting the women's AFCON. In return, the Ghana FA supported Chinese youth football development, including team visits and training matches. Not coincidentally, the Chinese media firm StarTimes then secured the broadcast rights to the Ghana Premier League, and under the terms of the deal China agreed to fund the construction of 10 artificial pitches in the country. StarTimes has become a significant player in the mediation of African football, with exclusive long-term rights deals in several countries. The company is also effectively a gatekeeper for foreign football in Africa through its broadcast rights to show European football in several African nations. StarTimes' involvement in African football must also be contextualized within the broader expansion of Chinese media operations on the continent (Jedlowski 2021; Lewis 2023).

China's emphasis on youth football development, and Africa's well-known credentials in international youth competition, has led to numerous connections between youth academies, involving tours, shared training resources and friendly matches. The China–Africa Youth Tournament (CAYT) launched in 2019 with four African FA representative teams from Nigeria, Ethiopia, Tanzania, and Kenya traveling to Hunan Province to face off against local representatives from Hunan, Guangdong, Shandong and Shanghai. This first iteration was hosted by Hunan Provincial Sports Bureau and linked to the China–Africa Economic and Trade Expo. The second edition scheduled to be held in Nigeria was canceled due to the COVID-19 pandemic but resumed in summer 2023. It is one of many youth exchanges. In a later chapter, Tobias Ross analyzes the 2001 Lion Cub Project initiated by the Chinese professional club Dalian Shide in Cameroon, the first large-scale player recruitment and naturalization program in Chinese sport. The Lion Cub project was launched at a time when attitudes toward naturalization in China were predominantly negative and it failed to deliver on its goal of developing 24 Cameroonian teenagers into CSL and national representative level players. Other migrations, in both directions, have led to the establishment of transnational communities and enriched cross-cultural fandoms. African communities based in Guangdong and Zhejiang have become fans of local teams, while Chinese fandoms have coalesced around individual African players like the Ivorian Didier Drogba, one of Africa's greatest players and a star for Shanghai Shenhua, and James Chamanga from Zambia, who enjoyed a decade-long career in the CSL. The presence of settled African communities in China's southern provinces has led to cross-national relationships and children of mixed heritage, some of whom are promising young football talents. Two players of mixed Nigerian and Chinese heritage, Su Yuliang and Huang Shenghao played for Guangzhou City FC youth teams, and the latter for China's under-17 national squad. The Tanzanian-Chinese player Eddy Francis and Gabon-Chinese Alexander N'Doumbou play for Shanghai Shenhua and Zhejiang Professional, respectively. African community establishment in China will thicken connections between China and African countries and, with CSL clubs and the Chinese national team actively scouting mixed heritage players, may lead to further talents emerging.

China–Africa Engagement

The People's Republic of China (PRC) has long considered itself as an actor in solidarity with other developing nations in the struggle against western imperialism. This orientation was entangled in the idiosyncrasies of Maoist Thought and complicated by the conceptual hybridity inherent in "market socialism with Chinese characteristics" that emerged in the Dengist reform era (Taylor 1998). It was further complicated by China's transformation into an economic superpower and integral motor of the globalized economy. However, China has not relinquished the idea that it shares the developing world's struggle against western domination of global systems, structures, and norms that fundamentally disadvantage, and often mistreat, developing nations (Yin 2023). How China manifests its self-image in its engagement with the developing world, including Africa, has changed as the country moved from socialist construction and the export of revolutionary ideas under Mao, to an economic superpower engaged in geopolitical "systemic rivalries" with the West. When China engages with African countries today, there is an inescapable power differential that cannot be masked by invoking legacies of solidarity or rhetorical commitments to "win-win" economic cooperation.

China's omni-lateral approach to diplomacy in the past two decades has produced a multitude of initiatives from FOCAC to the BRI and Asian Infrastructure Investment Bank (AIIB). Facilitated by diplomatic connections and governmental policies (on both sides), Chinese State-Owned Enterprises (SOE) and ostensibly private corporations are active across most economic sectors in Africa. The focus has been on extractive primary industries, for good reason, but Chinese firms are increasingly diversifying into telecommunications, logistics, agriculture, construction, trade, and media industries. Over the past 20 years China has become Africa's biggest trade partner, surpassing African trade with former colonial powers and the United States. China became Africa's biggest donor, surpassing the World Bank and former colonial powers' foreign aid. As a development partner, China's characteristic modus operandi foregrounds what it likes to frame as "win-win" economic cooperation. Chinese involvement in Africa has been welcomed by many African partners, not least when Western partners withdrew or downsized engagements in the early 2000s. Yet, the reality is that Chinese involvement in Africa is not driven by altruism: China pursues its own national interest in its dealings with African countries and often drives hard bargains. It also does not concern itself with promoting democratization, good governance or improving human rights. This is consistent with China's long-standing if selectively employed policy of "non-interference" (Aidoo and Hess 2015) and it has been welcomed by self-interested elites in some African countries. China has directly or indirectly bolstered repression in Zimbabwe, Equatorial Guinea, D. R. Congo, Angola, Sudan and several other African countries (Masunungure 2011). It has enriched and entrenched numerous illiberal regimes across the continent and sometimes refused to use its influence to intervene in the abuses that their partners inflict on African people and societies (Large 2008). On the other hand, China has participated in UN peacekeeping missions in Mali and South Sudan, anti-piracy operations in the Gulf of Aden (Coleman and Job 2021; Lanteigne and Hirono 2013) and contributed to African countries' COVID-19 pandemic response, supplying PPE and vaccines.

China's rapid industrialization has created a substantial appetite for African natural resources. An inexhaustive list might include oil, copper, coal, diamonds, gold, bauxite, iron ore, timber, lithium, and various rare earths. China buys these resources from African firms, where they exist, or negotiates access rights and operating concessions for SOEs specializing in extractive industries. Redolent of European colonial powers of old, China has also invested heavily in the physical infrastructure needed to mine, refine, transport and ship resources back to China, where they will fuel manufacturing and technological development, modernization, and urbanization on a scale mostly unknown in Africa. Across the African continent, Chinese SOEs in the construction and engineering sectors have built ports, roads, airports, railways, bridges, dams, mines, power plants, and refineries. These constructions are instrumental in that they support China's need to extract and deliver natural resources, but the same SOEs have also built hospitals, civic buildings and other facilities from which it doesn't directly benefit. Indirect benefits accruing to such contributions may come in the form of engendering positive views of China and their subsequent conversion into influence or soft power.

SOEs like China Petroleum & Chemical Corporation (Sinopec), China National Petroleum Corporation (CNPC), and China National Offshore Oil Corporation (CNOOC) are extracting substantial quantities of oil from Angola, Nigeria, Libya, and Sudan. China Nonferrous Metal Mining Group extracts copper from Zambia and D. R. Congo. Agribusiness and food conglomerate Beidahuang, the world's biggest soya producer, has acquired agricultural land in Namibia, Niger, and Zimbabwe for growing crops and cotton. China State Construction Engineering Corporation (CSCEC) is one of several state-owned construction companies building all kinds of physical infrastructure across Africa, from the African Union in Addis to the Great Mosque in Algiers and hundreds of smaller projects. China Railway Construction Corporation has laid thousands of kilometers of track across Algeria, Angola, Egypt, Libya, Mali, Nigeria, and Senegal. China Merchants Port Holdings Company has built four ports in the Horn of Africa, and linked the mega-port at Doraleh, Djibouti to landlocked Addis via a Chinese-built railway. Many Chinese projects are financially underwritten by state-backed "policy banks" like the Export–Import (Exim) Bank of China (Corkin 2011).

The scale and rapid increase in these projects led to an equation that purportedly explained China–African engagement: resources for infrastructure (Brautigam 2009). But China's ambitions—and African countries' ambitions—extend beyond that. African population growth, the youthful slant of its demographic composition and increasing levels of prosperity make the continent's current and future market attractive. Chinese companies are deeply involved in establishing market position in numerous sectors. In some sectors, like telecoms, vertical integration of hardware and software puts Chinese firms in a strong, and potentially dominant position, with concomitant risks (Gagliardone 2022). For example, China's national champion telecom firm Huawei, ostensibly private but with close government links, is building telecommunications networks across Africa, bringing broadband connectivity and phone networks on which its own devices and smartphones will operate on. Once connected, African users have shown an appetite for Chinese digital entertainment platforms like TikTok (international cousin of Douyin owned by Beijing-based ByteDance), Chinese fast fashion apps like Shein, wholesale and retail e-commerce platforms like Taobao, and "do everything" communication apps like WeChat. This is good for Chinese firms' ambition to go global. Setting aside valid concerns about what Chinese companies do with all the personal data it will collect on African users (Gravett 2022), it is also good for those

African consumers who were previously unable to access Wi-Fi and mobile internet, cheap smartphones and connected devices, abundant shopping and entertainment options, or take part in digital citizenship. It is not coincidental that TikTok sponsored a content partnership with the Confederation of African Football (CAF) in 2022 covering the men's and women's AFCON and the CAF Champions League. It is also consistent with the Chinese state's conception of domestic professional football as a driver of economic activity with a distinct social function (Hesketh and Sullivan 2020).

Reflecting its intensifying connections across the continent, Chinese migration has increased substantially in the past two decades (Sun 2014, 28). Many of these people are individual citizens with no connection to the Chinese state who come to Africa to pursue small-scale economic opportunities, often with little prior knowledge, connections or language skills (Sullivan and Cheng 2018). Some put down roots and become embedded in local economies. Others are sojourners, using Africa as a migration stepping-stone to Europe or North America, encouraged or forced by economic or personal circumstances to seek opportunities outside of China (Driessen 2016). Conflicts have arisen in some receiving societies as a result of the preferential hiring practices employed by Chinese SOEs, whereby Chinese workers are brought in to work on Chinese projects (Cardenal and Araujo 2013; Michel and Bevret 2009). The increasing number of Chinese living in Africa has prompted negative reactions in some countries' media and some host populations. Poor working conditions, labor abuses and the distortion of local economies by incoming Chinese actors have led to protests and political opposition in Zambia, action by trade unions in South Africa, and by business organizations in Uganda and Ghana. In some cases, notably Zambia, anti-Chinese sentiment has been instrumentalized by local politicians (Larmer and Fraser 2007; Mohan and Tan Mullins 2009). Chinese companies and migrants have been criticized for "unfair competition, smuggling, inferior quality, illegal immigration, ruining local industries, taking local jobs, and simply invading foreign countries by virtue of sheer numbers" (Nyiri 2011, 149). Chinese economic activity has been criticized for discouraging exchange with African populations in the form of employment opportunities, investment in local projects, assimilation into communities and knowledge exchange (Carmody 2011). The China–Africa engagement is replete with consequential issues, and by comparison football may appear frivolous. The intention of this book is not to sideline or minimize broader issues, but to use the political, economic, and social dimensions of sport as a site to illuminate the complexities of China–Africa and Africa-China engagement.

China–Africa Engagement in Sport

Sport in the Mao period was as politicized and ideological as it was in other Communist nations (Hong and Xiong 2002). Excellence in sporting competition was leveraged as a physical demonstration of the superiority of Communism and ideological supremacy over the capitalist bloc. Football in the early years of the PRC was "a symbol of modernity; a talisman of topicality; a statement of intent" (Dong and Mangan 2001, 79), and the Communist state saw utility in it for nation building internally and alliance building internationally. Irrespective of the fact that China's capacity in football was limited in every respect during the early Mao period, it provided a means to approach these ends. In 1955, a Chinese team was dispatched to socialist bloc ally Hungary, then one of the strongest teams in the world, to learn "modern football." Among the delegation was star player and captain Shi Wanchun. Having benefited from training and experience in Hungary, Shi was sent two years later to North Vietnam, another Communist bloc ally, to coach the national team. Further Chinese players sought training in Hungary, and in 1959 a Chinese national team beat a Hungarian team in a friendly match. During the Mao period, including the Cultural Revolution, China invited and hosted delegations of African athletes to expand relations at a time of domestic instability and international isolation. Demonstrations of solidarity were equally valuable on both sides, demonstrating the symbolic power of sporting exchanges under the most difficult political and economic conditions (Shuman 2017).

China's absence from FIFA and the International Olympic Committee (IOC) for political reasons (i.e., those institutions' recognition of the Republic of China (Taiwan) rather than PRC) until the 1970s was a hindrance to making advances on the pitch. The national team could not compete in international competitions, only friendlies and exhibition matches against mainly fellow Communist bloc countries. But that did not prevent the use of sport off the pitch. The idea of using foreign sports aid was conceived in the late 1950s and institutionalized with the founding of the Foreign Sports Aid office of the General Administration of Sport in 1965. This established a crucial mechanism for planning, budgeting, and executing sport-related projects among ideologically aligned or friendly countries in the developing world. By 1966, it had already delivered the first Chinese construction project in sports delivered overseas, in the form of multi-purpose facilities in Phnom Penh, Cambodia, where the second iteration of the Games of the New Emerging Forces was held. Later the same decade, funded by Chinese aid, Chinese architects and workers broke ground on the first football stadium China built overseas. Construction on Amaan Stadium in Zanzibar, part of Tanzania and home by the 1930s to Chinese diasporic communities (Hsu 2007), was completed in the early 1970s. Tanzania and China were closely aligned in the Maoist ideological orientation of their political regimes, and the stadium was one of many physical manifestations of the goodwill that existed between them.

Chinese SOEs possess substantial expertise and capacity in engineering and construction and Chinese governments have consistently shown a preference for aid projects that result in tangible physical infrastructure. However, the extent of China's support for African countries through football goes beyond the supply of infrastructure. One example is the long-standing pursuit of knowledge exchange, resource sharing and mutual support for football development, particularly at the youth level. Starting in the 1970s, China has sent elite players and coaches to numerous African countries to share their expertise and conduct knowledge exchange programs. Yan Dejun, a former national team player, was sent by the Chinese government to share his coaching expertise with the Mauritanian and Burundi men's national squads between 1974 and 1977. Yan was succeeded as Burundi coach by another former Chinese national team player, Gao Fengwen. After gaining valuable practical experience, Gao returned to China and entered the Chinese national team set-up, coaching age-group football in the early 1980s and helping China to qualify for the Seoul Olympics in 1988. Qi Wusheng was another former player to gain coaching experience in Africa before entering the Chinese national team management structure. Qi led the Somali national team from 1978, before returning to China to coach the Chinese national team from 1994 to 1997. Chinese coaches were active in the 1970s and 1980s in Tanzania, Rwanda and several other African nations. A similar story of knowledge and expertise exchange is evident in youth football, with long-standing training programs and competition between China, Cameroon, Mozambique and others (Zhou et al. 2022). These programs include the supply of pitches, equipment, and referee training. Unsurprisingly given these foundations, players from African nations constitute one of the largest cohorts of foreign talent throughout the professional era in Chinese domestic football starting in 1994.

The PRC has a history of using sport in the pursuit of national diplomacy. The most famous example was the "ping-pong diplomacy" that facilitated communications with the US and signaled a willingness to establish bilateral relations at a pivotal moment in the Cold War following the Sino-Soviet split. Table tennis matches helped pave the way for President Nixon's visit to China in 1972, which in turn facilitated the normalization of US-China relations and changed the course of world history (Hong and Sun 2000). Normalization was a win for both sides in the context of the Cold War, and the episode showed China's perceived utility in sport for the pursuit of its national interests, which in the early 1970s was rapprochement with the United States. There are other examples, including the stadium diplomacy referenced above. China's contribution of football stadiums across Africa has enabled numerous countries to develop football, host international competitions and showcase the contributions of local elites. It may also help to secure Chinese access to resources and markets. The evidence is circumstantial but suggestive. Were the four football stadiums that China built for Angola at a cost of $500 million in 2010, allowing that country to host the AFCON, an act of solidarity for a developing nation, or a means to consolidating Chinese access to Angolan oil? In the period after 2010 China became the biggest recipient of Angolan oil, and by extension Angola's biggest export partner. It may be coincidental, or it may reflect a Chinese approach to doing business in the developing world. After decades of civil war, Angola had little governance capacity, weak institutional oversight, emasculated media, fractured and marginalized civil society, and a regime that enriched itself by selling the nation's natural resources without redistributing the income or investing in the hard and soft infrastructure needed for the country's future development. China implemented a similar playbook in Gabon, Equatorial Guinea, and Cameroon, three AFCON host nations that would not have been able to hold that honor (with the glory reflected onto their ruling elites) without Chinese-gifted stadiums.

A less cynical reading of these exchanges might invoke the concept of "soft power." Soft power is salient in China and germane to discussion of global football (Connell 2018; Li and Feng 2021). As the world's most popular sport, with a lucrative assemblage of adjacent industries, football occupies a prominent position in the global cultural economy. Not surprisingly, many nations have attempted to leverage or develop capacities for using football to accrue socio-cultural, political, and economic capital, including China (Leite and Rodrigues 2023). Examples abound, from Brazil's "joga bonito" narrative and England's "home of football" self-image to accusations that Qatar and Saudi Arabia's respective investments in football are motivated to rehabilitate images damaged by the contribution of fossil fuels to the climate emergency and human rights issues (Chadwick and Widdop 2023). China has also been criticized for "sport washing," that is, using the spectacle of sport to detract from its record on human rights and other issues. Such efforts can be grandiose—such as hosting global mega-events like the Olympics—or banal, like the crude use of football imagery by under-fire Chinese mining corporations in D. R. Congo (Dubinsky 2023).

At the beginning of the 2000s, China recognized that its admirable development story had failed to resonate commensurately with its rapid economic and physical transformation. The Chinese government acknowledged openly in 2006 that soft power would henceforth be an indivisible part of its pursuit of "comprehensive power" (Li 2008). Substantial investment was directed into international media operations, an expanded cultural footprint overseas, expanded public diplomacy efforts, student exchanges and the supply of generous scholarships, and the establishment of Confucius Institutes. Such efforts, conceived as soft-power initiatives primarily led by the state, ultimately failed to yield the desired results (Shambaugh 2015). Negative views of China persisted in many countries, although with significant variation between developed and developing world publics (Xie and Jin 2022). Host nations in the west securitized Confucius Institutes as instruments of influence, and many cultural products failed to resonate and were literally and figuratively lost in translation. Given these setbacks, the attraction of sport is obvious, since it is widely resonant and does not require cultural interpretation. Football culture is enriched by its diverse, contextually specific articulations across the world, but on the pitch, and as beamed or streamed, football is football: Instantly recognizable, and for much of the world's population, instantly attractive. It is also particularly popular in the regions where China is most interested to pursue economic and political engagement, that is, Africa, South America, and Europe. Given China's pursuit of soft power, the global interest in football and its potential to generate positive responses, it is easy to understand why football appeals to Chinese state and commercial actors (Leite and Rodrigues 2020).

Structure of the Book

The brief synopsis of China–Africa connections through football set out above hints at the diversity and layers of complexity that pertain to this issue. This multiplicity is represented in the chapters collected in this volume. Simon Chadwick and Jonathan Sullivan begin by presenting a high-level perspective that examines Chinese football development and China–Africa sports networks from the perspective of the Geopolitical Economy of Sport (Chadwick 2022). On the question of stadium diplomacy, they argue that the deployment of stadium building and gifting was a response to geographic, political, and economic challenges faced by both Chinese and African states. The expansion of Chinese corporations' use of sport sponsorship is interpreted as a means to build industrial presence and strengthen political influence in Africa. However, it is not a one-way street, and the bilateral nature of such developments are examined through assessing the rollout of Chinese 5G telecommunications across Africa, which are in part enabled by sport sponsorships. The chapter highlights some of the key issues and challenges created by China–Africa networks in sport.

Leah Li and Alexandre Zhao Huang conceive football as a crucial vehicle to developing the "China brand" internationally, as well as advancing China's foreign policy goals. Analyzing football-related strategic narratives, their chapter unpacks the strategies the Chinese government adopts to brand the country for the purpose of thickening its involvement in Africa. Expanding on the geographical scope of the preceding chapters Mahfoud Amara and Youcef Bouandel's chapter focuses on China's interventions in sports in the Middle East and North Africa (MENA), situating Chinese policies in the context of the unique characteristics of the sub-region. By examining China's motives and the implications of its interventions, the chapter contributes to a broader understanding of the complexities of China-MENA relations in the context of sports, development, and geopolitics.

There follow four chapters on diverse aspects of African labor migration (Darby et al. 2022). The geographic mobility of African football players has been examined from historical, economic, geographical, social, cultural, and sporting dimensions, with the majority of these studies viewed from a European perspective. This is a lacuna given the extent of African migration to China as a significant dimension of the burgeoning relationship between Africa and China. Peizi Han thus explores how African players have become embedded in Chinese professional football, reviewing the history of African football migration to China. Most work on African football migration has focused on men, but Han's case studies of African women players reveals the important role they have played in China–Africa football engagement. Christopher Edyegu focuses on the motivations of various Chinese stakeholders to encourage African footballers to migrate to China to bolster the competitiveness and marketability of Chinese leagues. He also analyzes the volatility in Chinese government policy on foreign players, including CFA quotas on eligible foreign players, which has fluctuated from attracting foreign players to increase the CSL's competitiveness to implementing policies that appear to do the opposite. Moving away from economics, institutions and policy, Wycliffe W. Simiyu Njororai approaches African football labor migration through the lens of cultural exchange. This innovative approach turns African players in the CSL into vectors of transnational cultural exchange. Unwana Samuel Akpan, Chuka Onwumechili, and Kalema Elizabeth

Meggs complement Njororai's approach by examining the attitudes of Nigerian football fans toward Nigerian football migrants to China. Their findings suggest that football cannot be divorced from broader aspects and perceptions of China's political-economic activities in Africa.

Two subsequent chapters by Tokunbo Ojo and Angela Lewis, respectively, examine Chinese media operations in Africa, specifically the market entrance of StarTimes. As a major football broadcasting rights holder in the African pay-TV market, this Chinese company has played a major role in serving the increasing demand for European football and the emergence of transnational fans across the African continent (Onwumechili 2019). This popularity is largely fueled by the globalization of football, hyper-marketization of European football, and the deregulation of broadcasting sectors in many African countries since the late 1990s. Ojo's chapter thus examines StarTimes' corporate strategies of appropriating local and global football rights in its expansion into African pay-TV markets. In assessing the social-cultural ramifications and political-economic dimensions that underpin StarTimes' media-sports complex in the African context, the chapter argues that StarTimes' sponsorship of football leagues as well as broadcasting of local and global football are inextricably linked with the broader public diplomacy agenda of China on the continent. Taking a different angle to analyze StarTimes' operations, Lewis examines sponsorship of football in Ghana and Uganda, including women's football development. She locates the expansion of StarTimes to the establishment of FOCAC and its development assistance and public-private-partnership remit. She explains how in practical terms this has led to the Chinese firm owning broadcasting rights to domestic and international matches. Key interventions by StarTimes in African football include youth training opportunities with StarTimes' Bundesliga partner, sponsorship of national teams in Ghana and Uganda, broadcasting the Women's AFCON and the creation of a channel exclusively for women's competitions. Development objectives ultimately aim to produce lucrative football brands attractive to domestic and international audiences. However, numerous obstacles have arisen, including under-investment and power-asymmetries in agency and control.

To conclude the book, two chapters examine historical cases of football engagement. First, Tobias Ross presents the case of Dalian Shide FC's "Lion Cub" program. In 2001, the club recruited 24 Cameroonian teenagers to northern China in the hope that they would develop into professional players and possible candidates for Chinese national team representation. At the time Dalian Shide was one of China's most successful clubs, and the ambitious program was the first large-scale player recruitment and naturalization effort in Chinese professional football. Drawing on insights from protagonists, Ross provides a unique treatment of a largely forgotten and unique episode. Finally, architecture scholars Charlie Xue and Guanghui Ding provide a comprehensive account of Chinese stadium building in Africa in previous decades, going beyond general arguments about sports diplomacy to scrutinize the symbolic and practical relevance of the infrastructure. Employing a lens that draws on the concepts of cosmopolitanism and nationalism, and emphasizing the tangible ways in which stadiums are experienced, the chapter takes an interdisciplinary approach to the political roots and transcultural practices of China's sports diplomacy, analyzing the motivations, design, construction, and operations of China-built stadiums in Africa.

References

Aidoo, Richard, and Steve Hess. 2015. "Non-interference 2.0: China's Evolving Foreign Policy towards a Changing Africa." *Journal of Current Chinese Affairs* 44 (1): 107–139.

Brautigam, Deborah. 2009. *The Dragon's Gift: The Real Story of China in Africa*. Oxford University Press.

Brautigam, Deborah. 2020. "A Critical Look at Chinese 'Debt-Trap Diplomacy': The Rise of a Meme." *Area Development and Policy* 5 (1): 1–14.

Cardenal, Juan Pablo, and Araújo Heriberto. 2013. *China's Silent Army: The Pioneers, Traders, Fixers and Workers Who are Remaking the World in Beijing's Image*. Allen Lane.

Carmody, Pádraig. 2011. *The New Scramble for Africa*. Polity.

Chadwick, Simon. 2022. "From Utilitarianism and Neoclassical Sport Management to a New Geopolitical Economy of Sport." *European Sport Management Quarterly* 22 (5): 685–704.

Chadwick, Simon, and Paul Widdop. 2023. "Sport Washing and the Gulf Region." In *The Geopolitical Economy of Sport: Power, Politics, Money, and the State*, edited by Simon Chadwick, Paul Widdop and Michael Goldman. Taylor & Francis.

Chadwick, Simon, Paul Widdop, Christos Anagnostopoulos, and Daniel Parnell, eds. 2022. *The Business of the FIFA World Cup*. Routledge.

Cockayne, David, Simon Chadwick, and Jonathan Sullivan. 2022. "Chinese Football—from a State-Led Past to a Digital Future." *Journal of Global Sport Management* 7 (3): 345–354.

Coleman, Katharina P., and Brian L. Job 2021. "How Africa and China May Shape UN Peacekeeping beyond the Liberal International Order." *International Affairs* 97 (5): 1451–1468.

Connell, John. 2018. "Globalisation, Soft Power, and the Rise of Football in China." *Geographical Research* 56 (1): 5–15.

Corkin, Lucy. 2011. "Redefining Foreign Policy Impulses toward Africa: The Roles of the MFA, the MOFCOM and China Exim Bank." *Journal of Current Chinese Affairs* 40 (4): 61–90.

Darby, Paul, James Esson, and Christian Ungruhe. 2022. "The History, Geography and Regulation of African Football Migration." In *African Football Migration: Aspirations,*

Experiences, Trajectories, edited by P. Darby, J. Esson, and C. Ungruhe, 40–63. Manchester University Press.

Dong, Jinxia, and Tony Mangan. 2001. "Football in the New China: Political Statement, Entrepreneurial Enticement and Patriotic Passion." *Soccer & Society* 2 (3): 79–100.

Driessen, Mirriam. 2016. "Pushed to Africa: Emigration and Social Change in China." *Journal of Ethnic and Migration Studies* 42 (15): 2491–2507.

Dubinsky, Itamar. 2021. "China's Stadium Diplomacy in Africa." *Journal of Global Sport Management* 1–19.

Dubinsky, Yoav. 2023. *Nation Branding and Sports Diplomacy: Country Image Games in Times of Change*. Springer.

Hesketh, Chris, and Jonathan Sullivan. 2020. "The Production of Leisure: Understanding the Social Function of Football Development in China." *Globalizations* 17 (6): 1061–1079.

Hirono, Miwa, and Shogo Suzuki. 2014. "Why Do We Need 'Myth-Busting' in the Study of Sino–African Relations?" *Journal of Contemporary China* 23 (87): 443–461.

Hong, Fan, and Xiong Xiaozheng. 2002. "Communist China: Sport, Politics and Diplomacy." *The International Journal of the History of Sport* 19 (2–3): 319–342.

Hong, Zhaohui, and Yi Sun. 2000. "The Butterfly Effect and the Making of 'Ping-Pong Diplomacy.'" *Journal of Contemporary China* 9 (25): 429–448.

Gagliardone, Iginio. 2022. "China's Information Infrastructures in the Horn: A Laboratory for Experimentation?" In *Routledge Handbook of the Horn of Africa*, edited by Bach, Jean-Nicolas, 692–701. Routledge.

Gravett, William H. 2022. "Digital Neocolonialism: The Chinese Surveillance State in Africa." *African Journal of International and Comparative Law* 30 (1): 39–58.

Grix, Jonathan, and Barrie Houlihan. 2014. "Sports Mega-Events as Part of a Nation's Soft Power Strategy: The Cases of Germany (2006) and the UK (2012)." *The British Journal of Politics and International Relations* 16 (4): 572–596.

Hsu, Elisabeth. 2007. "Zanzibar and Its Chinese Communities." *Population, Space and Place* 13 (2): 113–124.

Jedlowski, Alessandro. 2021. "Chinese Television in Africa." *Theory, Culture & Society* 38 (7–8): 233–250.

Lanteigne, Marc, and Miwa Hirono, eds. 2013. *China's Evolving Approach to Peacekeeping*. Routledge.

Large, Daniel. 2008. "Beyond 'Dragon in the Bush': The Study of China–Africa Relations." *African Affairs* 107 (426): 45–61.

Large, Daniel. 2021. *China and Africa: The New Era*. John Wiley & Sons.

Larmer, Miles, and Fraser, Alastair. 2007. "Of Cabbages and King Cobra: Populist Politics and Zambia's 2006 Election." *African Affairs* 106 (425): 611–637.

Leite, Emanuel Junior and Carlos Rodrigues. 2020. "Belt, Road and Ball: Football as a Chinese Soft Power and Public Diplomacy Tool." In *The Belt and Road Initiative: An Old Archetype of a New Development Model*, edited by Francisco José BS Leandro and Paulo Afonso B. Duarte, 61–83. Springer Nature.

Leite, Emanuel Junior, and Carlos Rodrigues. 2023. *China, Football, and Development: Socialism and Soft Power*. Routledge.

Leslie, Agnes Ngoma. 2016. "Zambia and China: Workers' Protest, Civil Society and the Role of Opposition Politics in Elevating State Engagement." *African Studies Quarterly* 16 (3–4): 89–106.

Lewis, Angela. 2023. *Chinese Television and Soft Power in Africa*. Taylor & Francis.

Li, Mingjiang. 2008. "China Debates Soft Power." *Chinese Journal of International Politics* 2 (2): 287–308.

Li, Xiufang, and Juan Feng. 2022. "Nation Branding through the Lens of Soccer: Using a Sports Nation Branding Framework to Explore the Case of China." *European Journal of Cultural Studies* 25 (4): 1118–1138.

Masunungure, Eldred V. 2011. "Zimbabwe's Militarized, Electoral Authoritarianism." *Journal of International Affairs* 65 (1): 47–64.

Mawdsley, Emma. 2009. "Fu Manchu Versus Dr Livingstone in the Dark Continent? Representing China, Africa and the West in British Broadsheet Newspapers." *Political Geography* 27 (5): 509–529.

Mohan, Giles, and May Tan-Mullins. 2009. "Chinese Migrants in Africa as New Agents of Development: An Analytical Framework." *European Journal of Development Research* 21 (4): 588–605.

Negi, Rohit. 2008. "Beyond the 'Chinese scramble': The Political Economy of Anti-China Sentiment in Zambia." *African Geographical Review* 27 (1): 41–63.

Nyiri, Pal. 2011. "Chinese Entrepreneurs in Poor Countries: A Transnational "Middleman Minority" and Its Futures." *Inter-Asia Cultural Studies* 12 (1): 145–153.

Onwumechili, Chuka. 2019. "African Fandom: From Cape Town to Cairo." In *Africa's Elite Football: Structure, Politics, And Everyday Challenges*, edited by Chuka Onwumechili, 117–132. Routledge.

Sautman, Barry, and Yan Hairong. 2009. "African Perspectives on China–Africa Links." *The China Quarterly* 199: 728–759.

Skey, Michael. 2023. "Sportswashing: Media Headline or Analytic Concept?" *International Review for the Sociology of Sport* 58 (5): 749–764.

Shambaugh, David. 2015. "China's Soft-Power Push: The Search for Respect." *Foreign Affairs* 94 (4): 99–107.

Shuman, Amanda. 2017. "Giving 'Prominence to Politics': African Sportsmen Visit China in the Early Cultural Revolution." In *China–Africa Relations: Building Images through Cultural Co-operation, Media Representation, and Communication*, edited by Kathryn Batchelor and Xiaoling Zhang, 51–72. Routledge.

Sullivan, Jonathan, and Jing Cheng. 2018. "Contextualising Chinese Migration to Africa." *Journal of Asian and African Studies* 53 (8): 1173–1187.

Sun, Yun. 2014. *Africa in China's Foreign Policy*. Brookings.

Taylor, Ian. 1998. "China's Foreign Policy towards Africa in the 1990s." *The Journal of Modern African Studies* 36 (3): 443–460.

Taylor, Ian. 2014. *Africa Rising?* Boydell & Brewer.

Xie, Yu, and Yongai Jin. 2022. "Global Attitudes toward China: Trends and Correlates." *Journal of Contemporary China* 31 (133): 1–16.

Xue, Charlie Qiuli, Guanghui Ding, Wei Chang, and Yan Wan. 2019. "Architecture of 'Stadium diplomacy'-China-Aid Sport Buildings in Africa." *Habitat International* 90: 101985.
Yin, Zhiguang. 2023. "'World of Tomorrow' Afro-Asian Solidarity and the Great Leap Forward of Culture in the People's Republic of China." *Third World Quarterly* 44 (10): 2263–2280.
Zhou, Xinxiang, Li Yan, and Jianli Zhang. 2022. "Research on Football Development Cooperation between China and Cameroon." *Open Access Library Journal* 9 (7): 1–11.

2

A Geopolitical Economy of Sport Approach to China–Africa Engagement in Football

Simon Chadwick[1] and Jonathan Sullivan[2]

Introduction

Relations between China and various African countries in sport go back to the 1960s, but these connections have diversified and deepened significantly in the last two decades, coinciding with China's determined effort and greater capacity to expand its engagement in Africa. Among these connections is the migration of African football labor to Chinese professional football leagues and investment and sponsorship engagement by Chinese corporations in Africa. Crypto currency business Binance's sponsorship of the 2021 African Cup of Nations is one example of the latter, as was Huawei's similar arrangement with the 2019 version of the tournament. While the Binance deal appeared to be driven by opportunism, that is, a private sector firm seeking first-mover advantage in a new market, the Huawei deal was much more significant as Huawei used the tournament to launch the rollout of its 5G mobile network in Africa. Egypt, the host of the championships, was one of the continent's first markets to be targeted by the

1 Simon Chadwick, Professor, Skema Business School, simon.chadwick@skema.edu.
2 Jonathan Sullivan, Associate Professor, University of Nottingham, jonathan.sullivan@nottingham.ac.uk.

Chinese telecommunications business. This is not the first time we have seen Chinese state and non-state actors involved in the blue-ribbon event in African football. Indeed, at most editions of the African Cup of Nations in the twentieth century there has been a significant Chinese presence. This is evident in the presence of Chinese sponsors, but more tangibly in terms of the stadiums and adjacent physical infrastructure, including transportation. Much of the infrastructure needed to host football matches and tournaments has been funded by gift or loan and designed and built by Chinese state actors supplemented by state-guided private enterprise. This phenomenon, characterized by many observers as "stadium diplomacy," has a long history, but manifestations of it have increased in geographical scope and quantity during the past decade.

In crude terms, African nations benefit from stadium diplomacy by receiving new football, hospitality and transportation infrastructure in return for what the Chinese state hopes will lead to direct (e.g., natural resource concessions or access to markets) or indirect (e.g., deeper connections to local elites, reputational boost in public opinion, Chinese brand awareness) benefits. As the chapters in this volume demonstrate, stadium diplomacy is far from the only interaction in football between China and African nations. However, as one of the most long-standing, physically tangible and scrutinized forms of engagement, it is necessary to consider it seriously. This chapter therefore presents an analysis of stadium diplomacy using the case of the 2023 African Cup of Nations (AFCON). The analysis is set in the context of the geopolitical economy of sport, an approach that foregrounds sport as a tool and a vector for advancing state and state-corporate interests, in which the on-field action is subsidiary to more consequential off-field outcomes (Chadwick 2022). In addition, we set out in this chapter our contention that Chinese behavior in terms of stadium diplomacy can be understood as an extension of the state's instrumental understanding of football, and the modus operandi that it employs to football development domestically within China (Sullivan et al. 2019). Although there is an explicitly international dimension to stadium diplomacy, there are obvious consonances with the Chinese state's understanding of the utility of football domestically, with a similar modus operandi and shared cast of actors involved. We will demonstrate these consonances by setting out briefly the state's ambitions for football development within China and identifying a similar set of logical underpinnings to engagements with football in Africa, including, but not limited to, the financing and construction of stadiums. As with many other Chinese state behaviors, manifestations that emerge in international contexts can often be illuminated by appreciating how the state approaches the same issue or sector in China.

A Geopolitical Economy of Sport Approach

The geopolitical economy of sport is an approach, and a field of research, that takes sport seriously, that is, it is concerned with the activities, strategies, and implications of sport beyond the field of play. This alone does not make the approach novel or unique, since it has long been acknowledged that sport is such an embedded and resonant part of national and global cultural economies that it cannot help but have a political and economic dimension. What is distinct about the geopolitical economy approach is that it recognizes that the political and economic dimensions of sport play out in the context of competition between states on a global scale, that is, geopolitics. Acknowledging that sport has a role in geopolitics is also not novel and there are many examples, notably from the Cold War era, of this playing out (Rider 2016). What marks the geopolitical economy of sport approach out further, is a foundation in strategic reasoning rather than ideology; an explicit acknowledgment of the power of the networks and connectivity that structure contemporary global business and society; and an understanding of the multiplicity of actors involved (Chadwick et al. 2023). We can think of the approach as having three main elements. First, it is concerned with the way in which nations, states and other entities engage in, with or through sport with relevance to political economy. Second, it is concerned with identifying the motivations of the actors involved, and specifically considers whether they are attempting to build and exert power within the realm of international politics and economy. Third, it is concerned with relative strategic advantage, which states pursue through the control of physical, strategic, or symbolic resources within and via the networks in which sport is a constituent part. All this action takes place on a global scale, operating within the parameters of global finance, media, institutions of multilateral governance and international relations. From a geopolitical economy of sport perspective, in a contemporary world characterized by hyperconnectivity, multipolarity and rising authoritarianism, sport is a policy instrument that can be used by state actors to pursue both domestic and international goals. Although it emphasizes states in terms of motivations, behaviors and outcomes, the approach is clear that firms and other non-state actors are actively involved, either in service of the state or through the pursuit of their own benefits.

The geopolitical economy of sport approach emphasizes the importance of geography, politics, and economics in shaping the ways in which state entities (as principals) and private firms (often as agents) engage with sport. For China, stadium diplomacy has the potential for establishing or consolidating asymmetric power relationships with some African nations. By extension, these power relations and subsequent dependencies can have broader strategic dimensions to its geopolitical relevance. Africa offers access to an abundance of important natural resources that are needed to help sustain China's economic growth. This reality, and the opacity of China's authoritarian regime and that of many of its partners in Africa, means that diplomacy in sport has frequently been suspected of masking quid pro quo transactions in which stadiums are built in return for preferential access to natural resources. Politically, investing in stadium projects offers China the possibility of extending its influence in Africa, through *guanxi* (i.e., personalized reciprocal networks), corruption, economic leverage, or soft power. Critics condemn the asymmetries of China/Africa transaction relations as being redolent of neocolonialism. Yet, while China may derive benefits from the relatively low-cost diplomacy of stadium construction, there is little evidence that is seeking to interfere in the governance of African societies. And there are benefits for African recipients too. Sporting mega-events like the African Cup of Nations can produce positive local economic benefits, for example through tourism (Swart et al. 2018). The opportunity to expand bilateral exchange relations with the world's second-biggest economy is important too. There are concerns about the legacy of these stadiums once tournaments have finished. The comparative utility of large sports venues to the lives of African people—when the funds could be directed into more pressing needs like hospitals and education—is another question. China's defense is that the decision-making of African elites, post-construction usage and the failure of economic benefits to trickle down is not their responsibility.

Allied to the specific geographies, politics, and economics of stadiums, there are also broader notions of strategic positioning and power at play. For China, the popular appeal of football across Africa provides opportunities to build legitimacy, trust, and positive public attitudes. Given China's relatively weak presence in global football competition, stadium building, sponsorship and other adjacent activity facilitates China's involvement in global football irrespective of the strength of its players and teams. This is relevant to China given the growing interest in Africa displayed by other nations (including new entrants like Qatar), which are also using sport-related investments to establish strategic and exchange relationships in Africa. In this respect, China has already established first-mover strategic advantages that may prove to be an effective barrier to entry in potential rivalries with countries like Saudi Arabia or India.

China's Vision for Football

The relevance of football is not restricted to sporting performance and on-field action. Economically and industrially, football can generate national wealth, create jobs and boost export earnings. Socio-culturally, the sport can promote social cohesion, health, well-being, and active lifestyles. It is also a political instrument. Domestically, football development can be seen as an articulation of China's pursuit of modernization, buttressing the Party-state's narrative of national development and, ultimately, regime legitimacy (Hesketh and Sullivan 2020). Internationally, football is also a political instrument, illustrated by the incorporation of football-related political-economic activity into China's soft-power repertoire. China is not a traditional football nation. As an exotic import in the early twentieth century that was subsequently co-opted by the new Communist regime for its nation building potential, football does not have deep community roots in China. Since the mid-1990s Chinese football has undergone an uneven process of liberalization, professionalization, and commercialization, with continuing institutional and regulatory involvement by the state (Peng et al. 2019). Some clubs remain owned by SOEs, others by private firms with state connections. The Chinese Super League may have some of the assemblages and private economy excesses associated with European and American counterparts, but football in China remains an enterprise in which the state has a determinative structuring role (Ma and Kurscheidt 2019). This is evident in multiple state-led efforts to reform the organization of football. The most recent reform effort launched in the mid-2010s illuminates how the state sees football and what it hopes to derive from harnessing its power.

The reforms, and an explicit statement of China's ambitions, are laid out in three documents. In 2014, the State Council issued its opinion on "Accelerating the Development of the Sports Industry to Promote Sport Consumption," which set out an industrial vision for Chinese sport and aimed to create a domestic sports economy worth up to US$800 billion by 2025 (Goddard 2014). In 2015, there followed the "The Overall Reform Plan to Boost the Development of Football in China," which, among other things, proposed liberalizing and professionalizing the organization and operation of the game. In 2016, the government laid out its "Medium to Long Term Development Plan 2016–2050," containing a multi-sector roadmap and benchmarks for becoming a football power. Taken together, the reform policies were ambitious and holistic, incorporating reforms to governance structures, regulation of football industry actors, the national team set-up, youth training and education, public health and other elements (Sullivan et al. 2019). Underlyingly, and explicit in any reading of the reform policy documents, is an understanding of football's utility for pursuing broad economic and socio-political ends (Peng et al. 2023). These include promoting public health, well-being and active lifestyles, generating feelings of national unity and pride, stimulating the economic sectors adjacent to football (e.g., leisure, hospitality, shopping, entertainment, real estate) and encouraging middle-class consumption, inculcating social cohesion, patriotic citizenship and forging a shared national identity (Yu et al. 2019). The potential for football to produce such outcomes explains why the Chinese leadership under Xi Jinping was willing to invest significant financial, political and reputational capital in the reform project (Ma and Kurscheidt 2022).

The decline in the fortunes of the Chinese football project since the COVID-19 pandemic began does not change this analysis, although clearly football development has lost the priority status conferred on it in the mid-2010s. Chinese football has faced numerous serious setbacks in the past few years. Clubs suffered financially from the dynamic-zero-COVID regime that effectively neutered the Chinese Super League for three years. The broader economic downturn affected sectors of the economy like real estate and commerce, in which the majority of club owners operated, creating further constraints on the professional leagues. The Chinese men's national team once again failed to qualify for the FIFA World Cup. Facing a difficult economy and complex and deteriorating foreign policy environment, the Chinese government's focus and priorities turned away from football. Unquestionably, football has lost the political luster it enjoyed in the mid-2010s. Notwithstanding these setbacks, football retains potential to become a site and a vehicle for promoting domestic consumption, civic participation, public health, and national pride. As long as the state continues to recalibrate China's economic model through increasing consumption, Chinese society continues to face a looming obesity crisis and other public health issues, and the central leadership continues to be preoccupied with unifying the populace behind the elision of nation and the Communist Party, the potential contribution of football will remain salient to Chinese "cultural citizenship" (Newman et al. 2021).

Consonance between Domestic and Foreign Utilization of Football

China's engagement with football is complicated by its status as a reforming socialist economy, a rapidly modernizing country, and an authoritarian polity.

There are similarities between China's organization of sport during the Mao era and other Communist countries, notably the Soviet Union (Edelman 2007), and patriotism and propaganda are a feature of numerous Communist regimes' treatment of sport, like North Korea (Lee and Bairner 2009). But reform-era developments in Chinese football have relatively little in common with post-Soviet states, where uncontrolled liberalization led to endemic corruption and the emasculation of domestic football structures (Molnar 2007; Veth 2017). Football in China is not an incubator of violent nationalism or ethnic conflict as it has been in other reforming socialist nations (Mills 2009). Neither has football become a site for anti-state mobilization as it has in other developing nations like Brazil, despite sharing similar social conditions such as inequality and corruption (Goldblatt 2014). Other authoritarian regimes have sought soft power gains through association with football, particularly countries in the Gulf region (Thani and Heenan 2017), and many countries, including advanced economies in the west, have adopted policies to promote sport to tackle health issues and elite sporting success (Grix and Carmichael 2012). Other nations, notably Japan and the United States, have launched new football leagues and invested heavily in the recruitment of foreign expertise (Collins 2006; Horne 1999). Football in Europe and elsewhere is similarly no stranger to the involvement of political figures and the business-football-politics nexus embodied by figures like Silvio Berlusconi or Roman Abramovich (Doidge 2015; Porro and Russo 2000). Individual aspects of China's football experience thus have corollaries elsewhere. Yet, taken as a whole, China's experience retains a distinct character. The symbolic resonance of football in China goes beyond the appreciation of sport, notwithstanding Xi Jinping's purported affinity for it (Soderman 2023). At the domestic level, it is implicated in China's ongoing pursuit of modernity, the Party-state's narrative of national development and, ultimately, regime legitimacy. These elements together constitute "the Chinese Dream" of national strength and "moderate prosperity" for Chinese people under the leadership of the Communist Party. The effort to transform Chinese football since the mid-2010s illuminates the party-state's domestic aspirations and modus operandi. It also helps to contextualize China's approach to football internationally.

First, the view of football is equally utilitarian, strategic, and transactional in the domestic and international realms. Football, in short, is instrumentalized for promoting economic and political gains to the benefit of Chinese state objectives. Instead of the domestic issues noted above, in the international realm the gains sought are access to resources, markets and the thickening of relations that might be converted into political leverage or influence. Second, the state employs a similar playbook domestically and internationally. Initiatives are driven from top-down, networks engaged, transactions made, and finances provided through state-connected entities (Ross et al. 2023). Different actors within the state apparatus operate in foreign initiatives, finance may come from externally-focused "policy banks," and negotiations are between Chinese and foreign elites rather than between central, provincial and local governments. Yet, the operating procedures are similar. This includes the facilitation role of SOEs and ostensibly private, but state-connected or state-guided, firms. Third, the range of actors involved domestically and internationally includes state agencies, banks, SOEs, private industry and various intermediaries leveraging networked personal connections. We do not claim that there is a direct translation of domestic and international football initiatives, but the corollaries are distinctive enough to show that the underlying motivations, strategies, and methods are analogous not discrete.

Xi Jinping's vision for China to become a global sporting power and using football as vehicle, illustrates the maturation of China's global engagement strategy during the past two decades. Instead of the blunt instrument to reward ideological allies, transparently court local elites holding the key to natural resources, or marginalizing Taiwan as it once was, China's contemporary engagement with football in Africa is multifaceted, as the chapters in this book demonstrate. There continue to be instrumental and transactional elements, but the ambition has widened to include the search for investment opportunities in key industries, accessing and developing burgeoning African markets for Chinese goods and services, and thickening the exchange relationships needed to secure access to strategic assets such as ports and agricultural land. In the hybrid model the Chinese state has employed for football development domestically there are six key operating principles: top-down state investment, bottom-up private investment, external acquisition of football properties and expertise, network influence, football as driver of consumption and entertainment, and football as an instrument of soft power. These elements are also present across China's international football engagements in the developing world, for example in the transformation of China-Brazil relations (Leite et al. 2019). Having established the broader context and strategy of China's approach to football, we now turn to a case study of stadium diplomacy in the context of AFCON 2023.

The 2023 African Cup of Nations

Initially planned for summer 2023, the AFCON was postponed to early 2024, but retained the original name. The tournament began with a game between Côte d'Ivoire and Guinea-Bissau at the Alassane Ouattara Stadium in Abidjan. This state-of-the-art venue—otherwise known as the Olympic Stadium of Ebimpé—was opened in 2020 and is one of six stadiums being used during the tournament. Construction began in 2016 when then-Prime Minister Daniel Kablan Duncan broke ground accompanied by several Chinese embassy officials based in Côte d'Ivoire. This was no surprise, since the stadium was designed by the Beijing Institute of Architectural Design and built by the Beijing Construction Engineering Group, both of which are state entities. The Alassane Ouattara Stadium was not the only tournament venue with considerable Chinese involvement. In San Pedro, the Laurent Pokou Stadium was built by the state-owned China Civil Engineering Construction Corporation. China National Building Material, its senior directors enjoying links to the Chinese Communist Party, served as general contractor on the Amadou Gon Coulibaly Stadium in Korhogo.

China's role in the African Cup of Nations is not new. When Gabon co-hosted the AFCON in 2012 with Equatorial Guinea, China was involved in building both of its stadiums. Five years later, in 2017, when Gabon hosted the tournament again, China built a further two stadiums to accommodate the Gabon's role as sole host. In the meantime, Presidents Ali Bongo of Gabon and Xi Jinping of China met to agree a comprehensive cooperation partnership. Gabon now sends around 15 percent of all its exports to China, of which crude petroleum and manganese ore form the largest proportion. Just as construction of the Alassane Ouattara Stadium got underway, Côte d'Ivoire president of the same name visited Beijing to finalize details on a strategic cooperative partnership. By 2020, China had invested US$1.5 billion in Côte d'Ivoire and the African nation exported US$700 million worth of natural resources and goods to China, up from US$100 million in 2016. While circumstantial, critics of stadium diplomacy see these developments as evidence of the instrumentality of China's engagement with African nations: Provision of prestige infrastructure enables China to extend its sphere of influence in Africa, creating asymmetric dependencies that can be leveraged to source the raw materials to sustain China's economic growth and strategic advantage in sectors such as battery manufacturing.

Yet, China is far from the only country engaging with Africa in a transactional way. After all, the French utilities business Total Energies was the title sponsor of the 2023 AFCON and is involved in the exploitation of oil across the continent. Not motivated by access to African oil, countries from the Gulf region are also now engaging in football diplomacy. Countries like Saudi Arabia and Qatar, resource-rich but undergoing economic transformation and diversification, are investing billions of dollars in sport. The Saudi government plans to position the country as an Afro-Eurasian hub, which has already begun to impact upon football. In 2023, it appeared as though the kingdom would bid to host the 2030 FIFA World Cup in conjunction with Egypt and Greece, and as part of the proposed arrangement, it reportedly offered to build new stadiums for the two partner countries. Ultimately, Saudi Arabia became sole bidder for the 2034 edition of the competition, though the potential involvement of African nations should not be discounted. Indeed, in one of the country's many mega-projects that is under construction, Neom, entails collaboration with Egypt. The Visit Saudi Arabia tourist board campaign has signed on as sponsor of the African Football League, while the Saudi Arabia Football Federation has agreed a cooperation deal with the Mauritanian Football Association. As the latter was being signed, Prince Mohammed bin Salman received a written message from Mauritanian President Mohamed Ould Cheikh El-Ghazouani pledging to boost relations and bilateral coordination. Some critics claim that the government in Riyadh is trying to secure African markets for Saudi oil, in an attempt to offset decreasing demand for it elsewhere in the world. Others have observed that the kingdom needs access to African natural resources like lithium, cobalt, and copper to drive its economic reforms. We have already seen another Gulf nation, Qatar, setting out a template for engagement with Africa. Having won the right to stage the 2022 FIFA World Cup, Rwanda became a legacy partner that saw football development projects being funded by the government in Doha. Alongside this, state-owned Qatar Airways made a bid to acquire significant stakes in both Air Rwanda and Kigali's new international airport.

Conclusion

China's presence in Africa and the nature of its deployment of sport there is a matter of geopolitical economy born out of domestic concerns and global ambitions. Building stadiums is an illustration of this. The appeal for African nations is obvious—countries get much-needed infrastructure, a boost to national pride and secure Chinese investment. For China, it is a way to consolidate exchange relations, not just in terms of natural resources, but access to Africa's fast-growing markets in diverse economic sectors. Competition for these resources and markets is increasing, with non-traditional entrants like Turkey, South Korea, United Arab Emirates, and India increasing their activities in African countries. These countries each have numerous tools they can use to establish and expand ties with African partners, and sport is one of them. For that reason, it is necessary to treat football as one component of nation-states' geopolitical economy repertoire. As Africa's economies develop, and many African countries remain a rich repository of football talent and interest, the geopolitical economy approach to football activity with the continent will become an ever more useful analytical tool.

References

Chadwick, Simon. 2022. "From Utilitarianism and Neoclassical Sport Management to a New Geopolitical Economy of Sport." *European Sport Management Quarterly* 22 (5): 685–704.

Chadwick, Simon, Paul Widdop, and Michael M. Goldman, eds. 2023. *The Geopolitical Economy of Sport: Power, Politics, Money, and the State*. Taylor & Francis.

Collins, Sandra. 2006. "National Sports and Other Myths: The Failure of US Soccer." *Soccer & Society* 7 (2–3): 353–363.

Doidge, Mark. 2015. *Football Italia: Italian Football in an Age of Globalization*. Bloomsbury.

Edelman, Rob. 1993. *Serious Fun: A History of Spectator Sport in the USSR*. Oxford University Press.

Goldblatt, David. 2014. *Futebol Nation: A Footballing History of Brazil*. Penguin.

Grix, Jonathan, and Fiona Carmichael. 2012. "Why Do Governments Invest in Elite Sport? A Polemic." *International Journal of Sport Policy and Politics* 4 (1): 73–90.

Hesketh, Chris, and Jonathan Sullivan. 2020. "The production of leisure: understanding the social function of football development in China." *Globalizations* 17 (6): 1061-1079.

Horne, John. 1999. "Soccer in Japan: Is *wa* All You Need?" *Culture, Sport Society* 2 (3): 212–229.

Lee, Jung Woo, and Alan Bairner. 2009. "The Difficult Dialogue: Communism, Nationalism, and Political Propaganda in North Korean sport." *Journal of Sport and Social Issues* 33 (4): 390–410.

Leite Jr, Emanuel., Rodrigues, Carlos and Leite, Emanuel. 2019. "Chinese Soft Power and Public Diplomacy: Football as a Tool to Promote China-Brazil Relations." *Boletim do Tempo Presente* 8 (3):194–214.

Ma, Yang, and Markus Kurscheidt. 2019. "Governance of the Chinese Super League: A Struggle between Governmental Control and Market Orientation." *Sport, Business and Management: An International Journal* 9 (1): 4–25.

Ma, Yang, and Markus Kurscheidt. 2022. "Doing It the Chinese Way: The Politically-Led Commercialization of Professional Football in China." *Journal of Global Sport Management* 7 (3): 355–371.

Mills, Richard. 2009. "'It All Ended in an Unsporting Way': Serbian Football and the Disintegration of Yugoslavia, 1989–2006." *The International Journal of the History of Sport* 26 (9): 1187–1217.

Molnar, Gyozo. 2007. "Hungarian Football: A Socio-Historical Overview." *Sport in History* 27 (2): 293–317.

Newman, Joshua, Hanhan Xue, Ryan Chen, Yiming Chen and Nicholas Watanabe. 2021. "Football and Cultural Citizenship in China: A Study in Three Embodiments." *Sport in Society* 24 (12): 2222–2245.

Peng, Qi, James Skinner, and Barrie Houlihan. 2019. "An Analysis of the Chinese Football Reform of 2015: Why Then and Not Earlier?" *International Journal of Sport Policy and Politics* 11 (1): 1–18.

Peng, Qi, Zhisheng Chen, Juan Li, Barrie Houlihan and Nicolas Scelles. 2023. "The New Hope of Chinese Football? Youth Football Reforms and Policy Conflicts in the Implementation Process." *European Sport Management Quarterly* 23 (6): 1928–1950.

Porro, Nicola, and Pippo Russo. 2000. "Berlusconi and Other Matters: The Era of 'Football-Politics.'" *Journal of Modern Italian Studies* 5 (3): 348–371.

Rider, Toby. 2016. *Cold War Games: Propaganda, the Olympics, and US Foreign Policy*. University of Illinois Press.

Ross, Tobias, Jonathan Sullivan, and Hongyi Lai. 2023. "Private Investment in Chinese Football Clubs: Political Capital and State–Business Exchanges." *Journal of Current Chinese Affairs* 52 (3): 518–541.

Söderman, Sten. 2023. *The Footballization of China: Strategies for World Cup Glory*. Edward Elgar.

Sullivan, Jonathan, Simon Chadwick, and Michael Gow. 2019. "China's Football Dream: Sport, Citizenship, Symbolic Power, and Civic Spaces." *Journal of Sport and Social Issues* 43 (6): 493–514.

Swart, Kamilla, Tembi M. Tichaawa, Joelle-Desiree Odounga Othy and Tracy Daniels. 2018. "Stakeholder Perspectives of Sport Tourism Development in Gabon: A Case Study of the Africa Cup of Nations." *EuroEconomica* 37 (2): 177–189.

Thani, Salma, and Tom Heenan. 2017. "The Ball May Be Round but Football Is Becoming Increasingly Arabic: Oil Money and the Rise of the New Football Order." *Soccer & Society* 18 (7): 1012–1026.

Veth, K. Manuel. 2017. "Sovintersport and the Cashing in on Soviet Football." *Soccer & Society* 18 (1): 132–143.

Yu, Lin, Joshua Newman, Hanhan Xue, and Haozhou Pu. 2019. "The Transition Game: Toward a Cultural Economy of Football in Post-Socialist China." *International Review for the Sociology of Sport* 54 (6): 711–737.

3

China–Africa Relations: Intention, Aspiration, and a shared Future through the means of Football

Xiufang (Leah) Li[1] and
Zhao Alexandre Huang[2]

Introduction

China's economic involvement in Africa has attracted substantial attention over the last two decades, as China has emerged as one of the top trade partners to most African countries (Ojo 2022). China's ambition may indeed be to become the single biggest trade partner across the continent by 2030 (Ayeni 2022). The rapid expansion of China's economic engagement with the Global South, including aid and trade, has been subject to much critique, especially in Africa, where Chinese loan practices have provoked much controversy (Mlambo 2022). Scholarly and policy communities have argued that creditor-debtor relationships between China and numerous African countries have created "debt traps" (H. Zhang 2023) that afford the Chinese state influence or indirect control over socio-political and economic practices in the guise of development aid and support (Rapanyane 2023). Some analyses even suggest that debt traps have evolved into a deliberate strategy for advancing geopolitical interests (DeBoom 2020).

1 Xiufang (Leah) Li, Senior Lecturer, RMIT University, leah.li@rmit.edu.au.
2 Zhao Alexandre Huang, Associate Professor, University of Paris Nanterre, zhao.huang@parisnanterre.fr.

Notwithstanding these arguments, Chinese lending to African states has decreased substantially since 2020, when it fell by 77 percent compared to the 2019 level. Rather than simply reflecting the idiosyncrasies of the first pandemic year, it seems to be a deliberate recalibration of Chinese policy, and the value of future new Chinese loans to Africa are predicted to be less numerous and smaller scale (H. Zhang 2023). In response to the moral hazard accusation concerning the traditional sovereign load-based infrastructure engagement, a new model termed "integrated investment, construction, and operation" (IICO) and endorsed by the Chinese infrastructure industry, financial institutions, and policymakers, has emerged (H. Zhang 2023). Guided by IICO, Chinese companies would transition from their conventional role as engineering and construction contractors to developers and operators of infrastructure projects. This shift sends the signal that Chinese companies are seeking both industrial upgrade and accountability in the projects they are involved in, thereby enabling the transfer of greater economic rewards to China (H. Zhang 2023).

A microcosm of its broader economic engagement, China's investment in Africa's sports infrastructure has provoked skepticism about the intentions and influence of the Chinese state in the Global South. Investment in sports facilities, including gifting stadiums and training facilities, has been interpreted as being motivated by the ambition to acquire sustained economic benefits in African markets and support in international bodies of the United Nations, while creating only limited or temporary benefits for African countries (Mlambo 2022). As an antidote to short-termism and lack of mutual benefit, the China–Africa Cooperation Vision 2035 (hereafter "Vision") launched in 2021, aims to strengthen strategic partnerships and produce high-quality China–Africa cooperation in the mid and long term. With characteristic ambition and rhetorical flourish, the stated priority is to "promote a closer community with a shared future for China and Africa" (Ministry of Commerce of China 2021). One of the Vision's objectives is to facilitate shared cultural prosperity through creating more vibrant cultural and sports exchanges (Ministry of Commerce of China 2021). Football acts as a vehicle for national and local governments in both China and African countries to boost local economies, bolster local and national pride and seek international acclaim (Li and Feng 2022; Thabet 2022). The Chinese government itself foregrounded football development in the mid-2010s and aspires to elevate the country to a greater role in global football and become a regional football power by 2050 (Tan et al. 2016). Aside from more instrumental economic incentives, the stated belief is that the advancement of football can contribute to the enhancement of Chinese people's well-being and cultural life. In many African countries, football is the most popular sport, and it is used as a vehicle to achieve the goals of local governments. Nevertheless, the overall state of Chinese and African football, including women and girls' football, is underdeveloped and fails to deliver sporting success equivalent to potential (Li and Feng 2022; Njororai 2022a; Saavedra 2003).

Although China has a rhetorical commitment to partnerships of equals in Africa, common framings in Chinese media illustrate the structural inequalities involved in cooperation. One example is the common framing of China as "leading and teaching, while Africa follows and learns," showcasing China's self-conception as a development model for the continent (Batchelor 2022, 228). This framing raises questions about equality, paternalism and lack of respect (Batchelor 2022). Nevertheless, after a decade of investing in large-scale projects, bilaterally and under the auspices of the BRI, Chinese statements at FOCAC and other forums indicate a change in approach. In practical terms, it has resulted in China scaling back planned investment in Africa, some of it in much-needed sectors such as agricultural assistance, action to mitigate climate change and the transition to green energy (Sun 2021b). The reality of these spending cuts raises the question of sports cooperation between Africa and China.

Reflecting on challenges to the IICO model, we pose the following questions: Will China continue to support Africa's sports development? What new forms of support for African sport could emerge? To what degree can Chinese sports aid consolidate relations between China and recipient countries in Africa? Will the entanglement of politics and sporting activities increase or decrease? The purpose of this chapter is to address these questions through a broader examination of the role of sports in China–Africa relations, particularly highlighting football. The chapter starts by outlining the different stages of China–Africa relations, the diplomatic approaches China has adopted and how they have served the needs of China's growth. It then examines the role of sports in facilitating China–Africa relations, with specific reference to the deployment of football in the service of internally and externally oriented goals in Africa. Following that, it analyzes China's sports diplomacy approaches and unpacks the strategies Beijing adopts to increase engagement with Africa before connecting with the philosophy that guides Chinese foreign policy in Africa. The chapter concludes by providing an assessment of the degree to which China's diplomatic approaches to Africa using sports helps to foster mutually beneficial relations before speculating on future trends in China–Africa relations in football.

China–Africa Relations

Africa is composed of 54 sovereign nations and two disputed areas, Somaliland and Western Sahara. By November 2021, China had established diplomatic relations with 53 of these countries (Ministry of Foreign Affairs of the PRC 2021). The mode of contemporary China–Africa relations can be traced back to the 1950s (Mohan and Power 2008). Africa's pursuit of independence from colonial powers and China's willingness to stand up to perceived American militarism in Asia following its own liberation and nation building forged a common basis for developing bilateral connections from 1950 to the early 1970s (Khan 2006; Mohan and Power 2008). The Communist Party was staunchly anti-imperialist, anti-colonial and offered solidarity with African "socialist brothers" (Hutchison 1976). Based on the changes in China's leadership since the establishment of the PRC, the diplomatic relationship between China and Africa can be divided into the following four phases (Ochieng 2022).

The first phase (1949–1976) under the leadership of Mao Zedong focused on building political rather than economic relationships with Africa (Campbell 2008; Ochieng 2022). The priority was to overcome the isolation and economic blockade imposed by the West through offering financial, technological, and medical aid to Africa, coupled with scholarships for Africans to obtain an education in China. The second phase (1978–1992) led by Deng Xiaoping promoted economic policies that provided Africa with economic assistance in exchange for the political support of African countries aiding recognition of China on the international stage and marginalizing Taiwan (Ochieng 2022). After the Tiananmen crisis in 1989, Beijing accelerated its investment in Africa. It attempted to reshape the country's international image in the post-Tiananmen era and to gain support from African states in international affairs (Taylor 2006).

The third phase (1993–2002) under Jiang Zemin was marked by the institutionalization of China–Africa relations. This was evidenced by the founding of the China–Africa Cooperation Forum (FOCAC) dialogue mechanism. In this period, China extended assistance for social development beyond purely economic aid, such as African human resources development funds and the establishment of the Confucius Institute (Ochieng 2022). China–Africa relations after 2000 were restructured by the formal founding of FOCAC as a multilateral institution. As a structural means by which Beijing institutionalizes and reinforces its geopolitical and economic expansion in African states, FOCAC helps to operationalize and localize Beijing's "go-out" (*zou chuqu*) policy in Africa. The enactment of going out, formalized by the Chinese state in 2001, encouraged large-scale economic expansion overseas through Chinese enterprises investing in overseas markets (Haglund 2009). The initiative has gradually transformed China's African aid policy into a sustainable investment mode that seeks to deliver on China's self-declared foreign policy goals of "win-win cooperation" and mutually beneficial exchange relations (L. Zhang 2015).

The fourth phase (2002-2012) under Hu Jintao saw the growth of a robust relationship, with deepening economic linkages aligned to China's increasing reliance on African natural resources and the launch of soft-power initiatives in education, media, and cultural sectors (Ochieng 2022). Since Xi Jinping assumed power, the present phase (2012–present) has been characterized by China's ambition to modify elements of the existing global order in pursuit of Chinese interests. In part, this is organized through exercising sustained cooperation between China and Africa in the economic and political domains guided by new overarching programs like the Belt and Road Initiative (Ochieng 2022).

According to Jian and Donata (2014), the shift in China's role in Africa from a "political investor" to an "economic investor" started around 2000, marked by Beijing's going-out policy toward the end of the 1990s. This shift has benefited both sides politically and economically, while enabling China to emerge as an active player in Africa, rather than merely acting as a donor to the continent. Furthermore, the emerging relationship has helped both sides negotiate with the West and navigate a global order designed by Western powers. However, critics are concerned with the plundering of resources and unfair competition behind China's rapid rise in Africa, even though this does not involve military coercion (Breslin 2013; Gertz 2000). They view China's active involvement in Africa as a starting point for China to export its own political and economic models or exert the so-called Beijing Consensus (Ambrosio 2012). The Beijing Consensus symbolizes the growing influence of Chinese power strategies, where one of the aspirations is developing "asymmetric capacities in different domains to balance against the US" (Kennedy 2010, 468).

China's public diplomacy toward Africa, although focused on fostering a sense of mutual solidarity for the purpose of establishing shared identity and correcting perceived asymmetrical relations with Africa, has caused distrust and dissatisfaction toward China (Kim 2018, 2020, cited in Ochieng 2022). To ease international concerns about China's impact on Africa, the Xi Jinping administration sought to "create a new concept, new category and new expression which could be accepted by both Chinese and foreign audiences" (cited in Huang and Wang 2019, 2986). As a result, initiatives such as "Chinese Dream, African

Dream" (Embassy of the PRC in Nepal 2013), "Telling China's Stories well" (Liu 2023) and "Community with a shared future" (Ministry of Foreign Affairs of the PRC 2018) have been used to frame the Chinese government's orientation toward Africa. Since 2021, the Chinese government has emphasized the principle of "partnership of equals," which is said to be the foundation of China–Africa relations in the new era. It states that "China is committed to consolidating China–Africa political mutual trust, expanding pragmatic cooperation with Africa in various areas, and extending its help to boost peace and development in the continent" (Ministry of Foreign Affairs China 2021). Guided by this principle, China is building relationships with Africa using two instruments: non-intervention in African domestic politics and policy, and frequent and reciprocal visits by high-profile politicians from the central government. These instruments have informed Beijing's approach to developing and maintaining China–Africa relations, and are evident in many interactions, including modes of delivery of Chinese aid to Africa (Kalu 2021). Political leaders in Africa have praised the principle of non-intervention and the concepts of respect and recognition as a sign of equality and respect for African countries, including respect for sovereignty and the right to decide their own development model (All Africa 2016; Kalu 2021).

China's policies toward Africa manifest the following trends. First, they go beyond achieving earlier political goals like breaking Western sanctions to multi-dimensional goals spanning politics, economy, culture and the media to boost Chinese growth. Second, one-way assistance to Africa has transitioned toward two-way sustained cooperation, featuring "win-win" outcomes and mutual benefit. Third, it highlights the value of equality in forging partnerships and undertaking collaboration between China and African countries, a perceived deficiency in earlier modes of Sino-African relations that served China's political and economic goals while doing little to improve conditions in Africa (Ochieng 2022). This marks a significant shift from earlier strategic cooperation with Africa that was perceived as mainly reinforcing China's position as a rising global power (Hamdy 2015) and as a model the Chinese state could export to other regions in the pursuit of global leadership (Tomic et al. 2022).

Since 2012, the Chinese leadership has increased the level of resource available to exercising China's diplomatic strategies and accomplishing foreign policy goals in Africa through sport, especially football. With Beijing's reorientation toward "a partnership of equals," potential shifts in China–African relations through sport are illuminating.

Sport and Football in Africa: The Case of South Africa and Beyond

The role of sport in Africa is intertwined with domestic politics and foreign policies. This is well addressed in the scholarship on sports development in African countries, notably football in South Africa (Bogopa 2022; Giampiccoli and Nauright 2019; Ogunnubi 2019; Saavedra 2003), Kenya (Mary and Misiani 2017; Nasong'o 2022), Cameroon (Ayuk 2022a; Lawo-Sukam 2022), Nigeria (Onwumechili 2022; Saavedra 2003), D. R. Congo (Nlandu 2022; Storey 2019), Egypt (Rommel 2021; Tuastad 2014), Ghana (Dankwa 2022; Mehler 2008), Senegal (Diouf and Tine 2023; M'bayo 2022; Saavedra 2003), and Uganda (Manzo 2012; Njororai 2022b, 2014). Former president of South Africa, Nelson Mandela famously asserted the power of sport: "[Sport] has the power to change the world. It has the power to inspire [. . .] It has the power to unite people in a way that little else can. Sport can awaken hope where there was previously despair" (2000, np).

Sports competition and sporting mega-events are used by countries in Africa to boost their international profiles. In Kenya, sporting achievements in track and field have helped to convey a powerful image of the national brand internationally (Mary and Misiani 2017). Based on the achievement of remarkable results in international sporting competitions and increasing involvement in developing sporting programs, South Africa has established a reputation for excellence within the continent and beyond (Lepp and Gibson 2011; Ogunnubi 2019). Indeed, South Africa has emerged as the sporting powerhouse in Africa by staging a set of major global sporting events, including the cricket, rugby and football world cups (Tella and Labuschagne 2018), in addition to achieving a high level of success in athletics, cycling, tennis, boxing, shooting, swimming, rowing, canoeing, rugby and triathlon that surpasses most other African countries (Ogunnubi 2019). Hosting international events in South Africa has significantly contributed to growth in local employment, infrastructure, tourism, social cohesion, and nation building. The success of staging the 2010 FIFA World Cup exhibited South Africa's capacity to deliver infrastructure and leadership and challenged negative stereotypes about Africa (Tella and Labuschagne 2018).

Within African countries, football has become a political vehicle for consolidating or challenging ruling regimes, as well as playing an important role in shaping the collective identity of Africa. This is partly due to football being unequivocally the most popular sport in most African countries. The case of

Egypt is typical, where football diverts attention from domestic issues like corruption and bad governance (Rommel 2021; Thabet 2022). Politicians use football to grow revenues by selling match tickets and broadcasting rights, as well as to boost national pride, showcase national accomplishments, and legitimate the political regime. Egyptian ministries funded the construction of stadiums to exhibit their dominance in domestic politics and the ruling regime gained popularity and legitimacy by relying on the support of Egyptian football coaches, players and sports analysts (Thabet 2022). Simultaneously, social groups, including ultras, have used the mobilizing power of football to challenge the political system by protesting the corruption and poor governance that led to violence, instability, and political turmoil in the country (Thabet 2022).

As in other sectors, African engagement in football has been characterized by marginalization and outside influence. Football was first brought to Africa by European imperialists and the first football match in Africa was played by Europeans in 1862. FIFA has long been dominated by Europe and South America, with its attitudes toward Africa marked by various inequalities (Njororai 2022a). Africa was not involved in the governance of FIFA until 1954, with most of the African countries joining FIFA within the 60 years since independence (Njororai 2022a). Egypt was the first country invited to participate in World Cup competition in 1934, 30 years after the establishment of FIFA in 1904 (Ayuk 2022b). During the first half of the twentieth century, football was associated with colonial exploitation and cultural imperialism (Darby 2000).

In the last years of colonial rule in many African countries, football became a form of resistance and a vehicle for protesting European rule and economic and cultural imperialism. This is represented by the establishment of the Confederation of African Football (CAF) in 1957 by Egypt, Ethiopia, South Africa, and Sudan, which was critical to the continent in a political sense. The establishment of CAF "lent considerable weight to the use of the game as a tool for asserting African and pan-African identity and represented a highly visible podium for mediating that identity both throughout Africa and on a global basis" (Darby 2000, 78). The first African Cup of Nations, hosted by Sudan in 1957 and won by Egypt, raised national consciousness throughout the continent (Darby 2000). Through these events, football has contributed to building African national identities and communicating them to the world (Darby 2000).

Regarding the contribution of football to forging the collective identity of Africa, the 2010 FIFA World Cup hosted by South Africa was treated as a sporting mega-event for the people of the entire African continent (Ndlovu 2010). It was a diplomatic tool showcasing South African leadership credentials but was equally a demonstration of African unity and the Pan-African identity of this event: In short, an African event to be shared with people of African descent (Ndlovu 2010). Likewise, the success of Nigeria and Cameroon winning the Olympic men's football tournaments in 1996 and 2000 represented the continent as much as the individual nations (Njororai 2022a), and consolidated the competitive arrival of African football on the international stage following Cameroon's performance at the 1990 FIFA World Cup (Armstrong and Giulianotti 2004).

Despite the popularity of football across Africa and an exceptional talent base, no African country has won the FIFA World Cup. Only three African countries have reached the quarterfinal stage: Cameroon in 1990, Senegal in 2002, and Ghana in 2010 (Njororai 2022a). The relative underperformance of African football is due to several linked factors. Poor governance of domestic leagues has caused a shortfall in the revenues needed to develop organized grass-root football. Talented local players with limited opportunities for a career in Africa have migrated *en masse* to clubs in Europe and elsewhere. Fans have lost interest in domestic leagues owing to the exodus of the most talented players (Chiweshe 2014; Njororai 2022a). Underpinning these factors is the debilitating issue of corruption (Sugden and Tomlinson 1998, cited in Zahid 2018).

The underdeveloped state of football development in Africa has many similarities with China. The introduction and popularization of modern football in China was also attributed to Europeans. It is recorded modern football was first played by the British in Hong Kong, prior to arriving in mainland China in the late nineteenth century (Fan and Mangan 2003). Leveraging the mass appeal of football to local and international audiences, coupled with its social impact on individual well-being and social solidarity (Birdsall-Strong 2022; Cook et al. 2023), the Chinese state has committed to football development. It does so for the purpose of bolstering national pride, social cohesion and the state's legitimacy, while exhibiting the country's success and influence on the international stage (Li and Juan 2022). However, the failure of Chinese men's national team to qualify for a succession of international tournaments does not match China's emerging superpower status, and a rigid administration system and corruption have hindered progress (Li and Feng 2022).

China's Football Diplomacy in Africa

Sports diplomacy involves using sports people and sporting events to create a favorable image of a country among foreign publics and organizations in support of a state's foreign policy goals (Murray 2012). Sport has been widely acknowledged as a diplomatic tool that serves to bring people, nations, and states together, as well as exhibiting collegial relationships between them (Murray 2012). Sporting mega-events, such as the World Cup and the Olympic Games, attract global media attention and boost tourism and trade in the host city, region, or country, while showcasing a country's accomplishments (Li 2017). Shared values conveyed through sports, such as mutual respect, tolerance, compassion, discipline, equality of opportunity and the rule of law, provide governments with resources to build relationships with foreign stakeholders that can cut across cultural and ethnic barriers (Cook et al. 2023).

The strategies of China's sports diplomacy in Africa have changed from offering tangible assistance with the construction of infrastructure toward initiating cooperation and partnerships. Within the context of the Cold War, Beijing offered funding (e.g., grants, loans, and foreign-aid assistance) to support the construction and renovation of stadiums in Africa to forge political solidarity and alliances with friendly African countries (Ojo 2022). China's stadium diplomacy began in 1958 with the construction of the 12,500-seat National Sports Stadium in Mongolia (Chang and Xue 2019; Song 2021; Wang 2023, cited in Ojo 2022). The substantial number of China-built stadiums in Africa are large and visually prominent, becoming landmarks symbolizing political equality, citizen health and emancipation (Xue et al. 2019), as well as serving as a constant and tangible reminder of China's contribution to the local population (Will 2012). Their presence exemplifies China's international influence, its intention to seek alliances with recipient countries, and the advantages of Chinese firms' access to low-cost and disciplined labor, advanced technologies and materials (Xue et al. 2019). Chinese-built stadiums in Kenya, Tanzania and Senegal have improved bilateral relations between China and these recipient countries (Xue et al. 2019), notwithstanding critics pointing to instrumentalism and self-interest (Tomic et al. 2022; Will 2012).

For most of the 1990s, stadium diplomacy was not the focus of China's diplomatic strategy. It returned to governmental priority due to the quest for enhancing diplomatic cooperation and resource acquisition overseas at the beginning of the 2000s (2000–2020) (Ojo 2022). Following the establishment of FOCAC in 2000, the construction of new China-funded stadiums occurring in the 17-year period (2001–2018) reached at least 34, meaning two stadiums on average per year. This exceeds the total number in the 31-year period prior (1968–1999) (Ojo 2022). This shows the impact of FOCAC as a platform for strengthening consultation and cooperation as well as promoting political dialogue with the aim of achieving mutual reinforcement and cooperation among developing countries (African Union 2023). Again, China's contribution to these stadium projects in Africa is criticized for prioritizing a self-interested agenda and serving the interests of political elites over national interest and the public's socio-economic needs.

Since 2020, aid from China to Africa has decreased. It has also shifted from money for infrastructure to soft cooperation on trade and human capital (Cichocka and Gavas 2021). China's financial commitment dropped from US$60 billion in 2018 to US$40 billion in 2021, including investment, credit lines, trade finance and special drawing rights, signaling Beijing's increasing concern about African indebtedness (Pilling and Hille 2021). The number of committed projects in agricultural assistance, climate and environment, health, peace and security, and trade promotion decreased from 50 in 2018 to just 10 in COVID-disrupted 2021. Opportunities for education and training have declined by 90 percent, from 50,000 government scholarships and 50,000 training opportunities three years ago to a combined 10,000 training opportunities for high-end talents in 2021 (Sun 2021b). Significantly, the word "infrastructure" was absent from President Xi's keynote speech delivered to the eighth FOCAC meeting in 2021. In the corresponding keynote in 2018 it was mentioned four times in the context of enhancing connectivity via building hard infrastructure projects on the ground (Sun 2021b). Infrastructure investment has now been replaced by digital innovation, poverty reduction and agricultural development and trade, marking the shift in China's priorities for cooperation with Africa (Cichocka and Gavas 2021).

Within the context of reducing monetary investments in Africa, the China–Africa Cooperation Vision 2035 was jointly formulated by China and Africa and launched in 2021. The Vision lays out the directions and objectives for cooperation in the medium and long term (Ministry of Commerce of China 2021). It states that the goal of cooperation is to "promote a closer community with a shared future for China and Africa" (Ministry of Commerce of China, 2021). One objective of the Vision is to create common cultural prosperity by improving people-to-people exchanges, especially through generating more vibrant cultural exchange and strengthening practical cooperation in sports. Among other initiatives, this will include China sponsoring the Dakar 2026 Youth Olympic Games (Ministry of Commerce of China 2021).

Guided by the Vision, the narrative pertaining to "friendship" and "cooperation" in connection with "youth" frames numerous partnerships in sport between Africa and China. The meeting between the Association of National Olympic Committees of Africa (ANOCA) and the Chinese Olympic

Committee took place in Hammamet, Tunisia, in June 2023. It articulated key areas of cooperation between China and the African countries with the focus on advocating for the values of sincerity, friendship and progress (APO Group 2023). These include athlete preparation for international events (e.g., the Dakar 2026 Youth Olympic Games), training for coaches, improvement of governance within African National Olympic Committees, mutual support during elections (e.g., for the presidency of the International Olympic Committee), promotion of Olympic values, maintenance and development of sports facilities, and compliance with the Olympic Charters (APO Group 2023). The Vision also highlights mutual support in athletics and football, which are strengths in numerous African countries, and gymnastics and table tennis, in which China excels. Facilitated by the Vision, South Africa and Fujian province, famous for its badminton, have formed a partnership in sports. Chinese representative teams participated in the BRICS Games held in South Africa in October 2023 (SA News 2023). These actions serve to consolidate sport and cultural ties between China and Africa.

The Vision demonstrates a clear alignment with the domestic version of China's "Vision 2035," with its emphasis on collaborative development, including security and governance. Through economic cooperation, China not only bolsters its own economy but addresses domestic demand and enhances the quality of life for the Chinese populace. Furthermore, the emphasis on people-to-people exchanges is integral to China's broader soft-power initiatives on the global stage (Sun 2021a). Since Xi Jinping became the General Secretary of the CCP in 2012 Beijing has released several plans to speed up football development, including prioritizing football education in schools (Tan et al. 2016). Connecting with these state-sponsored programs, the Vision has become a pathway for China to achieve its aspirations internationally.

Discussion

The four stages of the China–Africa relations going back to the 1950s reveal the significant shift in China's policies toward Africa, from the accomplishment of political goals based on one-way assistance to broader socio-economic and political-economic goals using two-way sustained cooperation. These changes are determined by the persistent and pragmatic purpose of strengthening China's domestic growth and international influence. Aligning with the direction of China's foreign policies toward Africa, the analysis of Beijing's diplomatic strategies to engage Africa using sports demonstrates similar trends. This means the transition from donating money for infrastructure toward multi-tiered support for sports development in the hope of creating mutual benefits. This transition is in line with China's ambition to emerge as a major sports country by 2050 (Cockayne et al. 2022).

Although China's relations with Africa have sparked ongoing controversy over Chinese self-interest and negative externalities, sports engagement has the potential to help development. For instance, in Nigeria, the demand for investment and sponsorship of youth sports is high, and participation has been shown to reduce youth crime and increase social stability (Ani 2023). From this perspective, implementing the objectives contained in the Vision would allow Nigeria to overcome economic barriers to developing sports participation, and thereby facilitating social development. The Vision for a shared future for China and Africa based on friendship and cooperation, using sport as a vehicle and guided by the principle of "a partnership of equals" is meaningful, despite mainly Western skepticism. According to Renger et al. (2017), equality-based respect increases perceived autonomy, contributing to satisfaction and social cooperation. Following this logic, "countries that feel respected by others are likely to respond to the respecter in a more cooperative way than they would to others who are disrespectful" (Kalu 2021, 344). Kalu makes the further point that China's non-intervention approach positively contributes to China–Africa relations while validating China's commitment to exercising the principle of a partnership of equals.

The discussion above shows commonalities between China and African countries, including the history and the current state of football development, in addition to the contribution of football in the promotion of governmental agendas, such as the construction of national identity, social cohesion and international influence. This points to the ties in the sports and football fields between China and African counterparts. China and African countries also exhibit complementarities. Africa possesses natural resources but is constrained by the shortage of infrastructure, skills, education, jobs, unity, and stability. China has a demand for the same resources combined with a wealth of "skills, monetary muscle, human capital, a strong work ethic and the historical experience of conquering poverty and attaining the skills that can be used in a liberal market economy to its advantage" (Du Toit 2015, 2). These complementary assets fuel growing interdependence between China and Africa and can act as the foundation for lasting and fruitful relationships between China and its partners in Africa (Du Toit 2015).

We also argue that Sino-African relations have a basis in shared values, specifically the consonances between African humanism (*ubuntu*) and Confucianism. Both sets of values underscore the role of communalism and human solidarity in contributing to collective goals through the shared efforts of individuals in society. These values are manifest in the foreign policies of China and African countries to regulate international relations (Du Toit 2015). The African philology of *ubuntu* underpins long-standing pan-Africanist thought and Africa's quest for the integration of the continent (Ndlovu 2010, 146). It is manifest in South Africa, Nigeria, and Cameroon's performance in football mega-events being framed as belonging to all the peoples of the African continent, conveying the collective identity of Africa to the world through football. Similarly, Confucianism promotes harmonious relations through the universalizing idea that "all human beings are born and brought up in the family, and the world is nothing but an enlarged family" (Chun 2012, xi). Drawing on the tenets of Confucianism, China is keen to be perceived as "a responsible member of the global community working to promote harmonious international relations defined by mutual benefits, equality-based respect, partnership, dialogue, and cooperation" (Kalu 2021, 337). This philosophy forms the basis of "a partnership of equals" in nurturing China–Africa relations, as well as the enactment of the Vision in the sports realm.

Conclusion

The analysis set out in this chapter shows commonalities and mutual reliance between China and African countries. This includes the history and current state of football development disadvantaged by institutionalized problems with administration; the contribution of football to governmental goals; the strategy of embracing youth participation; and the underlying values defining foreign policy; and the consonant philosophies of Chinese Confucianism and African *ubuntu*. Notwithstanding these commonalities, collective memories of colonialism have evoked negative emotions among some Africans (Bobowik et al. 2018), which is likely to affect interpretations of China's foreign policies and economic practices in Africa (Kalu 2021. Indeed, Africans express mixed perceptions about Chinese activities in their countries. Angolans, Kenyans and Nigerians have expressed concerns about the employment of Chinese labor in Africa creating job insecurity for locals and Chinese firms' dominance of Africa's manufacturing industry (Ezirim 2007; Faucon and Su 2010; Le Pere 2006, cited in Kalu 2021). Conversely, Africans have also expressed positive perspectives on China's investment in local infrastructure, economic growth and the respect-based relationship (Besada and O'Bright 2017; Bräutigam 2009; Vhunmbunu 2016, cited in Kalu 2021). While there are unfolding challenges for China's engagement with Africa, collaboration in football as discussed in this chapter represents an opportunity for mutual gains.

References

African Union. 2023. "China–Africa Cooperation Forum (FOCAC)." Accessed October 10. https://au.int/en/partnerships/africa_china.

All Africa. 2016. "Africa: China's Growing Presence in Africa Wins Positive Popular Reviews." *All Africa*, October 24, 2016. https://allafrica.com/stories/201610241620.html.

Ambrosio, Thomas. 2012. "The Rise of the 'China Model' and 'Beijing Consensus': Evidence of Authoritarian Diffusion?" *Contemporary Politics* 18 (4): 381–399.

Ani, Kelechi Johnmary. 2023. "Sports, Youth and Diplomacy: The Social-Economy and Driver of Societal Development in Africa." In *Political Economy of Colonial Relations and Crisis of Contemporary African Diplomacy*, edited by John Chimezie Onu and Reuben Edafenene Ojighoro, 245–253. Palgrave Macmillan.

APO Group. 2023. "Africa and China Fortify Friendship and Cooperation in the Realm of Sports." Accessed October 6. https://guardian.ng/apo-press-releases/africa-and-china-fortify-friendship-and-cooperation-in-the-realm-of-sports/.

Armstrong, Gary, and Richard Giulianotti. 2004. *Football in Africa: Conflict, Conciliation, and Community*. Springer.

Ayeni, Tofe. 2022. "China to Overtake the EU as Africa's Biggest Trade Partner by 2030." Accessed October 06. https://www.theafricareport.com/229297/china-to-overtake-the-eu-as-africas-biggest-trade-partner-by-2030/.

Ayuk, Augustine E. 2022a. "Football in Cameroon, Best of Times, Worst of Times: Exploring the Paradox of Africa's Venerable Football Nation." In *Football (Soccer) in Africa: Origins, Contributions, and Contradictions*, 77–101. Springer.

———. 2022b. "Introduction: Football (Soccer) in Africa: Origins, Contributions, and Contradictions." In *Football (Soccer) in Africa: Origins, Contributions, and Contradictions*, 1–23. Springer.

Batchelor, Kathryn. 2022. "Images of 'Africa'in China–Africa Cooperation." *China Information* 36 (2): 221–240.

Birdsall-Strong, Lottie. 2022. "S01–3 Determining the Social and Economic Value of Football in England." *European Journal of Public Health* 32 (Supplement 2). https://doi.org/10.1093/eurpub/ckac093.004.

Bobowik, Magdalena, Joaquim Pires Valentim, and Laurent Licata. 2018. "Introduction to the Special Issue: Colonial Past and Intercultural Relations." *International Journal of Intercultural Relations* 62: 1–12. https://doi.org/10.1016/j.ijintrel.2017.10.003.

Bogopa, David L. 2022. "Contradictions and Inconsistencies Facing the South African Football Association and the Premier Soccer League." In *Football (Soccer) in Africa: Origins, Contributions, and Contradictions*, 231–252. Springer.

Breslin, Shaun. 2013. "China and the Global Order: Signalling Threat or Friendship?" *International Affairs (London)* 89 (3): 615–634. https://doi.org/10.1111/1468-2346.12036.

Campbell, Horace. 2008. "China in Africa: Challenging US Global Hegemony." *Third World Quarterly* 29 (1): 89–105. https://doi.org/10.1080/01436590701726517.

Chiweshe, Manase Kudzai. 2014. "The Problem with African Football: Corruption and the (under) development of the Game on the Continent." *African Sports Law and Business Bulletin* 2.

Chun, Shan. 2012. *Major Aspects of Chinese Religion and Philosophy: Dao of Inner Saint and Outer King*. Springer.

Cichocka, Beata, and Mikaela Gavas. 2021. "Europe, Take Note: A New Course for China–Africa Relations Set Out at FOCAC 2021." Accessed October 10. https://cgdev.org/blog/europe-take-note-new-course-china-africa-relations-set-out-focac-2021.

Cockayne, David, Simon Chadwick and Jonathan Sullivan. 2022. "Chinese Football—from a State-Led Past to a Digital Future." *Journal of Global Sport Management* 7 (3): 345–354.

Cook, David, Rui Biscaia, Karolos Papadas, Lyndon Simkin, and Libby Carter. 2023. "The Creation of Shared Value in the Major Sport Event Ecosystem: Understanding the Role of Sponsors and Hosts." *European Sport Management Quarterly* 23 (3): 811–832. https://doi.org/10.1080/16184742.2021.1931394.

Dankwa, Kwame B. 2022. "The History and Development of Football in Ghana." In *Football (Soccer) in Africa: Origins, Contributions, and Contradictions*, 165–187. Springer.

Darby, Paul. 2000. "Football, Colonial Doctrine and Indigenous Resistance: Mapping the Political Persona of FIFA's African Constituency." *Culture, Sport Society* 3 (1): 61–87.

DeBoom, Meredith J. 2020. "Who Is Afraid of 'Debt-Trap Diplomacy'? Geopolitical Narratives, Agency and the Multiscalar Distribution of Risk." *Area Development and Policy* 5 (1): 15–22.

Diouf, Djibril, and Cheikh Tidiane Tine. 2023. "Conflicts, Sport, and Proximity in Senegal." *The International Journal of Sport and Society* 15 (1): 29–47. https://doi.org/10.18848/2152-7857/CGP/v15i01/29-47.

Du Toit, Cornel. 2015. "The Rise of China and the Time of Africa: Gauging Afro-Sino Relations in the Light of Confucian Philosophy and African Ideals." *Hervormde Teologiese Studies* 71 (1): 1–10. https://doi.org/10.4102/hts.v71i1.2864.

Fan, Hong, and JA Mangan. 2003. "Will the 'Iron Roses' Bloom Forever? Women's Football in China: Changes and Challenges." *Soccer & Society* 4 (2–3): 47–66. https://doi.org/10.1080/14660970512331390825.

Gertz, Bill. 2000. *The China Threat: How the People's Republic Targets America*. Regnery Publishing.

Giampiccoli, Andrea, and John Nauright. 2019. "Beyond the Reach of FIFA: Football and Community 'Development' in Rural South Africa, towards a Politics of Inclusion and Sustainability." *Soccer and Society* 20 (2): 288–306. https://doi.org/10.1080/14660970.2017.1302937.

Haglund, Dan. 2009. "In It for the Long Term? Governance and Learning among Chinese Investors in Zambia's Copper Sector." *The China Quarterly* 199 (199): 627–646. https://doi.org/10.1017/S0305741009990130.

Hamdy, A. Hassan. 2015. "Contending Hegemony and the New Security Systems in Africa." *African Journal of Political Science and International Relations* 9 (5): 159–169. https://doi.org/10.5897/AJPSIR2015.0772.

Huang, Zhao Alexandre, and Rui Wang. 2019. "Building a Network to "Tell China Stories Well": Chinese Diplomatic Communication Strategies on Twitter." *International Journal of Communication* 13: 2984–3007.

Hutchison, Alan. 1976. *China's African Revolution*. Westview Press.

Jian, Junbo, and Frasheri Donata. 2014. "Neo-colonialism or De-colonialism? Chinas Economic Engagement in Africa and the Implications for World Order." *African Journal of Political Science and International Relations* 8 (7): 185–201. https://doi.org/10.5897/AJPSIR2014.0687.

Kalu, Kenneth. 2021. "'Respect' and 'Agency' as Driving Forces for China–Africa Relations." *Place Branding and Public Diplomacy* 17 (4): 336–347. https://doi.org/10.1057/s41254-020-00178-z.

Kennedy, Scott. 2010. "The Myth of the Beijing Consensus." *The Journal of Contemporary China* 19 (65): 461–477. https://doi.org/10.1080/10670561003666087.

Khan, Humayoun. 2006. "A Historical View of China's Foreign Policy towards Big Powers." *Strategic Studies* XXVI (2): 73–99.

Lawo-Sukam, Alain. 2022. "Vicious Cycle: Cameroon(ization) and/or Foreign(ization) of the Indomitable Lions' Head Coaching." In *Football (Soccer) in Africa: Origins, Contributions, and Contradictions*, 275–297. Springer.

Lepp, Andrew, and Heather Gibson. 2011. "Tourism and World Cup Football amidst Perceptions of Risk: The Case of South Africa." *Scandinavian Journal of Hospitality and Tourism* 11 (3): 286–305. https://doi.org/10.1080/15022250.2011.593361.

Li, Xiufang. 2017. "From Beijing to Rio: Rebranding China via the Modern Olympic Games." *Journal of International Communication* 23 (2): 252–271. https://doi.org/10.1080/13216597.2017.1347101.

Li, Xiufang, and Juan Feng. 2022. "Nation Branding through the Lens of Soccer: Using a Sports Nation Branding Framework to Explore the Case of China." *European Journal of Cultural Studies* 25 (4): 1118–1138. https://doi.org/10.1177/13675494211011179.

Liu, Guangyuan. 2023. "Telling China's Stories Well Is a Glorious Diplomatic Mission." *China Daily*, May 31, 2023. https://www.chinadailyhk.com/article/333551.

M'bayo, Tamba E. 2022. "Soccer in Senegal: National Identity, Commercialization, and Acquisition of Wealth." In *Football (Soccer) in Africa: Origins, Contributions, and Contradictions*, 213–230. Springer.

Mandela, Nelson. 2000. "Nelson Mandela: 'Sport Has the Power to Change the World' Laureus Lifetime Achievement Award—2000." *Speakola*. https://speakola.com/sports/nelson-mandela-laureus-lifetime-achievement-award-2000.

Manzo, Kate. 2012. "Development through Football in Africa: Neoliberal and Postcolonial Models of Community Development." *Geoforum* 43 (3): 551–560. https://doi.org/10.1016/j.geoforum.2011.10.006.

Mary, Mugo, and Mwencha Peter Misiani. 2017. "Applying Anholt's National Branding Model: The Case of Kenya." *Business and Economics Journal* 8 (335): 2.

Mehler, Andreas. 2008. “Political Discourse in Football Coverage—the Cases of Côte d’Ivoire and Ghana.” *Soccer and Society* 9 (1): 96–110. https://doi.org/10.1080/14660970701616787.

Ministry of Commerce of China. 2021. “China–Africa Cooperation Vision 2035.” Accessed October 06. http://www.focac.org/eng/zywx_1/zywj/202201/t20220124_10632442.htm.

Ministry of Foreign Affairs China. 2018. “Beijing Declaration-Toward an Even Stronger China–Africa Community with a Shared Future.” Ministry of Foreign Affairs. Last modified September 5. Accessed December 6. https://www.fmprc.gov.cn/mfa_eng/wjdt_665385/2649_665393/201809/t20180910_679540.html.

Ministry of Foreign Affairs China. 2021. *China and Africa in the New Era: A Partnership of Equals*, edited by Ministry of Foreign Affairs of the People’s Republic of China. Ministry of Foreign Affairs of the People’s Republic of China.

Mlambo, Courage. 2022. “China in Africa: An Examination of the Impact of China’s Loans on Growth in Selected African States.” *Economies* 10 (7): 154. https://doi.org/10.3390/economies10070154.

Mohan, Giles, and Marcus Power. 2008. “New African Choices? The Politics of Chinese Engagement.” *Review of African Political Economy* 35 (115): 23–42. https://doi.org/10.1080/03056240802011394.

Murray, Stuart. 2012. “The Two Halves of Sports-Diplomacy.” *Diplomacy & Statecraft* 23 (3): 576–592. https://doi.org/10.1080/09592296.2012.706544.

Nasong’o, Wanjala S. 2022. “The Politics of Soccer Management in Kenya: The Rise and Decline of a Popular Sport.” In *Football (Soccer) in Africa: Origins, Contributions, and Contradictions*, 189–212. Springer.

Ndlovu, Sifiso Mxolisi. 2010. “Sports as Cultural Diplomacy: the 2010 FIFA World Cup in South Africa’s Foreign Policy.” *Soccer & Society* 11 (1–2): 144–153.

Nepal, Embassy PRC. 2013. “Chinese Dream, African Dream: Achieving Common Development.” Embassy of the People’s Republic of China in Nepal. Last modified August 28. http://np.china-embassy.gov.cn/eng/News/201308/t20130828_1582201.htm.

Njororai, Wycliffe W. Simiyu. 2014. “The History and Identity of East African Football within the African Context.” In *Identity and Nation in African Football: Fans, Community, and Clubs*, 67–80. Springer.

———. 2022a. “FIFA and Football Development in Africa.” In *Football (Soccer) in Africa: Origins, Contributions, and Contradictions*, edited by Augustine E. Ayuk, 25–54. Springer.

———. 2022b. “The Origins, Status, Contributions and Contradictions of Association Football in Uganda.” In *Football (Soccer) in Africa: Origins, Contributions, and Contradictions*, edited by Augustine E. Ayuk, 253–273. Springer.

Nlandu, Tamba. 2022. “Football in DR Congo: A Critical Account of ‘Congolese Football.’ ” In *Football (Soccer) in Africa: Origins, Contributions, and Contradictions*, 125–146. Springer.

Ochieng, Haggai Kennedy. 2022. “China’s Public Diplomacy towards Africa: Strategies, Economic Linkages and Implications for Korea’s Ambitions in Africa.” *East Asian Economic Review* 26 (1): 49–91.

Ogunnubi, Olusola. 2019. “Soft Power and the Currency of Sports: (Re)imagining South Africa’s Rising Hegemony in Africa.” *Global Society* 33 (4): 520–540.

Ojo, Tokunbo. 2022. "Sino-African Sport Diplomacy? 'New' Wave of Chinese Stadiums in African Cities." In *China's International Communication and Relationship Building*, edited by Xiaoling Zhang and Corey Schultz, 216–232. Routledge.

Onwumechili, Chuka. 2022. "Historicizing Football Nigeria: Disciplinary, Governmentality, and Resistance Within Football Labor's Struggle." In *Football (Soccer) in Africa: Origins, Contributions, and Contradictions*, 103–124. Springer.

Pilling, David, and Kathrin Hille. 2021. "China Cuts Finance Pledge to Africa amid Growing Debt Concerns." *Financial Times*, November, 2021. https://www.ft.com/content/b7bd253a-766d-41b0-923e-9f6701176916.

Rapanyane, Makhura B. 2023. "China's International Relations with Africa: A Comparative Analysis of Neo-Colonial Practices in Angola and the DRC." *Journal of African Foreign Affairs* 10 (1): 51.

Renger, Daniela, Sophus Renger, Marcel Miché, and Bernd Simon. 2017. "A Social Recognition Approach to Autonomy: The Role of Equality-Based Respect." *Personality & Social Psychology Bulletin* 43 (4): 479–492. https://doi.org/10.1177/0146167216688212.

Rommel, Carl. 2021. *Egypt's Football Revolution: Emotion, Masculinity, and Uneasy Politics*. University of Texas Press.

SA News. 2023. "SA, China Strengthen Sport Relations." Last modified September 19. Accessed October 6. https://www.sanews.gov.za/south-africa/sa-china-strengthen-sport-relations.

Saavedra, Martha. 2003. "Football Feminine—Development of the African Game: Senegal, Nigeria and South Africa." *Soccer and Society* 4 (2–3): 225–253. https://doi.org/10.1080/14660970512331390925.

Storey, David. 2019. "National Allegiance and Sporting Citizenship: Identity Choices of 'African' Footballers." *Sport in Society* 23 (1): 1–14.

Sun, Yun. 2021a. "An Examination of the 2035 Vision for China–Africa Cooperation." Brookings. Last modified December 27. https://www.brookings.edu/articles/an-examination-of-the-2035-vision-for-china-africa-cooperation/.

———. 2021b. "FOCAC 2021: China's Retrenchment from Africa?" Brookings. Last modified December 6. https://www.brookings.edu/articles/focac-2021-chinas-retrenchment-from-africa/.

Tan, Tien-Chin, Hsien-Che Huang, Alan Bairner, and Yu-Wen Chen. 2016. "Xi Jin-Ping's World Cup Dreams: From a Major Sports Country to a World Sports Power." *International Journal of the History of Sport* 33 (12): 1449–1465. https://doi.org/10.1080/09523367.2016.1243103.

Taylor, Ian. 2006. *China and Africa: Engagement and Compromise*. 1st ed. Vol. 10. *Routledge Contemporary China Series*. Routledge.

Tella, Oluwaseun, and Pieter Labuschagne. 2018. "Sport, Politics, and Diplomacy: Perspectives on Durban's (South Africa) Bid to Host the 2022 Commonwealth Games." *Politikon* 45 (3): 408–425.

Thabet, Hala. 2022. "Football in Egypt: Between Joy and Politics." In *Football (Soccer) in Africa: Origins, Contributions, and Contradictions*, edited by Ayuk Augustine E., 147–163. Springer.

Tomic, Dusko, Eldar Saljic, and Mohamed Badine El Yattioui. 2022. "Specific Projection of China's Soft Power in Africa: A New Security Paradigm." *Journal of Liberty and International Affairs* 8 (3): 368–377. https://doi.org/10.47305/JLIA2283368t.

Tuastad, Dag. 2014. "From Football Riot to Revolution. The political Role of Football in the Arab World." *Soccer and Society* 15 (3): 376–388. https://doi.org/10.1080/14660970.2012.753541.

Will, Rachel. 2012. "China's Stadium Diplomacy." *World Policy Journal* 29 (2): 36–43. https://doi.org/10.1177/0740277512451487.

Xue, Charlie QL, Guanghui Ding, Wei Chang, and Yan Wan. 2019. "Architecture of "Stadium Diplomacy"-China-Aid Sport Buildings in Africa." *Habitat International* 90: 101985.

Zahid, Mustafa. 2018. "Corruption and Soccer in Africa: Empirical Evidence on the Determinants of Association Soccer Success in the Continent." BA thesis, University of San Francisco. https://repository.usfca.edu/honors/19/.

Zhang, Hong. 2023. *From Contractors to Investors? Evolving Engagement of Chinese State Capital in Global Infrastructure Development and the Case of Lekki Port in Nigeria* (Working Paper). Johns Hopkins University, China Africa Research Initiative. https://www.econstor.eu/handle/10419/268870.

Zhang, Lili. 2015. *A Brief History of Contemporary Chinese Diplomacy*. Shanghai People's Publishing House.

4

China's Comprehensive Engagement with North Africa and Middle East: Economic, Political, and Sports Relations

Mahfoud Amara[1] and Youcef Bouandel[2]

Introduction

Over the past several decades the geopolitical landscape has experienced significant shifts, particularly marked by the resurgence of Russia and the rise of China as a global economic power. In this context, China's historical ties with the Middle East and North African (MENA) countries have evolved substantially. Originally rooted in support for independence struggles and anti-imperialist causes, China has recently intensified its role in the region through significant investment and cooperative initiatives such as the China-Arab States Cooperation Forum (2004) and the China-Gulf Cooperation Council Strategic Dialogue (2010).

China's multifaceted engagement in the MENA region, primarily driven by its energy needs and the desire for market expansion under initiatives like the Belt and Road, aims to ensure regional stability. Concurrently, MENA countries have shown a growing openness to China's approach, particularly attracted by its principle of non-interference, allowing them to pursue economic growth independently from traditional Western powers. China's influence extends beyond

1 Mahfoud Amara, Associate Professor, Qatar University, mamara@qu.edu.qa.
2 Youcef Bouandel, Professor, Qatar University, ybouandel@qu.edu.qa.

oil, leveraging soft power through medical aid during the COVID-19 pandemic, cultural exchanges and educational collaborations.

A noteworthy aspect of this engagement is China's utilization of sports diplomacy as a strategic tool. This modern approach, rooted in historical ties, encompasses not only economic investments and infrastructure development but also fosters political dialogue. Sports have become a conduit for market expansion, relationship-building with MENA decision-makers, and access vectors to essential resources. China's investments in sports infrastructure are particularly significant, enhancing the MENA region's capacity to host major events and furthering its geopolitical and economic influence.

This chapter assesses China's strategic and multifaceted engagement with the MENA region, covering economic, political, cultural, and sports aspects. It will analyze China's goals and the proactive role of MENA countries in shaping their interactions to fulfill regional and international objectives. The focus will be on China's extensive involvement in sports and soft power, with specific attention to North African countries like Algeria, Tunisia, and Morocco, to understand the growing presence and influence of China in the region.

Historical Background

Diplomatic relations were initially established with Egypt in 1956, and later the same year relations were established with Algeria, Iraq, Morocco, North Yemen, Syria, and Sudan (Rózsa 2021). After the establishment of the People's Republic of China (PRC) in 1949 and subsequent Cold War period, China sought to consolidate the new regime and navigate foreign relations in a divided world. Mao Zedong's adopted a diplomatic strategy of leaning to one side, that is, establishing close ties to the Soviet Union and the socialist camp, but he also emphasized developing relations with Third World countries in Africa, Asia, and Latin America. At the heart of this policy was opposition to the imperialist and capitalist bloc headed by the USA. The Bandung Conference in Indonesia in 1955, which laid the foundation for the creation of the Non-Aligned Movement (NAM) and its future role in a bipolar world, provided the setting for China to develop and enhance its relations with African countries, including those in the MENA region (Lu 2012, 38).

Given China's anti-imperialist stance, along with like-minded countries such as newly independent Egypt, India, and Indonesia, it came as no surprise that representatives of colonized countries were invited to the Bandung Conference.

Furthermore, in the sports sector, China defied football's highest authority, FIFA, by disregarding threats against any country that played against Algeria's FLN football team. In 1958, several high-profile Algerian players operating in France, such as Mekhloufi, answered the FLN's call and fled to Tunisia. There, the FLN football team was assembled and played almost 100 games to raise awareness about Algeria's struggle for independence. These games were played against teams from friendly countries, including China. China was the first non-Arab country to recognize the Provisional Government of the Republic of Algeria (GPRA) shortly after its establishment in 1958 (Lafargue 2008). China's issues with international sport were exacerbated by its unilateral decision to withdraw from the International Olympic Committee (IOC) and other sporting organizations in 1958 over the IOC's decision to allow athletes from both the PRC and the Republic of China (Taiwan) to compete, despite efforts by the PRC to have Taiwan expelled. Avery Brundage, Secretary-General of the IOC, reminded the Chinese that a distinct and internationally recognized government existed in Taiwan, whereas the United Nations did not at that time recognize the PRC. Throughout the 1960s, the PRC did not participate in the Olympic Games, leaving the door open for Taiwan to participate in international sports events (Chan 1985).

In its pursuit of a prominent position in the Third World, China helped Indonesia to organize the first Games of Newly Emerging Forces (GANEFO) in 1963. High-ranking members of the Chinese leadership, including Prime Minister Zhou Enlai, frequently met with athletes from friendly countries when they visited China (An et al. 2012, 274). Several Arab and North African countries, including Algeria, Iraq, Lebanon, Morocco, Palestine, Saudi Arabia, Somalia, The United Arab Union (Egypt and Syria) and Tunisia, participated in the event.

Technology, Infrastructure Development, and Energy Cooperation

China's interests in MENA extend beyond natural resources to encompass trade, security, and diplomatic influence (Xinhua 2023). It intervenes in a shifting regional order in the Arab world, marked by changes in power dynamics and divergent developments among Arab states, which according to Rózsa suits China's tendency "to not perceive the Middle East and North Africa as one unit, and fits its practice of maintaining bilateral relations with the regional states, instead of a regional approach" (2021, 68). Since the beginning of the twenty-first century, China's presence, notably its economic footprint, has witnessed substantial growth in the MENA region. First and foremost, China's increasing need for energy resources, primarily from the MENA region, is driven by the imperative to support its ongoing economic growth. The region's energy reserves are of paramount importance to China's energy security. Second, China's Belt and Road Initiative (BRI) extends its influence through various MENA countries, facilitating infrastructure development and economic connectivity along these strategic routes. Third, the Chinese central government has initiated numerous mega-investment projects in the region, making it an attractive destination for other sources of Chinese capital. The comprehensive analysis of these dynamics is vividly depicted in the infographics crafted by the Centre for Strategic and International Studies, as presented in the report Dire Straits: China's Pursuit of Energy Security in the Middle East (Fuaiole et al. 2023). This report assesses China's multifaceted approach, encompassing both commercial and military strategies, aimed at ensuring the safety of its oil imports and the unobstructed flow of energy resources. Related investments, such as in ports at Ain Sokhna in Egypt and Hamdania in Algeria, have significantly impacted the economic landscape of these countries and raised concerns about potential military uses in the future (Andersen and Lons 2020, 94–95). Fourth, the MENA region encompasses some of the world's most critical maritime routes, including the Strait of Hormuz, the Suez Canal, and Bab el Mandeb. These routes are vital for the continuous flow of energy resources to China and the success of its BRI projects (Fuaiole et al. 2023). Furthermore, the growing engagement of China in the Middle East and its strategic alliances with the MENA region are underscored by the landmark events of the inaugural China-Arab States Summit and the inaugural China-Gulf Cooperation Council (GCC) Summit, both convened in 2022 (Eslami and Papageorgiou 2023).

It is important to recognize that some governments in the MENA region are contemplating China as a potential alternative or counterbalancing force to the United States. This consideration extends to initiatives aimed at addressing global conflicts, exemplified by the recent rapprochement between Saudi Arabia and Iran as part of their involvement in the Global Security Initiative (Hale 2023). Furthermore, China's sustained presence and expansion in the MENA region, often at the expense of Western countries, can be attributed to its adherence to the principle of non-interference and respect for national sovereignty in its foreign relations (Chaziza 2021). Unlike Western nations, which often condition foreign aid and investment on human rights considerations and influence in the domestic affairs of other countries, China typically adheres to a non-interference policy when it comes to the internal affairs of other nations, seeking reciprocation in terms of respecting its own sensitivities. China emphasizes a policy of "developmental peace" in the belief that economic development is essential for stability and peace (Wong 2021). This approach underpins China's primary focus on trade and investment, avoiding direct involvement in issues pertaining to human rights, governance and liberalization. Critics argue that reliance on China may ultimately compromise the sovereignty of recipient countries and limit their capacity to address governance and human rights concerns. Yet, it is indisputable that China's strategy has produced concrete benefits, particularly in the realm of infrastructure development. Numerous countries have witnessed substantial improvements in their infrastructure, courtesy of Chinese investments and projects. Consequently, this has not only bolstered China's economic influence but also enhanced its geopolitical standing in the MENA region and elsewhere in the developing world.

China's economic influence in North Africa and the Middle East region continues to expand. China's trade volume with MENA countries reached approximately US$368.4 billion in 2022 (Every CRS Report 2023; Sidlo 2020). The massive investment in infrastructure has not only stimulated economic growth but has also facilitated increased regional trade. It is estimated that between 2013 and 2021, MENA countries received approximately US$152.4 billion in investment and construction financing from China. From 2005 to 2022, Chinese investments and contracts in the MENA region totaled US$273 billion (Foreign Affairs Committee 2022). Notably, the region has become an important partner in China's energy strategy. China's commitment to addressing the region's energy needs is exemplified by initiatives like the US$30 billion North Field natural gas expansion project in Qatar. Through such investments in energy projects, China ensures a stable and sustainable energy supply. Beyond physical infrastructure and energy projects, China's involvement in the MENA extends to technology transfer, including in the military sector. There have been reports of China sharing sensitive ballistic missile technology to support domestic production capabilities in MENA countries (Materson 2022). This technology transfer underscores China's dedication to bolstering the military capabilities of its regional partners while promoting collaboration in defense and security. This approach places China in competition with Europe and the USA, traditionally the main suppliers in this domain, and there is apprehension among these traditional suppliers regarding the proliferation of ballistic missile technology in a region already marked by volatility. Table 4.1 provides an overview of China's volume of investment in MENA and Turkey.

China's Sport Diplomacy and Soft Power

Over the years, sport diplomacy has played a significant role in China's foreign relations strategy. The early 1970s famously marked the inception of ping-pong diplomacy, that led to a series of diplomatic exchanges between China and the United States. China in this period also advanced the idea of "friendship first, competition second," to emphasize the importance of building international rapport through sports. The concept underscores the significance of fostering friendships and facilitating mutual understanding through sports, placing greater emphasis on these aspects than on competitive outcomes. It facilitated exchanges with socialist nations and enhanced China's global presence, particularly during periods of relative isolation in the 1950s and 60s (An et al. 2021).

Former Chinese Foreign Minister Qian Qichen formally conceptualized sports diplomacy in 2005, defining it as foreign sports exchanges orchestrated by a country's sports authorities to bolster international relationships. This definition underscores the strategic importance of sports in Chinese diplomacy and the significance of sport as a tool to achieve diplomatic objectives, strengthen foreign relations and advance national interests (Lu 2012; Wang 2023; Zhao 2022). In their comprehensive analysis, Lu et al. chronicle the various phases of China's sporting diplomacy journey, starting from its early use of sports to consolidate the new regime and learn from the Soviet Union. This trajectory culminates in the contemporary strategy of "major country diplomacy" with Chinese characteristics (Wang 2019).

A turning point in China's sports diplomacy narrative unfolded with the hosting of the 2008 Beijing Olympics. This mega-event left an indelible mark on the country's global standing across multiple dimensions. The 2008 Summer Olympics showcased China's exceptional organizational capabilities and positioned it as a dominant force across diverse sports disciplines, ultimately leading the medal table. Culturally, the Olympics provided an expansive platform for China to showcase its rich cultural heritage. Economically, the event triggered substantial infrastructural development in Beijing, fostering economic growth and urban transformation. Furthermore, the successful execution of the Olympics contributed significantly to enhancing China's reputation as a global economic powerhouse. Politically, the Olympics afforded China a strategic opportunity to

Table 4.1 Chinese volume of investment in the MENA region

Aspect	Details
China's Influence on MENAT	
Oil Imports	PRC imports half of its oil from the Middle East; top oil customers of Saudi Arabia and Iran
BRI Investments	MENAT accounts for 28.5 % of BRI investments in 2021
Strategic Partnerships	Comprehensive strategic partnerships with Algeria, Egypt, Iran, Saudi Arabia, and UAE; Strategic partnerships with Iraq, Jordan, Kuwait, Morocco, Oman, Qatar, and Turkey
Huawei's Presence	12 5G contracts in the Middle East
China's Foreign Investment in MENAT	
Total Investments (2005–2022)	$273 billion
Investment Growth (2021)	Increased by an estimated 360 %
Construction Growth (2021)	Rose by 116 % relative to 2020
Industrial Park Plans (2018)	Link industrial parks with ports in Saudi Arabia, UAE, Oman, and Egypt
Most Exposed Countries to PRC	Jordan, Oman, and Iraq
China and the Energy Sector in MENAT	
Total Investment (2005–2022)	Over $126 billion in the MENAT energy sector
Energy's Share of Investment	46 % of PRC investment in the region
Key Energy Partnerships	Iraq (Al-Khairat heavy oil power plant and Mansuriya gas field); Qatar (North Field natural gas expansion project); Saudi Aramco and Sinopec refinery in Yanbu
Security and Research Partnerships	
Ballistic Missile Technology	Transferred to Saudi Arabia

Continued

Table 4.1 *Continued*

Aspect	Details
Military Exercises	Egypt hosted the PLA Navy and Russian Navy in a counter-piracy training exercise; the PLA Navy conducted port calls in every GCC country, Israel, Egypt, and Iran
Research Centers	Defense research center in Abu Dhabi in partnership with UAE defense company
China's Weapons Sales in MENAT	
Total Arms Export (2005–2021)	$307.7 billion to 12 MENAT countries
Top Recipients	Algeria ($1 billion), Morocco ($478 million), Saudi Arabia ($318 million), Turkey ($252 million), Egypt ($221 million)
Drone Purchasers	UAE (22.1 %), Saudi Arabia (19.3 %), and Egypt (15.5 %)
China's Diplomacy in MENAT	
China-Arab States Cooperation Forum	Biennial meetings between China and 22 Arab League members
UN Security Council Vetoes	Eleven of the 16 vetoes since 2011 have been on Syria
China's Soft Power in MENAT	
Tourism	Increased tourism from the PRC in the Middle East
Confucius Institutes	22 institutes in 12 MENAT countries
Expos and Events	China-Arab States Expo; Huawei's GITEX Technology Week in Dubai
China's Broadcasts and Media Cooperation in MENAT	
Collaborations	China Intercontinental Communication Center with Image Nation in UAE
Publications	Arabic version of China Today in the Middle East
Social Media	CGTN's Arabic-language Facebook account has 14.4 million followers
Media Agreements	Xinhua's exchange agreement with Daily News Egypt

Source: Adapted from Foreign Affairs Committee. 2022. "China Regional Snapshot: Middle East and North Africa—Committee on Foreign." Last Modified May 30. https://foreignaffairs.house.gov/china-regional-snapshot-middle-east-and-north-africa/.

assert itself on the global stage. It not only demonstrated the nation's capacity to host a significant international event but also emphasized its growing influence in international geopolitics, marking a shift in global perceptions of China's role in world affairs.

China's sports diplomacy has evolved from being a tool for political confrontation during the Cold War to a means of enhancing international relations in the contemporary globalized world. This evolution mirrors China's transition from traditional to new diplomacy, with sports diplomacy viewed as a more socially embedded form of diplomacy, often involving grassroots movements, civil society organizations, and young people. This transformation reflects broader changes in international relations, where non-state actors and individual citizens play increasingly pivotal roles (Zhang 2013).

China's Engagement in Sports Diplomacy and Enterprise across MENA

China's sport engagement in the MENA region has been characterized by a series of infrastructure and construction projects, particularly under the auspices of the BRI. PowerChina, a prominent Chinese construction entity, has played a leading role in these endeavors, contributing to the development of roads, bridges, power plants, and other critical infrastructure components. When it comes to the geopolitics of sport in the region China is in competition with Turkey, which enjoys proximity and historical ties to the region. Both China and Turkey are striving to expand their influence and economic connections. Despite a brief slowdown between 2013 and 2020, Turkey's trade with the Gulf has roared back, hitting US$22 billion, while Gulf nations have become major investors, injecting US$15.8 billion and accounting for 7.1 percent of Turkey's foreign direct investment since 2020 (Çubukçuoğlu and Almarzouki 2023). Unlike China, Turkey can leverage its unique position in the region beyond geographical and cultural proximity. Its membership in NATO grants it additional influence, particularly in the realm of security and defense cooperation. Both countries, however, are actively seeking investment opportunities in sports infrastructure across the region. They were involved in the construction of stadiums for the Qatar World Cup. China Railway Construction Corporation (CRCC) was Hamad Bin Khalid Contracting Company Contracting's joint venture partner for Lusail Stadium in Qatar. Aljaber Engineering and Turkish contractor Tekfen Construction partnered for the construction of the 40,000-seater Al-Thumama Stadium (Iqbal

2023). This highlights the competitive nature of their involvement in a region that is increasingly gaining significance as a hub for global sporting events. Countries like Qatar, UAE and Saudi Arabia are expanding their influence as direct investors in the sports industry. These countries are hosting international sport events, investing in and sponsoring football clubs for nation branding, soft power and economic diversification domestically and internationally (Al-Arian 2022; Chadwick et al. 2023; Chavanat et al. 2017; Rieche and Brannagan 2022). This will continue, with major sporting events being held in both Qatar and Saudi Arabia, including the 2023 Asian Football Confederation (AFC) Asian Cup, the 2030 Asian Games, the Asian Winter Games in 2029, and the 2034 FIFA World Cup. This model is also being pursued by other North African countries, such as Morocco, which is set to host the 2025 African Cup of Nations, co-host the 2030 FIFA World Cup, and has expressed interest in bidding to host the FIFA Women's World Cup.

Through sports diplomacy, China positions itself as a partner for development and cooperation, gaining the favor of nations in Africa and the Middle East (Liu 2023). It has formalized cooperation agreements in various sports with countries such as Algeria, Morocco, and Tunisia. These agreements encompass a wide range of sports which will be the focus of the subsequent section.

Algeria

In recent years, China has been involved in sports infrastructure projects in Algeria as part of its broader economic cooperation with the country, following Algeria's participation in the BRI in 2019. According to Belguidoum (2023), the number of Chinese companies operating in Algeria increased from 480 in 2007 to 1,200 in 2020, accounting for 9 percent of total foreign companies. A Chinese enterprise completed the Oran Multifunctional Sports Center in Algeria in 2022, featuring a 40,000-seat stadium and a multifunctional training facility. This center is expected to play a significant role in promoting sports development and hosting major sporting events in the country, including the 2022 Mediterranean Games and the 2023 Arab Games. These tournaments mark Algeria's return to the international sports arena after a decade of turmoil in the 1990s, signaling its ambition to host regional and international sports events. The last major tournament organized by Algeria was in 1990, when it coincidentally secured its first AFCON title. Following FIFA World Cup qualifications in 1982 and 1986, Algerian national team fans had to wait until 2010 and 2014 for another World

Cup qualification, and it was not until 2019 that they witnessed Algeria winning AFCON for the second time. The Pan-Arab Games, rebranded as the Arab Sports Games, were held in July 2023 in cities across Algeria, including Algiers, Oran, and Constantine. This edition marked the resumption of the Arab Games after a decade of interruption: The previous edition was hosted in Qatar in 2011, coinciding with the Arab Spring.

China's participation in sports infrastructure projects in Algeria is a component of its wider economic cooperation with the country. In 2022, China committed to investing US$36 billion in Algeria across multiple sectors, including manufacturing, new technologies, the knowledge economy, transportation, and agriculture. This investment is anticipated to stimulate economic growth, create employment opportunities in Algeria, and thereby support its stated ambition to join BRICS. In August 2023 in a meeting in Johannesburg, the BRICS group of emerging economies agreed to invite Argentina, Saudi Arabia, Egypt, Ethiopia, the UAE and Iran to join the bloc. The expansion of BRICS is testament to the importance China attaches to multilateralism, and a forum in which it is the major actor. That important regional actors like Algeria aspire to join BRICS is a signal of its resonance among emerging economies, and a level of comfort in engaging with China.

Tunisia

In 2018, China provided aid and technical support for the construction of a youth center in Tunisia. It offered Tunisian youth a space and activities, while also becoming a prominent venue for culture and sports. In 2021, Tunisia and China signed an economic and technical cooperation agreement encompassing various fields, including sports. Building on this collaboration, in 2022, China completed the Ben Arous Sports and Cultural Center for Youth in northeastern Tunisia. This new facility has now been delivered and is poised to provide increased opportunities for cultural and sports activities for Tunisian youth. During a meeting in 2022, Chinese President Xi Jinping expressed China's willingness to expand exchanges in human resources, sub-national interactions, and non-governmental exchanges with Tunisia, including in the field of sports. In 2021, Huawei announced a collaboration with the large retail chain GO Sport, which specializes in the distribution of sports equipment and clothing and has four points of sale in La Marsa, Azur City, Mall of Sousse and Downtown. This collaboration offers a comprehensive range of clothing, shoes, accessories, and sports equipment for women, men and children (Radio IFM 2021). The same company has been actively involved in sponsoring sports events and sports clubs in Tunisia, including the funding of a friendly match between Etoile Sportive du Sahel (ESS) and Ligue 1 club Olympique Marseille held in July 2015 to commemorate the 90th anniversary of the Tunisian Club's founding. In 2021, the Chinese Basketball Association signed a Memorandum of Understanding with the Tunisian Basketball Federation to promote basketball development in Tunisia. The Tunisian Olympic Committee and its Chinese counterpart signed a partnership agreement in June 2023 in Hammamet, Tunisia, marking a significant advance in sports development and bilateral relations. This agreement, signed by Mehrez Boussayene, the President of the Tunisian Olympic Committee, and Gao Zhidan, the Chinese Minister of Sports, focuses on fostering youth support and advancing Tunisian sports. High-level officials, including Kamal Deguiche, the Tunisian Minister of Youth and Sports, and Mustapha Berraf, the President of the Association of National Olympic Committees of Africa, were in attendance, underscoring the agreement's importance. It promises material and logistical benefits, such as providing sports equipment, facilitating expertise exchange, and training sports personnel. The agreement, marking Tunisia the first African nation to engage with China on this scale, aims to leverage Tunisian athletic achievements to boost the country's international image and sports diplomacy. It envisions establishing Tunisia as a prime sports destination in Africa, reinforcing its role in hosting global athletes (Tunisian Ministry of Sport 2023).

Morocco

China and Morocco established diplomatic relations in November 1958, and their political ties have grown stronger over the years. Morocco has traditionally been considered an ally of the US in the region, especially when compared to neighboring Algeria, which maintained closer ties with the communist bloc. Nevertheless, in 2016, Morocco established a strategic partnership with China, signaling its intent to seek political and economic partners beyond its traditional market in Europe. This shift is noteworthy given the European Union's trade relations with Morocco, concerns over the unresolved Western Sahara issue, and disputes over the exploitation of phosphate and fisheries in contested territories.

In August 2022, Morocco reaffirmed its commitment to the One-China policy, recognizing the People's Republic of China as the sole legitimate government of China. This move appears to be aimed at securing China's support and recognition of Western Sahara as an integral part of Moroccan territory, contrary to UN resolutions supported by the United States, Spain, and Israel in favor of Western Sahara's autonomy under Moroccan sovereignty. Bilateral exchanges between China and Morocco have seen substantial growth, increasing by 50 percent from US$4 billion (€3.5 billion) in 2016 to US$6 billion in 2021. Over 80 Chinese investment projects are currently in progress in Morocco, with Chinese direct investment reaching US$380 million (AFP 2022).

Chinese companies have actively engaged in sports development projects in Morocco, displaying a growing partnership in this sector. In 2019, the Chinese government committed US$10 million to support Moroccan sports initiatives, including the provision of telecommunication equipment for Casablanca's Mohammed V Stadium. The following year, Huawei formed a partnership with the Moroccan government to foster the growth of the country's digital sports industry, signifying a shift toward modernizing sports through technology. Further solidifying this trend, in 2022, Anta Sports, another Chinese company, entered a sponsorship deal with the Moroccan Olympic Committee. This collaboration gains particular significance in light of Morocco's expanding role in the global sports arena, highlighted by its hosting of the 2025 AFCON and its joint bid with Spain and Portugal for the 2030 FIFA World Cup. These developments present lucrative opportunities for Chinese companies to further their involvement in various sports-related ventures in Morocco, aligning with the country's evolving sports landscape and its growing international sports prominence. Other projects related to the construction of football stadiums in Morocco and in the MENA region are illustrated in Table 4.2.

Conclusion

China's expanding presence in the MENA region, driven by its quest for energy and substantial regional investments, is not only reshaping the political landscape but also the world of sports, signaling a significant shift in global politics and economics. This presence positions MENA as a key market for Chinese goods, challenging traditional Western influence. The shared principle of noninterference has fortified China-MENA ties, aligning China's need for stability with MENA's pursuit of economic growth as well as the region's growing ambitions in international sport. Sports diplomacy has emerged as a significant component of China's multifaceted engagement in the region. This contemporary approach, deeply rooted in historical ties, encompasses not only

Table 4.2 Selection of major past, current, and future projects involving Chinese construction companies

Chinese Company	MENA Country	Sports Arena Project	Completion Date
China State Construction Engineering Corporation (CSCEC)	Qatar	Lusail Iconic Stadium	2022
China National Technical Import & Export Corporation (CNTIC)	Egypt	New Cairo Stadium	2019
China Railway Group Limited (CREC)	Saudi Arabia	King Fahd International Stadium	2014
Beijing Construction Group (BCG)	United Arab Emirates	Hazza bin Zayed Stadium	2013
Shanghai Construction Group (SCG)	Morocco	Stade Mohammed VI	2011
China State Construction Engineering Corporation (CSCEC)	Qatar	Ras Abu Aboud Stadium	2022
China National Technical Import & Export Corporation (CNTIC)	Egypt	New Administrative Capital Stadium	2023
China Railway Group Limited (CREC)	Saudi Arabia	King Abdullah Sports City Stadium	2023
Zhejiang Construction Investment Group Co., Ltd.	Algeria	Stade de Douera	2023
China State Construction Engineering Corporation (Cscec)	Saudi Arabia	Jeddah Superdome	2026
China National Technical Import & Export Corporation (Cntic)	Egypt	New Cairo International City Stadium	2025
China Railway Group Limited (Crec)	Morocco	Casablanca Grand Stadium	2024

Source: Authors' own compilation.

economic investment and infrastructure development but also facilitates political dialogue. Sport serves as a conduit for market expansion, relationship-building with MENA decision-makers, and access to essential resources. Moreover, China's investments in sports infrastructure boost the region's capability to host major events, furthering its own geopolitical and economic influence. The strategic depth of China's involvement in the MENA region is significant. By integrating various elements China's engagement reflects its global ambitions, while MENA countries strategically use this relationship to meet their own objectives. This interplay is not only shaping regional dynamics but also global trends, necessitating ongoing study to understand its evolving implications for international relations.

References

AFP. 2022. "Nouvelles Routes de la Soie: Le Maroc et la Chine Scellent Leur Partenariat." 6 January, 2022. Available at: https://www.bfmtv.com/economie/international/nouvelles-routes-de-la-soie-le-maroc-et-la-chine-scellent-leur-partenariat_AD-202201060049.html Accessed 7 September, 2023.

Al-Arian, Abdullah. 2022. *Football in the Middle East, State, Society, and the Beautiful Game.* Oxford University Press.

Andersen, Lars Eerslev, and Camille Lons. 2020. "The Geopolitical Implications of China's Presence in the MENA Region." In *The Role of China in the Middle East and North Africa (MENA). Beyond Economic Interests? Euromesco Joint Policy Paper 16*, edited by Katarzyna W. Sidlo. European Institute of the Mediterranean.

An, Yalun, Wang Xueshuang, and Fujun Xiang. 2021. "The Evolution of China's Sporting Diplomacy since 1949: The History, Experience and Promotion Strategies." *Journal of the Croatian Anthropological Society* 45 (3): 271–283.

Belguidoum, Saïd. 2008. "Algérie: fantasmes et réalité de la présence chinoise" [Algeria: Fantasies and Reality of the Chinese Presence]. *Moyen-Orient* 58: 42–46.

BF MTV. 2023. "Nouvelles routes de la soie: Le Maroc et la Chine scellent leur partenariat." Last modified 7 September. https://www.bfmtv.com/economie/international/nouvelles-routes-de-la-soie-le-maroc-et-la-chine-scellent-leur-partenariat_AD-202201060049.html.

Chadwick, Simon, Widdop, Paul, and Michael M. Goldman. 2023. *The Geopolitical Economy of Sport: Power, Politics, Money, and the State.* Taylor & Francis.

Chan, Gerald. 1985. "The 'Two Chinas' Problem and the Olympic Formula." *Pacific Affairs* 58 (3): 473–490.

Chanavat Nicolas, Desbordes Michel, and Lorgnier Nicolas. 2017. *Routledge Handbook of Football Marketing.* Routledge.

Chaziza, Mordechai. 2021. "China's Strategy to Maintain its Non-interference Policy: The Safety of Chinese Travellers in the Middle East." *China: An International Journal* 19 (1): 50–67.

Çubukçuoğlu, Serhat S., and Mouza H. Almarzooqi. 2023. "What's Behind Growing Ties Between Turkey and the Gulf States." Atlantic Council. Last modified July 21. https://www.atlanticcouncil.org/blogs/turkeysource/whats-behind-growing-ties-between-turkey-and-the-gulf-states/.

Eslami, Mohammad, and Maria Papageorgiou. 2023. "China's Increasing Role in the Middle East: Implications for Regional and International Dynamics." *Georgetown Journal of International Affairs*. Last modified June 2, https://gjia.georgetown.edu/2023/06/02/chinas-increasing-role-in-the-middle-east-implications-for-regional-and-international-dynamics/.

Every CRS Report. 2023. "China and the Middle East and North Africa (MENA)." Last modified August 4. https://www.everycrsreport.com/reports/IF12469.html.

Foreign Affairs Committee. 2022. "China Regional Snapshot: Middle East and North Africa—Committee on Foreign." Last modified 30 May. https://foreignaffairs.house.gov/china-regional-snapshot-middle-east-and-north-africa/.

Foster, Scott. 2022. "Belt & Road Reaching Far and Wide in the Middle East." *Asia Times*, March 7, 2022. https://asiatimes.com/2022/03/belt-road-reaching-far-and-wide-in-middle-east/.

Funaiole, Matthew P., Brian, Hart Brian, and Lily McElwee. 2023. "Dire Straits: China's Push to Secure Its Energy Interests in the Middle East." Last modified February 23. https://features.csis.org/hiddenreach/china-middle-east-military-facility/.

Hale, Erin. 2023. "Can China Replace the US in the Middle East?" *Aljazeera*, April 25, 2023. https://www.aljazeera.com/features/2023/4/25/can-china-replace-the-us-in-the-middle-east.

Hindustan Times Tech. 2023. "Chinese Contractors Win Over 50% of MENA Sports Stadium Contracts." *International Construction*. Last modified 6 September. https://tech.hindustantimes.com/photos/170foot-wide-asteroid-2023-qe8-to-get-frighteningly-close-to-earth-nasa-says-check-speed-size-more-71694000745525.html.

Iqbal, Yasir. 2023 "The Frontrunners for the Saudi World Cup 2034 Stadiums." Middle East Business Intelligence. Last modified October 31. https://www.meed.com/the-frontrunners-for-the-saudi-world-cup-2034-stadiums.

Sidlo, Katarzyna W. 2020. "The Role of China in the Middle East and North Africa (MENA). Beyond Economic Interests?" European Institute of the Mediterranean. Last modified July 20. https://www.iemed.org/publication/the-role-of-china-in-the-middle-east-and-north-africa-mena-beyond-economic-interests/.

Lafargue, Francois. 2023. "China in North Africa." In *IEMed Mediterranean Yearbook*, 64–68. IEMed Publisher.

Liu, Linzhi. 2023. "China Constructs New Ties with the Middle East." *China Daily*, September 19, 2023. https://www.chinadaily.com.cn/a/202309/19/WS65094baca310d2dce4bb6871.html.

Fan, Hong, and Zhouxiang Lu. 2012. "Sport, Militarism, and Diplomacy: Training Bodies for China (1960–1966)." *The International Journal of the History of Sport* 29 (1): 30–52. https://doi.org/10.1080/09523367.2012.634983.

Masterson, Julia. 2022. "Saudi Arabia Said to Produce Ballistic Missiles." *Arms Control Today*, January/February 2022. https://www.armscontrol.org/act/2022-01/news/saudi-arabia-said-produce-ballistic-missiles.

Preethi Amaresh. 2020. "China's Stadium Diplomacy: All That Glitters Is Not Gold." *Diplomatist.* Last modified November 3. https://diplomatist.com/2020/11/03/chinas-stadium-diplomacy-all-that-glitters-is-not-gold/.

PR Newswire. 2022. "PowerChina's Construction Projects in the Middle East and North Africa under the Belt and Road Initiative." Last modified November 4. https://www.prnewswire.com/news-releases/powerchinas-construction-projects-in-the-middle-east-and-north-africa-under-the-belt-and-road-initiative-301668647.html.

Radio IFM. 2021. "Huawei annonce son partenariat avec l'incontournable sportive GO Sport" [Huawei Announces Partnership with Leading Sports Retailer GO Sport]. Last modified February 22. https://www.ifm.tn/fr/article/economie/huawei-annonce-son-partenariat-avec-l-incontournable-sportive-go-sport/33829.

Reiche, Danyel and Paul Michael Brannagan. 2022. *Routledge Handbook of Sport in the Middle East.* Routledge.

Rózsa, Erzsébet N. 2021. "China's Interests in the Middle East and North Africa." In *IEMed Mediterranean Yearbook*, 68–73. IEMed Publisher.

Silk Road Briefing. 2002. "China's Belt & Road Initiative and Qatar." Last modified November 22. https://www.silkroadbriefing.com/news/2022/11/22/chinas-belt-road-initiative-and-qatar/.

Statista. 2023. "Sports & Outdoor—China." Accessed January 27, 2024. https://www.statista.com/outlook/dmo/ecommerce/toys-hobby-diy/sports-outdoor/china.

Tunisian Ministry of Youth and Sport. 2023. "Hammamet 2023: CNOT and its Chinese Counterpart Sign Partnership Agreement." 25 June, 2023. Available at tap.info.tn/en/Portal-Sports/16405522-jap-hammamet-2023. Accessed 15 March, 2024.

Wang, Jianwei. 2019. "Xi Jinping's 'Major Country Diplomacy:' A Paradigm Shift?" *Journal of Contemporary China* 28 (115): 15–30.

Wang, Youfeng. 2023. "Research on Sports Diplomacy between China and Southeast Asia and South Asia under the New Situation." In *2nd International Conference on Education, Sport, Arts, and Management Engineering.* Last modified May 20. https://download.atlantis-press.com/article/25877270.pdf.

Wong, K. C. 2021. "The Rise of China's Developmental Peace: Can an Economic Approach to Peacebuilding Create Sustainable Peace?" *Global Society 35* (4): 522–540.

Xinhua. 2023. "Cooperation with China Brings Better Infrastructure, More Jobs, and Sustainable Development to Africa." *Xinhua*, December 13, 2023. https://english.news.cn/20221213/f6993d13f1914b97a4bdd07989b0ea90/c.html.

Xu, Chunyang, Yan, Li, and Jianli Zhang. 2022. "Research on a Complete Set of Sports Stadium Projects Assisted by China and Africa." *Open Access Library Journal* 9 (7): 1–13.

Zawya. 2022 "PowerChina Is Implementing 59 Projects in MENA under Belt and Road Initiative." Last modified November 4. https://www.zawya.com/en/projects/bri/powerchina-is-implementing-59-projects-in-mena-under-belt-and-road-initiative-haee5prc.

Zhang Qingmin. 2013. "Sports Diplomacy: The Chinese Experience and Perspective." *The Hague Journal of Diplomacy* (8): 211–233.

Zhao, Jinghui. 2023. "Sports Diplomacy of Socialism with Chinese Characteristics in the New Era: Opportunities and Challenge." *MATEC Web of Conferences* 365: 01035. https://doi.org/10.1051/matecconf/202236501035.

5

Sport, Migration and History: An Examination of African Female Football Migrants in China

Peizi Han[1]

Introduction

Women's football has witnessed substantial growth in terms of its global fan base, sponsorships, broadcasting, and professional league development over the past decade (FIFA 2021). Outside of earlier developing North American and Western European contexts, women's football in Africa has now come into the global spotlight. African women's football delivered an historic performance in the 2023 FIFA Women's World Cup in Australia and New Zealand, with three teams advancing to the round of 16 (CAF 2023). In recent decades, the international migration of African female players has become increasingly conspicuous. African women footballers now ply their trade in Western professional leagues and in Asia, notably China and Japan (Agergaard and Botelho 2014). Chrestinah Thembi Kgatlana, Asisat Oshoala, and Barbra Banda stand out as prominent figures among African female footballers due to their high-profile performances and transnational migration experiences (Norrito 2022). All three of these footballers have had associations and involvements with Chinese women's professional football at various points. For example, Barbra Banda had an impactful tenure

1 Peizi Han, Lecturer, Beijing Sport University, hanpz@bsu.edu.cn.

at Shanghai Shengli since the 2020 season, characterized by international fame, controversies, and a transfer fee that made her one of the most expensive women players in the world at the time. Despite scoring 17 goals in the Chinese league, she was banned from participating in the Women's Africa Cup of Nations Finals due to elevated testosterone levels. Despite Banda's high profile, African women footballers in China represent a relatively uncharted research area marked by a significant dearth of scholarly investigation.

In the broader context of African football migration studies, research has predominantly focused on the perspective of men's football. With the dramatic surge in the number of African footballers migrating to Europe over the past two decades, scholars have examined the mobility of African football players through economic, geographical, socio-cultural and sporting lenses (Darby et al. 2007, 2022; Magee and Sugden 2002; Poli 2006). Agergaard and Botelho (2014) have explored the migration of African women footballers, with a specific focus on their motives. However, most studies have adopted a Euro-centric perspective and are limited in scope to European host countries.

China offers a rich source of experiences and narratives concerning African female football migration. The presence of African migrants in China, including footballers, has become increasingly conspicuous, particularly after the expansion of China–Africa trade relations (Bodomo 2010; Monson and Rupp 2013). African migration to China represents a significant dimension within the burgeoning relationship between Africa and China. Surprisingly, there has been limited exploration of football-related migration at macro, meso, and micro levels, despite the shared enthusiasm for football in both China and Africa (Darby et al. 2022; Norrito 2022). And the migration of specifically female footballers to China has largely been overlooked. This chapter therefore investigates how female African players have integrated into Chinese professional football within the context of the China–Africa relationship.

This chapter provides a review of the history of African women footballer migration to China following the professionalization of the Chinese Women's Super League. Multiple clubs and specific players in the Chinese Women's Super League will be examined in terms of their affiliations with Chinese football and relationship to China. Two players—Asisat Oshoala from Nigeria and Tabitha Chawinga from Malawi—will be the focal points of this study. The narratives of their experiences highlight the profound impact of African women in the Chinese Women's Super League, depicting them not merely as athletes but also as cultural ambassadors bridging China and Africa. Their journeys pave the way for future opportunities for other African girls aspiring to realize their football dreams.

The Migration of African Women's Footballers

Football has long been perceived as a pathway to social mobility through individual skill and determination, a belief held by many young people in Africa (Norrito 2022; Poli 2010). Moving to play for European clubs has emerged as a means to fame, wealth, sporting success and attaining self-realization (Poli 2006; Norrito 2022). The weakening of political and other constraints in Africa related to player departures, combined with the relaxation of quota regulations in Europe, led to a surge in the migration of African players to European countries. The trend commenced in the 1980s and gained momentum in the 2000s (Darby et al. 2022; Poli 2006). Consequently, this period has witnessed an increasing body of research, encompassing numerous disciplines and approaches (Darby et al. 2022, 20). Nevertheless, research in this domain has overwhelmingly focused on the migration of male African footballers to Europe, while the study of African women's football migration has remained a neglected field (Agergaard and Botelho 2014; Botelho and Agergaard 2011; Darby et al. 2022).

Norrito (2022) persuasively argues that shifting the lens toward African female migrants is worthy of scholarly attention and requires identifying the gender-specific aspects of African football migration. Scholars in this field have concentrated on diverse issues, including the incentives driving African women's migration, the lived experiences of playing abroad, the challenge of pursuing a football career, the implications of gender-related issues in women's football, and the development of women's football in Africa (Agergaard and Botelho 2014; Botelho and Agergaard 2011; Clark and Burnett 2010; Darby et al. 2022; Saavedra 2003).

The development of women's football in Africa faces numerous obstacles, encompassing cultural norms that restrict female participation in sports, a scarcity of material resources such as pitches, equipment, transportation, professional leagues and coaching, and non-material resources like media coverage, sponsors and public support (Agergaard and Botelho 2014; Pelak 2010; Saavedra 2003). Despite these formidable challenges, football has played a transformative role in shifting gender power dynamics and relationships, which in turn may influence how families perceive women and girls' involvement in sports (Clark and Burnett 2011). Consequently, this has fueled the migration of African women footballers from their homelands to regions including Northern Europe and the USA to pursue professional football careers (Agergaard and Botelho 2014).

While economic gains are undoubtedly a significant motivation in the contemporary football landscape, Botelho and Agergaard (2011, 815) suggest that the incentives driving African women's migration extend beyond financial considerations. Factors such as football experience, career ambitions, and love for the game are also integral elements. König and de Regt (2010) further contend that the patriarchal family system represents a key push factor in motivating the migration of African women. In essence, the overarching objective of African female footballers has been identified as the pursuit of the "dream of social mobility" (Botelho and Agergaard 2011).

An Overview of Chinese Women's Super League

Exploring the dynamics of African women footballers' migration to China first requires a comprehensive understanding of the host site and its contextual background. This section thus provides an overview of the development of Chinese women's professional football, laying the foundation for a closer examination of the migration of African footballers to the country. Initially, Chinese women's football teams were established under the auspices of their respective provincial or city sports commissions (Fan and Mangan 2003, 52). In 1981, the first national women's football league was inaugurated (Valenti et al. 2021). Following the commercialization and professionalization of Chinese men's football, Chinese women's football underwent professionalization reforms and the inaugural professional football league was established in 1997 (Dong and Mangan 2002; Fan and Lu 2013). The inaugural season included the top four clubs from the previous season's National Women's Football League, expanding to eight clubs in its year, with matches played on a home and away basis (Fan and Mangan 2003).

Despite the Chinese women's team second place finish in the 1999 FIFA Women's World Cup, the new Chinese Women's Super League faced a crisis marked by inadequate parental and financial support, deficient facilities, gender bias, and chronic shortages of coaches, players, sponsors, and spectators (Dong and Mangan 2002; Fan and Mangan 2003). To address these challenges, the Chinese Football Association undertook significant reforms. In 2002, the league was opened to foreign women footballers for the first time . In addition, the China Women's Football Development Plan (2005–2012) was formulated, with the goal of establishing commercial women's leagues featuring promotion-relegation systems (Valenti et al. 2021). Consequently, the National League became the second-tier league of the Super League from 2004 onward. Another major change was that the home and away system was replaced by a short tournament to save money. The insufficient number of teams competing in the two leagues soon led to the abandonment of the open league system. In addition, the decision was made to cancel the National Women's Football League in 2006, ostensibly to aid national team preparations for the upcoming World Cup and Beijing Olympic Games. As a result, the National league was integrated into the Super League from 2007 to 2010 (Valenti et al. 2021). The setbacks in the commercialization and professionalization of Chinese women's football prompted the reorganization of the Super League into a double round-robin system with matches played in four regions from 2010 to 2015 (Beijing Youth Daily 2010).

The issuance of the Overall Plan for Chinese Football Reform and Development by the State Council in 2015 marked a turning point for Chinese women's football. Amid the general enthusiasm for football at the time, a new corporate sponsor was found, which reinvigorated the Chinese Women's Super League. This revival led in turn to the National League being split into two professional leagues: The top eight finishers of the 2014 National Women's Football League participated in the 2015 Chinese Women's Super League, while the bottom eight competed in the CFA Women's Football League (GAS 2015). The reorganization and momentum shift led to foreign women footballers, notably African and Brazilian, making their return to the professional leagues in China from 2016.

In 2019, the Chinese Football Association introduced a policy aimed at improving women's football. It stipulated that all Chinese Super League men's clubs must establish women's teams, in order to be eligible for participate in league competition from 2020 (Valenti et al. 2021, 328). The commitment to enhancing Chinese women's football gained further momentum after the women's national team won the Asian Cup in 2022, culminating in the release of the Reform and Development Plan for Chinese Women's Football 2022–2035 (GAS 2022). One immediate consequence was another increase in the number of teams in the Women's Super League, reaching 12 by 2023.

One of the prominent initiatives outlined in the reform plan involves improving the environment and infrastructure for developing Chinese women's football, with a focus on enhancing youth training and the professional league system (GAS 2022). The women's football league system is slated for gradual expansion, with 50 teams eventually expected to participate across three professional divisions: Women's Super League, Women's League One, and Women's League Two (GAS 2022). This expansion will provide further opportunities for Chinese women footballers to turn professional and opportunities to attract more overseas players.

Despite these efforts, the Chinese women's professional football league continues to encounter challenges on various fronts. Despite the introduction of reform policies in 2019 and 2022 mandating men's clubs invest in women's football, there remains uncertainty about whether men's clubs are the right vehicle for advancing the professionalization of Chinese women's football. This question has been emphasized by the post-COVID financial difficulties and waning enthusiasm among investors in the men's game.

African Migrations in China

It is useful to situate African football migration within the broader context of China's engagement with African countries. While the PRC's relationship with African countries was established in the 1960s, scholarly attention to African migration to China is relatively recent (Zhou et al. 2016). Prior research predominantly focused on China's economic presence in Africa, as well as Chinese migration to African countries (Liang and Le Billon 2018, 603). These studies explored various aspects of interactions, encompassing economic endeavors, social dynamics in workspaces, and the political dimensions of Chinese activities in Africa (Monson and Rupp 2013).

Adams Bodomo (2012) is a prominent figure in the field of research on African migration to China, with a primary focus on the social networks among African traders and their impact on the communities of African migrants in Guangzhou. He views African migrant communities as a cultural bridge between China and Africa (Bodomo 2010) despite countervailing observations of racial prejudice experienced by African migrants (Liang and Billon 2020, 603). Liang and Billon (2020) investigate the intimate social encounters related to housing, mobility, food, gender, and trade between African migrants and Chinese residents in Guangzhou. Their findings reveal that Africans are often subjected to "Othering" and racialization in contexts like public transport, food, and intimate relationships. Zhou et al. (2016) similarly identify ambivalence in the attitudes of Chinese residents in Guangzhou toward African migrants. While many Chinese express negative views about Africans, some also exhibit openness and a positive outlook on the overall presence of Africans (Zhou et al. 2016, 2016).

Several factors have contributed to the increasing number of African immigrants in China, particularly concentrated in the cities Guangzhou and Yiwu. First, African traders sought new markets following the Asian financial crisis in 1997/1998, prompting them to exit Southeast Asia (Bodomo 2010). Second, China–Africa trade has strengthened, notably with the inauguration of FOCAC in 2000 (Lan 2015), a new historical juncture in China–African friendship (Taylor 2018). China has maintained its position as Africa's top trading partner for over a decade, replacing the USA in 2011 (Lan 2015). Thirdly, China's accession to the World Trade Organization (WTO) enhanced China's role in global economic integration, attracting not only traders and diplomats, but artists, students and sports professionals seeking career development and economic opportunities in China (Bodomo 2010; Lan 2014). Some African entrepreneurs arrived in China as students with Chinese scholarships in the 1980s and 1990s, and thanks to their mastery of Chinese language established their own businesses or acted as intermediaries between China and Africa (Le Bail 2009). Although natural resources make up the majority of African exports to China, African imports from China include a diversity of manufactured products, electronics and machinery (Coface 2017). Many Africans are involved in this trade.

The city of Guangzhou hosts a remarkably diverse African population, representing various nationalities from across the African continent, particularly Nigeria, Senegal, Mali, Guinea and Ghana (Bodomo 2010). Official records indicate that approximately 16,000 Africans were registered with the government in 2014 (Liu 2014), but there is no official census data on the African population in China (Lan 2015, 294; Yang 2012). Chinese media often state that the number of African residents is underreported, with many undocumented Africans living in Guangzhou. Exaggerated numbers and increased media attention to crimes involving individuals of African descent has contributed to a negative perception of African migrants among some Chinese citizens (Lan 2015). This includes concerns related to issues such as drug trafficking, sexual assault and the spread of HIV/AIDS (Huang 2019). Higher levels of attention have prompted Chinese authorities to address related challenges. In 2019, the establishment of the National Immigration Administration underscored the recognition of transnational migration as a serious and practical issue facing China (Zhu and Qian 2021). Regulation and governance of African communities in China involves multiple authorities at different levels (Lan 2015). Immigrants who enter, stay, and work in China illegally have been the primary concern for both the Ministry of Public Security and the Ministry of Foreign Affairs. The issue is encapsulated by the Chinese term *sanfei*, meaning "triple illegal," in reference to people who enter, stay and work in the country without appropriate documentation (Lan 2015). Although this term does not directly refer to the African communities in China, media outlets have constantly linked it to African immigrants, leading to a new term "Black sanfei" (Huang 2019). African football labor migration does not fall into the *sanfei* category, but it occurs within this broader context.

The History of African Women Footballers' Migration to China

The Chinese Women's Super League began accepting foreign players in 2002 (Dong and Mangan 2002). During this initial phase, Tianjin signed three South Korean women, while Beijing extended invitations to three Nigerian players ahead of the upcoming season (Dong and Mangan 2002). Chinese clubs did not have the autonomy to sign foreign players directly. Instead, the introduction of foreign athletes into the league was centrally coordinated by the Chinese Football Association (CFA; Xinhuanet 2002). As part of this process, the CFA introduced 10 foreign women players from Australia, New Zealand, Ghana, Portugal, and Japan. The selection of these athletes took the form of a draft, allowing clubs a degree of flexibility in selecting their preferred players (Xinhuanet 2002). Athletes signed three-month contracts with the China Women's Super League Committee and competed in the league from June 30 to August 17 (Dong and Mangan 2002; Wang 2002). The draft involved participation from six Super League clubs, namely Sichuan, Dalian, Jiangsu, Guangdong, Shanghai, and Beijing (Sohu 2003).

The controlled, top-down approach to introducing foreign athletes faced criticism from several clubs, notably Beijing and Shanghai, who believed they could secure more accomplished women footballers through their own recruitment efforts (Xinhuanet 2002). This dissatisfaction extended to other clubs when the sporting performance of the imported foreign players did not meet the standard of domestic athletes (Qiu 2002). Compounding the issue, the CFA mandated that each club field a foreign athlete in their starting lineup during matches. Owing to subpar foreign player performances, substituting foreign starters for stronger Chinese counterparts within the first minutes of games became a common practice (Qiu 2002). Consequently, Qiu (2002) argued that empowering clubs and embracing the full professionalization and marketization of the women's football league should be a priority for the CFA. African female footballers initiated their entry into the Chinese women's league in 2002, with two Ghanaian players being selected by Sichuan and Shanghai (Xinhuanet 2002).

Also in 2002, the CFA introduced two policies aimed at promoting women's football. First, they sought to expand the scale of the women's league by introducing six additional clubs to the Super League. Second, the CFA acceded to club demands by permitting the direct recruitment of foreign players, which fundamentally transformed the landscape of women's professional football in China. Reflecting the CFA's cautious modus operandi, certain limitations remained in place. The number of foreign players was restricted to two, and clubs were prohibited from recruiting foreign goalkeepers (Lu 2002). In 2003, following the implementation of the new policy, Beijing signed the Nigerian Perpetua Nkwocha and Efioanwan Ekpo. After securing a victory against Tianjin, the media showered praise on the players, with headlines like "Black foreign athletes have captured the attention of Beijing, shining like black pearls" (Sohu 2003). Perpetua Nkwocha stood out among the foreign athletes signed during the 2002/2003 season for her goalscoring record that led Nigeria to multiple women's AFCON titles and secured her multiple African Women's Footballer of the Year awards (LCFC 2023). Her tenure in China spanned five years from 2003 to 2008, with successful stops in both Beijing and Tianjin.

Notwithstanding the attraction of higher-level foreign talent like Nkwocha, the women's continued to suffer from a lack of sponsorship and television coverage and an unsettled competitive format that moved between home-away matches and a short-term tournament. Yet this did not deter clubs from introducing more African female athletes into the Super League. For the 2004/2005 season, Tianjin recruited two Nigerian women footballers, Stella Mbachu and Rita Nwadike, whom local media lauded for their performances and affectionately referred to as "black roses on green" (Chen 2004). In their quest for a higher ranking in the Super League, Tianjin consistently pursued foreign athletes, despite not renewing Rita Nwadike's contract (Sina 2007). In 2005, Perpetua Nkwocha transferred from Beijing to Tianjin. Following that, Tianjin signed two more African women footballers, both of whom departed after just one season. Then, in 2007, Kikelomo Ajayi, a player from the Nigerian women's national team, joined the club (Zheng 2007). With three Nigerian national team players (Ajiayi, Nkwocha and Mbachu) on the team, Tianjin emerged victorious in the Chinese FA Cup during the 2007/2008 season (Sohu 2007). Tianjin was typical in pursuing competitive success by signing economically viable African footballers, and in the brevity of contracts it offered them. Contractual insecurity is a symbol of the unstable nature of African women's professional careers.

It is useful to interrogate why these Nigerian women players chose to join Tianjin, a major industrial city in northern China. In an interview with Oriental Sports Daily, Stella Mbachu and Perpetua Nkwocha cited the absence of coaching infrastructure in Nigeria, despite the women's national team's dominance in Africa (Chen 2006). Nigerian women footballers often had to rely on themselves due to the lack of coaching resources. Moreover, Nigeria lacked an independent women's football league and professional clubs. As a result, women's football matches were not played regularly in Nigeria, making it challenging for players to maintain their competitive edge and improve their skills. Moving to China, with its improving organization and facilities, thus became an appealing option for them (Chen 2006). Personal networks were also important. Stella Mbachu enjoyed her time in Tianjin and introduced the city to her good friend, Perpetua Nkwocha. Similarly, Kikelomo Ajayi came to Tianjin based on the recommendation of Stella and Perpetua (Sina 2007). As Ajayi put it: "Before, I didn't know much about Tianjin Huisen Women's Football Club, but through the introduction of my friends Nkwocha and Stella, I began to long for playing here!" (Xie 2007).

While financial remuneration was undoubtedly a factor, Stella and Perpetua's experience corroborates Botelho and Agergaard's (2011) finding that the motivations behind the migration of African women go beyond simple economic factors. Essential elements include the quality of the footballing experience, career aspirations, and a genuine passion for the game. According to Chen (2006), these two players' families did not face extreme financial hardship and did not come to China solely for monetary reasons. Nevertheless, they were content with their salaries, which exceeded CNY4,000 per month. Their earnings not only covered their living expenses in Tianjin but also allowed them to purchase electronics and affordable clothing as gifts for their families and friends in Nigeria (Chen 2006). They seemed to have adapted well to life in China, relishing the local hotpot cuisine, traditional Chinese culture and architecture, which they apparently missed while temporarily back home in Nigeria. Stella also praised the infrastructure in Tianjin, considering the stadium and training facilities far superior to what she was used to in Nigeria.

When the Chinese Women's Super League was suspended in 2008, African players had to leave their Chinese clubs, but when the league resumed in 2015, the CFA relaxed its restrictions on foreign players. The new regulations permitted clubs in the top two professional divisions to register up to three foreign athletes, with two allowed to participate in each match (Yuan 2015). Foreign athletes gradually began returning to China, with several African and Brazilian athletes choosing to make China their destination. Dalian recruited three Brazilian women footballers in 2016 (Ding 2016) and the season after secured the services of two Confederation of African Football (CAF) players, Asisat Oshoala and Gaelle Enganamouit, thanks to increased investment in the club. The club went on to win three consecutive Women's Super League titles, signifying the second wave of African female athletes' involvement in Chinese professional football. In 2017, a Cameroonian female player joined Changchun, and thereafter the migration of African women athletes accelerated significantly. Clubs like Beijing, Jiangsu, Shanghai, Henan, Wuhan and Changchun have all actively signed African women players since 2018, including South Africans Thembi Kgatlana and Linda Motlhalo, the Ghanaian Elizabeth Addo, and Tabitha Chawinga from Malawi.

The Shanghai women's football club, which had initially resisted recruiting foreign players, signed the Nigerian Francisca Ordega. Henan recruited two Nigerian players, Chinwendu Ihezuo and Onome Ebi. Tianjin Huisen, the pioneer of signing African women players in the early 2000s, exited the Super League in 2017 due to financial difficulties. Dalian Quanjian faced a similar situation when the club's owner came under suspicion of involvement in corporate scandals (Pu 2019). However, these developments did not impede the ongoing migration of African women athletes to China. Zambian players Barbra Banda and Margaret Belemu represented Shanghai for more than three seasons from 2019. From the 2019/20 season to 2023/2024 season, Malawians Tabitha Chawinga and Temwa Chawinga and Nigerian Désiré Oparanozie played for Wuhan. Beijing, which had temporarily ceased signing African women athletes, welcomed Genevieve Ngo Mbeleck from Cameroon and Jentrix Shikangwa from Kenya ahead of the 2023/24 season. Nigerian player Joy Jerry is now into her third season with Changchun. Nigerian Chinwendu Ihezuo and Charlene Meyong from Cameroon represented Guangdong. The Henan squad currently includes Nigerians Yetunde Adeboyejo and Ramat Ohunene Abdulkareem. Table 5.1 shows the current African players in the Chinese Women's Super League in the 2023/2024 season.

Table 5.1 African women footballers in the CWSL 2023/2024 season

Name	Club	Nationality	Position	Age
Yetunde Adeboyejo	Henan Zhongyuan F.C.	Nigeria	Midfield	27
Ramat Abdulkareem	Henan Zhongyuan F.C.	Nigeria	Midfield	23
Jentrix Shikangwa	Beijing Women F.C.	Kenya	Forward	21
G.Ngo Mbeleck	Beijing Women F.C.	Cameroon	Midfield	30
Joy Jerry	Changchun Dazhong F.C.	Nigeria	Forward	20
Barbra Banda	Shanghai Nongshang F.C.	Zambia	Forward	23
Margaret Belemu	Shanghai Nongshang F.C.	Zambia	Forward	26
Temwa Chawinga	Wuhan Chegudajiang F.C.	Malawi	Forward	23
Tabitha Chawinga	Wuhan Chegudajiang F.C.	Malawi	Forward	27
D. Oparanozie	Wuhan Chegudajiang F.C.	Nigeria	Forward	29

Source: Author's own compilation.

The Case of Asisat Oshoala and Tabitha Chawinga

The preceding section provides an overview of African women players' participation in Chinese professional football. However, examining the players' connections with the Chinese Women's Super League, their experiences as footballers in China, and their portrayal by Chinese media is required for a deeper contextualization. To facilitate this, I focus on two specific players, Assisat Oshoala from Nigeria and Tabitha Chawinga from Malawi.

Nigerian immigrants constitute one of the largest expatriate communities in China (Bodomo 2012) and Nigerians have dominated the contingent of foreign athletes in the Chinese Women's Super League. Asisat Oshoala holds the distinction of being regarded as one of the most successful African women footballers of all time (Karoney and Duarte 2023). In 2017, she transferred from Arsenal to Dalian Quanjian, a move that sparked considerable media debate (Abayomi 2021). From the perspective of fans and media, the primary motivation behind the player's decision to swap London for China's post-industrial northeast appeared to be financial (Abayomi 2021). Oshoala was candid about her decision and acknowledged the substantial increase in her salary, which multiplied her earnings 10-fold (Abayomi 2021). However, she also invoked a more profound personal motivation, seeing the move as an opportunity for personal and professional renewal having lost confidence in her abilities at Arsenal. The transfer was facilitated by Farid Benstiti, the French-Algerian former coach of French Ligue 1 club Paris Saint Germain, who had moved to Dalian himself to take the head coaching position. He personally extended an invitation to Oshoala to join the Dalian club. Oshoala later commented: "China was like a blessing for me. I keep saying it every day. I left Arsenal for China. I knew what I wanted then. I needed a coach and an organization that believed in me and could provide me with the confidence I needed, and China gave it to me" (Abeyomi 2021).

The decision of standout African players like Asisat Oshoala to join the Chinese Women's Super League was met with skepticism by some other African players, among whom there was limited knowledge about football and conditions in China (Wang 2018). In sporting terms, Oshoala silenced the doubts with her exceptional performances as the league's top scorer and leading her team to the league title in the 2017/2018 season (Wang 2018). In a 2022 interview, she expressed her deep affinity for China and the club she played for:

> I had a great experience in China; it's one of the best places I've ever played. My time in China was one of the highlights of my life. I had some problems to

> overcome in my career, and the Chinese team gave me a chance. I accepted the offer and rebuilt my self-confidence in a way that will always stay in my memory. I still follow some of my teammates on social media. I'm still in touch with some of my teammates. We're friends, and that's one of the things that football brings to the table: The sport connects us even though we don't speak the same language. (Hou 2022)

In 2018, CCTV Channel 9 produced a short film titled "For the Dream" depicting Oshoala's football journey and her experiences in China (CCTV 2022). Interviewed for the documentary, she mentioned that her initial communication concerns were quickly resolved, emphasizing that in football, speaking the same language is less important than understanding teammates' movements on the field. Her transition to Dalian, her positive impact on the team, and her personality led to her rapid acclimatization. It resonated with Chinese fans and media, who praised her professionalism and openness.

Oshoala's success in China was a turning point for her career, which culminated in a transfer to Barcelona FC in 2019 and the subsequent distinction of becoming the first African woman to win the UEFA Women's Champions League (Abayomi 2021). She explained that her experiences had inspired numerous Nigerian female footballers to consider China as a viable destination (Wang 2018). Back in Nigeria, Oshoala established her own football academy in 2015, and inspiring girls and young women to pursue their football dreams (Wang 2018). Her experiences as a professional athlete resonated with many African girls, including her defiance of her parents' wishes for her to attend university instead of pursuing a career in football (Wang 2018).

During Dalian Quanjian's three-year dominance of the Women's Super League, led Oshoala, rival clubs like Jiangsu Suning sought to emulate their success by recruiting the Malawian player Tabitha Chawinga. After Oshoala's departure from China, Chawinga led Jiangsu to their first Women's Super League title. A year later, she left Jiangsu to join her sister at Wuhan, marking the start of that club's dominance of the Chinese Women's Super League. Chawinga's journey paralleled Oshoala's in terms of overcoming family objections and cultural resistance to women and girls playing football. Her talent was eventually discovered, leading to an invitation to play for DD Sunshine in the Malawian capital Lilongwe (. She spent four years there from the age of 14, before moving to Sweden. Following her recognition as the best striker in the Swedish league, she candidly expressed her motivation to generate income for her family and support football development in Malawi (Wang 2018). The move to China followed.

Chawinga's dedication and talent demonstrated in the Chinese league gradually positioned her as a bridge between China and Malawi. On December 19, 2018, Ambassador Liu Hongyang hosted a reception for Chawinga with the theme "My Chinese Dream" in recognition of Tabitha's active role in China-Malawi cultural exchange (Sundu 2018). Ambassador Liu remarked that:

> I got to know about her through the media and that motivated me and the embassy to organize this celebration. We call her the "ambassador of friendship" between Malawi and China, not just in the world of football but more. She is the first Malawian woman football player in China and the best player. Many Chinese now know Malawi because of her. (Sundu 2018)

Tabitha expressed gratitude to the Chinese embassy for organizing the event and has praised the support that the Chinese government has provided for women's football. In her speech, she appealed for more stakeholders to become involved in women's football in Malawi, emphasizing that the government could draw inspiration from China (Sundu 2018). Minister of Industry, Trade and Tourism of Malawi, Francis Kasaila, seconded Tabitha's sentiments and acknowledged the mutual benefits of Malawi's engagement with China in football. The director of DD Sunshine was also in attendance, and he committed to organizing a Chinese tour focusing on cultural and sports exchanges (Manda 2018). Tabitha's experience as a sporting success and cultural ambassador demonstrates the opportunities open to African athletes to achieve success in China, and to share that success with their home communities.

Tabitha shared her knowledge of Chinese culture, society, and football development with Malawian players (Jiangsu 2018) and acted as a conduit for her Chinese employers to provide material support to local clubs in Malawi, such as donations of football equipment. Tabitha inspired her younger sister Temwa to leave Malawi to pursue her career in Sweden and then on to China (Musembi 2020) for a substantial transfer fee (Ruszkai 2021).

Conclusion

This chapter explores the under-researched topic of African female football migration to China in the context of expanding China–Africa relations and shows how female African players have integrated into Chinese professional football. The dynamics of African female footballers and their careers in the Chinese league have been primarily influenced by the development and professionalization of the

Chinese Women's Super League itself, rather than by the African communities in China (curiously there are no African players on the Guangzhou club, despite the city having the largest African population in China). Key African athletes like Barbra Banda, Margaret Belemu, Temwa Chawinga, and others have contributed significantly to their respective teams and the growth of the Chinese Women's Super League. However, as Chahadovali (2023) points out, the "careers of women footballers are often short, insecure, and precarious" (54), an argument substantiated by the experiences of many African footballers in China. Due to the challenges in various aspects of women's professional football in China, the majority of contracts are short and lack guarantees. Nonetheless, the pull factors from the Chinese side continue to exert their influence, with the promise of financial gain, career advancement and upward social mobility. The Chinese government's Reform and Development Plan for Chinese Women's Football 2022–2035 promises a continuing growth trajectory in women's football, with associated opportunities for African athletes. The stories of Oshoala and Chawinga underscore the transformative power of football for African women in China and in their home countries, not just as athletes but as cultural ambassadors, supporting Clark and Burnett's (2010) argument that football has a role in changing gender power dynamics and relationships within communities.

References

Abayomi, Anita. 2021. "Asisat Oshoala: 'As Much as Education Is Important, Sport Is Also Important.'" *The Athletic*. Last modified July 19. https://theathletic.com/2717486/2021/07/19/asisat-oshoala-as-much-as-education-is-important-sport-is-also-important/.

Agergaard, Sine, and Vera Lucia Botelho. 2014. "The Way Out? African Players' Migration to Scandinavian Women's Football." *Sport in Society* 17: 523–536.

Beijing Youth Daily. 2010. "Nüchao gaizhi Zhong zaoxue zuxie meinian luoshi 600zhi 800wan feiyong" [Women's Super League Restructuring to Re-create the Football Association to Implement the Cost of 6 to 8 Million Per Year]. Sports QQ. Last modified September 22. https://sports.qq.com/a/20100922/000378.htm.

Bodomo, Adams. 2010. "The African Trading Community in Guangzhou: An Emerging Bridge for Africa–China Relations." *The China Quarterly* 203: 693–707. https://doi.org/10.1017/S0305741010000664.

CAF. 2023. "A Look at Africa's Performance at the FIFA Women's World CupTM." CAF Online. Accessed December 21, 2023. https://www.cafonline.com/womens-football/news/a-look-at-africa-s-performance-at-the-fifa-women-s-world-cup/.

CCTV. 2022. "zhuimeng zhongguo: wei mengxiang ben paoba" [Run for Your Dreams]. CCTV-9 video, 4:49. July 2, 2022. https://tv.cctv.cn/2022/07/02/VIDEDtkxhRIeTcBd7felA0xg220702.shtml.

Celestine, Karoney, and Fernando Duarte. 2023. "Women's World Cup 2023: Asisat Oshoala's Journey from Rebellious Teenager to Africa's Star Player." BBC Sport. Accessed October 31, 2023. https://www.bbc.co.uk/sport/africa/66407312.

Chahardovali, Tarlan. 2023. "The Precarious Labour of Women Footballers: A Shadow in the Light of the 2023 FIFA Women's World Cup." In Adam Beissel, Verity Postlethwaite, Andrew Grainger and Julie E. Brice (eds) *The 2023 FIFA Women's World Cup*. London: Routledge, 52–67.

Chen, Jing. 2006. "Feizhou waiyuan chuang dang nüchao sai chang heimei qiangqiang tian jin san ren xing" [African Foreign Player to Break into the Women's Super League, the Black Girl Medaka Tianjin Trio]. Sohu. Last modified September 15. https://sports.sohu.com/20060915/n245362916.shtml.

Chen, Yu. 2004. "Zouguo kunnan (taida zhongchaobei)" [Walking Through Difficulties (TEDA Super Cup)]. Tianjin TV Station. Last modified June 10. http://tjtv.enorth.com.cn/system/2004/06/10/000800154.shtml.

Clark, C., and Cora Burnett. 2011. "Upward Social Mobility through Women's Soccer." *Journal of Physical Activity and Health* 16 (4): 834–849.

Coface. 2017. "China-Sub-Saharan Africa Trade Relations: Still Unbalanced." Coface. Last modified November 14. https://www.coface.ca/News-and-Publications/News/China-Sub-Saharan-Africa-Trade-Relations-Still-Unbalanced.

Darby, Paul, Gerard Akindes, and Matthew Kirwin. 2007. "Football Academies and the Migration of African Football Labor to Europe." *Journal of Sport and Social Issues* 31 (2): 143–161. https://doi.org/10.1177/0193723507300481.

Darby, Paul, James Esson, and Christian Ungruhe. 2022. "The History, Geography and Regulation of African Football Migration." In *African Football Migration*, edited by Darby, Paul, James Esson, and Christian Ungruhe, 40–63. Manchester University Press.

Ding, Xu. 2016. "Quan jian nüzu dashoub yinjin nei waiyuan mubiao zhi zhi guonei san guan wang" [Quanjian Women's Football Team Spends a Lot to Bring in Internal and External Supporters]. NetEase. Last modified March 18. https://www.163.com/sports/article/BIEUL8VC00051C8L.html.

Dong, Jinxia, and J. A. Mangan. 2002. "Ascending Then Descending? Women's Soccer in Modern China." *Soccer & Society* 3: 1–18.

Le Bail, Helene. 2009. "Foreign Migration to China's City-Markets: The Case of African Merchants." *Asia Visions* 19: 1–21.

Fan, Hong, and J. A. Mangan. 2003. "Will the 'Iron Roses' Bloom Forever? Women's Football in China: Changes and Challenges." *Soccer & Society* 4 (2–3): 47–66. https://doi.org/10.1080/14660970512331390825.

Fan, Hong, and Zhouxiang Lu. 2013. "The Professionalisation and Commercialisation of Football in China (1993–2013)." *The International Journal of the History of Sport* 30 (14): 1637–1654. https://doi.org/10.1080/09523367.2013.828710.

GAS. 2022. "Reform Plan to Boost the Development of Soccer in China, General Administration of Sports." Available at: https://www.sport.gov.cn/jts/n4998/c24847501/content.html Accessed: 28 December 2023.

Hou, Yichen. 2022. "Zhuanfang basa nüzu aoshaoala: nüzu zhengbian de yuelaiyue hao; xiangnian zhongguo pengyoumen" [Interview with Barcelona's Oshoala: Women's Football Is Getting Better and Better; Misses Chinese Friends]. Dongqiudi. Last modified March 8. https://m.dongqiudi.com/article/2623191.html.

Huang, Guangzhi. 2018. "Policing Blacks in Guangzhou: How Public Security Constructs Africans as Sanfei." *Modern China* 45 (2): 171–200. https://doi.org/10.1177/0097700418787076.

Jing, Liu. 2014. "118,000 Foreigners Reside in Guangzhou, with Africans Making Up Only 10%." *China Daily.* Last modified December 17. http://www.chinadaily.com.cn/dfpd/gd/2014-12/17/content_19105518.htm.

König, Reinhilde Sotiria, and Marina de Regt. 2010. "Family Dynamics in Transnational African Migration to Europe: An Introduction." *African and Black Diaspora: An International Journal* 3 (1): 1–15. https://doi.org/10.1080/17528630903368232.

Lan, Shanshan. 2014. "State Regulation of Undocumented African Migrants in China: A Multi-Scalar Analysis." *Journal of Asian and African Studies* 50 (3): 289–304. https://doi.org/10.1177/0021909614531903.

LCFC. 2022. "Football's Pioneers: Perpetua Nkwocha." Leicester City FC. Last modified January 2. https://www.lcfc.com/news/2434758/footballs-pioneers-perpetua-nkwocha?lang=EN.

Liang, Kelly, and Philippe Le Billon. 2018. "African Migrants in China: Space, Race and Embodied Encounters in Guangzhou, China." *Social & Cultural Geography* 21 (5): 602–628. https://doi.org/10.1080/14649365.2018.1514647.

Lin, Jian. 2015. "China Football Association Women's Super League Officially Launched." GAS. Accessed October 30, 2023. https://www.sport.gov.cn/n315/index.html.

Magee, Jonathan, and John Sugden. 2002. "'The World at Their Feet.'" *Journal of Sport and Social Issues* 26 (4): 421–437. https://doi.org/10.1177/0193732502238257.

Manda, Solomon. 2018. "DD Sunshine to Tour China." The Nation Online. Last modified December 22. https://mwnation.com/dd-sunshine-to-tour-china/.

Monson, Jamie, and Stephanie Rupp. 2013. "Africa and China: New Engagements, New Research." *African Studies Review* 56 (1): 21–44.

Musembi, Peter. 2020. "The Sisters Putting Malawi Women's Football on the Map." BBC Sport. Last modified August 16. https://www.bbc.co.uk/sport/africa/53779887.

Norrito, Alessio. 2022. "African Football Migration: Aspirations, Experiences, Trajectories." *Sport in Society 26* (6): 1133–1135.

Poli, Raffaele. 2010. "African Migrants in Asian and European Football: Hopes and Realities." *Sport in Society* 13 (6): 1001–1011.

———. 2006. "Migrations and Trade of African Football Players: Historic, Geographical and Cultural Aspects." *Africa Spectrum* 41 (3): 393–414.

Pu, Yaolei. 2019. "The League's Triple Champion Dalian Women's Football Team Disbanded, Who Can Help the Girls Who Are Owed Wages?" *The Paper*. Available at: https://www.thepaper.cn/newsDetail_forward_5346267. Accessed: 28 December 2023.

Qiu, Jiangjia. 2002. "Nüzu chaoji liansai zhi sikao: yang waiyuan kan shangqu hen mei" [Women's Super League for the First Time to Introduce the System of Attracting Foreign Aid Draft Football Association Will Be Responsible for the Introduction of High-Level Foreign Aid].

Sina Sport. Last modified August 7. https://sports.sina.com.cn/c/2002-08-07/1427296765.shtml.

Ruszkai, Amee. 2021. "Oshoala, Banda, Huge Salaries and Record-Fees: Inside the Chinese Women's Super League." GOAL. Last modified August 16. https://www.goal.com/en-gb/news/oshoala-banda-huge-salaries-and-record-fees-inside-the-chinese-womens-super-league/zkb7khftw2k013oq2yzzay28s.

Saavedra, Martha. 2003. "Football Feminine—Development of the African Game: Senegal, Nigeria and South Africa." *Soccer & Society* 4 (2–3): 225–253. https://doi.org/10.1080/14660970512331390925.

Sina. 2007. "Tianjin nüzu waiyuan rongru qiudui conghe kaishi yingqiu hui qu jiuba changyin" [Tianjin Women's Football Foreign Aid to Integrate into the Team from the Beginning of the Win Will Go to the Bar Drink]. Sina. Last modified April 4. http://sports.sina.com.cn/c/2007-04-06/15172852400.shtml.

Sohu. 2003. "Heiren waiyuan yinren zhu mu chengji an nüzu "heizhenzhu" defang yicai" [Black Foreign Athlete Attracts Attention]. Sohu. Last modified July 7. https://sports.sohu.com/30/05/news210800530.shtml.

Sundu, Yvonnie. 2018. "Tabitha Magic." *The Nation*, Last modified December 21. https://mwnation.com/tabitha-magic/.

Taylor, Ian. 2018. "Africa's Natural Resource Corner and BRICS." In *Handbook of African Development,* edited by Tony Binns, Kenneth Lynch, and Etienne Nel, 313–326. Routledge.

Valenti, Maurizio, Qi Peng, and Claudio Rocha. 2021. "Integration between Women's and Men's Football Clubs: A Comparison between Brazil, China and Italy." *International Journal of Sport Policy and Politics* 13 (2): 321–339. https://doi.org/10.1080/19406940.2021.1903967.

Wang, Yu. 2018. "Feizhou zuqiu xiaojie 'zhumeng zhongguo' " [African Women Player of the Year Chasing Football Dream in China] Sohu, Last modified October 9, 2018. https://www.sohu.com/a/258321073_115239.

Xie, Liqiang. 2007. "Nüzu xin waiyuan: jizhuwo ai tiqiu huiwan nengfeng de a jiayi" [Women's New Foreign Aid: Remember Me: Ajayi, Who Loves to Play Football, Can Play and Can Be Crazy!]. Enorth. Last modified April 4. http://sports.enorth.com.cn/system/2007/04/04/001596402.shtml.

Xinhuanet. 2002. "Zhongguo zuxie yuedi gongbu nüzu chaoji liansai waiyuan yinjin fangan" [CFA to Announce Women's Super League Foreign Aid Introduction Plan at the End of the Month]. Sohu. Last modified November 5. https://sports.sohu.com/88/81/sports_news165268188.shtml.

Yang, Yang. 2012. "African Traders in Guangzhou: Routes, Reasons, Profits, Dreams." In *Globalization from Below*, edited by Gordon Mathews, Gustavo Lins Ribeiro, and Carlos Alba Vega, 164–180. Routledge.

Yuan, Xuejing. 2015. "2016 nian nüzu liansai xin zhengguan shang xing tisheng keyin waiyuan" [New Women's Football League Policy for 2016 to Improve Spectatorship Can Attract Foreign Players]. General Administration of Sport. Last modified December 30. https://www.sport.gov.cn/n20001280/n20745751/n20767274/c22097260/content.html.

Zheng, Dengchun. 2007. "Niriliya nüzu guojiadui duizhang jiameng tianjin huisen nüzu" [Nigeria Women's National Team Captain Joins Tianjin Huisen Women's Football Team].

CCTV News Website. Last modified February 28. http://news.cctv.com/sports/football/woman/20070228/104898.shtml.

Zhou, Min, Shabnam Shenasi, and Tao Xu. 2016. "Chinese Attitudes toward African Migrants in Guangzhou, China." *International Journal of Sociology* 46 (2): 141–161.

Zhu, Hong, and Junxi Qian. 2021. "New Theoretical Dialogues on Migration in China: Introduction to the special issue." *Journal of Ethnic and Migration Studies* 47 (12): 2685-2705.

6

Transient African Male Football Players: Participation and Impact in Chinese Super League

Wycliffe W. Simiyu Njororai[1]

Introduction

There has been a burgeoning of African male football players moving abroad to play professionally. Although the initial regions that attracted African players were the USA, Europe, Middle East and even Southeast Asia (Acheampong et al. 2019; Darby et al. 2022; Poli 2006a, 2010), over the last 15 years the Chinese Super League (CSL) has emerged as a competitive destination (Delgado and Villar 2020; Yang and Wang 2022). China's sustained economic growth over the last two decades has contributed to an intense and multifaceted global engagement that includes the game of football. As China has opened up to the world, its rising disposable incomes, expanding middle-class, dynamic digital environment and burgeoning e-commerce sector, and the appetite of Chinese fans for foreign football products, have collectively contributed to significant market growth in the sector. These developments have attracted investment from foreign clubs, governing bodies, and corporate interests from across the world (Cockayne et al. 2022). These political, social, economic, and technological changes, coupled with

1 Wycliffe W. Simiyu Njororai, Professor, Stephen F. Austin State University, wycliffe.njororai@sfasu.edu.

renewed efforts to consolidate and develop Chinese football and China's influence on football globally has stimulated academic interest (Cockayne et al. 2022), and attracted corporate, practitioner and playing talent from the African continent (Yang and Wang 2022).

The CSL was established in 2004, and several African players including Kwame Ayew (Ghana), Kola Adams, Samuel Ayorinde, Prince Ikpe Ekong (Nigeria), Djima Oyawole (Togo) and Clement Lebe (Cameroon) competed in the league soon after its inception. However, the first high-profile African player to join the league was Nigerian striker Yakubu Aiyegbeni, who signed for Guangzhou City football club in 2012 (Fottrell 2012). Subsequently, the CSL attracted numerous high-profile African players, including Didier Drogba and Yaya Toure from Côte d'Ivoire, Asamoah Gyan from Ghana, and John Obi Mikel and Obafemi Martins from Nigeria (Agbaje 2020). These players have helped to raise the profile of the league and increase its competitiveness as well as advertising the attractiveness of the Chinese market to other potential African players. The presence of popular African players in the CSL has helped to enhance the growing cultural exchanges between China and Africa. The diverse representation of African countries embodied by these players has strengthened connections with China and how it is perceived on the African continent. This chapter will discuss the theoretical perspectives that explain African male football labor migration and identify the factors that underpin it. The chapter will then explain the emergence of the CSL as a competitive destination, citing data on annual participation rates and the range of African countries represented. It will then discuss the impact of African players in the context of China's football development and broader issues around China's engagement with African countries.

Theoretical Underpinnings for African Transnational Mobilities

Transnational labor mobility is a significant factor in today's global economy, with more people living and working outside their countries of birth than ever before (Horowitz and McDaniel 2015). Elite athletes are among a select group of workers seeking employment on a global market level. The transnational migration trends in association football, where players move to play the game abroad, are characteristic of a modern sport that is best understood through the lens of globalization (Maguire 1999). Globalization processes include the emergence of a globally connected economy, transnational cosmopolitan cultures, and a range of international social movements. Maguire (1999) argues that modern sport is an example of cultural and geographical globalization and a part of a global homogenization process. He further argues that there are both decreasing contrasts between and increasing varieties of cultures manifest within globalization processes. One illustration of the transnational nature of modern sport is the attempt by countries like China and Saudi Arabia to attract foreign players into their national football leagues. African players, who previously aspired to play in the European leagues, now have an extended range of career options, including playing in Asia. The growing trend of African football labor migration, especially concerning male players, is a complex and multifaceted issue that attracts scholarly attention. A review of the different theoretical explanations shows that there are underlying socio-economic, political, and cultural factors that drive this migration from Africa to established regions in Europe and North America and emerging ones in the Middle East and East Asia (Acheampong et al. 2019; Akindes 2018, 2013; Alegi 2010; Darby 2002; Darby et al. 2022; Poli 2006a, 2006b, 2010).

Various authors have asserted that the development of sporting organizations such as Federation of International Football Associations (FIFA) and the International Olympic Committee (IOC) among others, reflects the broader globalization processes that led to the conceptualization of the world as an interconnected space (Maguire 1999). In footballing terms, it is the mission of FIFA to establish and grow the game of football into a "global family" (Njororai 2022). This aspiration, however, continues to be undermined by the enduring inequalities and disparities grounded in political and socio-economic circumstances that shape the world. The inequalities and disparities in terms of access and availability of economic resources and opportunities incentivize transnational mobilities, as people seek to improve their livelihoods and prospects. African male football players are active participants in the search for opportunities to improve their livelihoods (Acheampong et al. 2019; Darby et al. 2022). A transnational African football migrant is therefore an active social navigator, who must negotiate economic, socio-cultural, interpersonal, familial and football terrain challenges to initiate, execute, and accomplish the pursuit of a better future (Darby et al. 2022; Onwumechili and Akpan 2020; Poli 2010). African migrant players are reflective beings, with agency, who engage in practices, and maneuver, strategize and actively pursue opportunities that might lead to entry into the professional playing ranks of the football industry (Darby et al. 2022). It is this agency that enables them to overcome challenges to make the dream of playing professionally abroad come true (Darby et al. 2022; Engh and Agergaard 2015).

Male players are also driven in part by the intergenerational contract prevalent in African culture, where the son is nurtured to be a breadwinner for the nuclear and extended family (Acheampong 2019; Acheampong et al. 2019; Darby et al. 2022; Onwumechili and Akpan 2020).

Theorization of the mobilities of African players has elicited different perspectives. One of the insightful early theories is that of Immanuel Wallerstein's (1974) world system theory which attempted to analyze and interpret global economic, political, and social processes to construct an explanation of the development of the world economy. According to Wallerstein (1974), the world system coheres around four interdependent sectors whose position vis-à-vis the global capitalist economy has been determined through a combination of colonial history, and economic power. The world economy is therefore divided into four sectors including the core (northwest Europe, North America, and Japan); the semi-periphery (Southern Europe and the Mediterranean region); the periphery (Eastern Europe, north Africa, and parts of Asia); and the external arena comprising most of Africa, parts of Asia and the Indian sub-continent, which, given the advance of colonialism and transnational corporate activity, can now be classified as being periphery (Darby 2002). One of the central tenets of the world system theory is that peripheral regions like Africa are heavily dependent on the core countries. Given the dominance of the world economy by the core countries, they exploit and bankrupt the underdeveloped periphery via skewed organization of world trade that suits their interests (Darby 2002; Darby et al. 2022; Rodney 1972). The world system theory shares some structural approaches with the dependency theory regarding the global inequalities and power imbalances that drive economic and labor migration (Frank 1967). Interpreted through this structuralist theoretical lens, the global football industry, primarily controlled by wealthy countries and clubs in Europe, exploits the talent and resources of less developed/prosperous countries. In the context of African football migration, it could be argued that African nations' dependency on the global football market, primarily controlled by European clubs, pushes talented male players to seek opportunities abroad due to limited local resources and opportunities (Darby et al. 2022). African footballers migrate to Europe, and elsewhere around the world, seeking better wages and opportunities due to the economic disparities between their home countries and the host nations (Darby and Solberg 2017).

The global mobilities of people, goods, and ideas across borders have been facilitated by globalization processes (Maguire 1999). These transnational mobilities of people, goods and services have been accentuated by neoliberal economic policies adopted by many countries, international economic agencies, and multinational organizations. The commercialization of sport, particularly association football, led to the change in the management and organization of the game as a business (Held and McGrew 2007). Whereas African football administrators lagged in embracing the commodification and professionalization of the sport, the players were quick to embrace the notion of selling their services and talents to the highest bidder. African players therefore migrate to other continents as part of the global football market, driven by market forces, privatization, and the pursuit of profit especially by football clubs. Globalization, driven by neoliberal ideologies and economic policies, has therefore facilitated the movement of human capital to areas and regions offering the greatest rewards. African footballers, like other professionals, move to places where their skills and talents are most valued. African players migrate to Europe, North America, Asia and within the continent to enhance their skills, gain experience, and improve their marketability, which can lead to higher wages and better career prospects. This movement of African football players is therefore instigated and sustained by socio-economic and political factors, collectively referred to as push factors and corresponding attractions or pull factors. The push-pull factors paradigm argues that migration of African footballers revolves around economic hardships, political instability, and limited opportunities in their home countries, which contrast with the allure of better salaries, advanced training facilities, and the prestige associated with moving to play abroad (Darby and Solberg 2017). Thus, as per Wallerstein's (1974) theorization, the structural inequalities that are evident within African countries and the global football industry play a significant role in this transnational mobilities. Many African nations lack the infrastructure and investment in football development to nurture, retain and reward talented players on home soil which pushes them abroad where they can find better prospects. In contrast, leagues in Europe, North America and emerging regions like the Middle East, Southeast Asia and now China, have resources and opportunities that attract African talent.

Factors Underpinning African Football Labor Migration

The improved international travel, technology and harmonized international football calendar has made it easier for players playing abroad to maintain contact with families and their national teams back home. The transnational mobility of many African footballers creates a win–win situation for the player and the country of birth and residency. This works well when the player maintains strong ties to their home countries while playing abroad. Such a player often engages in transnational practices, such as supporting development projects in the local home community, representing the country in international competitions when called up, and preserving the cultural identity. The transnational nature of football has evolved in tandem with the regulatory framework instituted by football authorities like FIFA and regional bodies such as Confederation of African Football (CAF), national governments, and other international agencies that deal with issues of citizenship and legal provisions for international travel of people. These regulations influence the migration patterns of African players, including issues related to work permits and player eligibility (Darby et al. 2022).

Talented young people are exposed to the successes of role models plying their trade abroad, especially in Europe. African players in leagues abroad are admired and celebrated in Africa. Their stardom and improved material status are enticing to youth aspiring to make a breakthrough in professional football (Alegi 2010; Darby 2002; Darby et al. 2022). Europe's attractiveness has been accentuated by the establishment of the lucrative Champions League, the Marc Bosman case that introduced freedom of contract and brought an end to foreign player quota systems in European Community (EC) countries, and a rapid upward surge in revenue accrued from media and sponsors (Magee and Sugden 2002). For example, national leagues increasingly export (sell abroad) their TV rights to attract foreign TV viewers—through foreign broadcasters—to pay for their supply of high-quality matches. The English Premier League (EPL), which is the market leader in football, secured TV rights revenues from abroad amounting to 26.2 percent of TV rights revenues earned on the domestic market, compared with 23.7 percent for the Spanish Liga, 14.1 percent for the Italian Serie A, 6.1 percent for the German Bundesliga, and 1.2 percent for the French Ligue 1, in 2006–2007 (Gratton and Solberg 2007). Since 2007, these percentages have increased substantially as European leagues have become more popular abroad. Today, EPL matches are watched worldwide, including in China and Asia where sports betting on matches is common (Andreff 2021). EPL TV rights revenues earned in the domestic market were £1706 million in 2007–2010, £1773 million in 2010–2013, £3018 in 2013–2016, and £5136 million in 2016–2019 while those earned abroad reached 64.3 percent of the domestic market magnitude in the last sub-period. EPL matches are broadcast in 200 countries with over one billion viewers' audience. The French Ligue 1 lags behind, although TV rights exports grew from 4.5 percent of domestic TV rights revenues before 2018 to 6.9 percent in 2018–2024 (Andreff 2021). Apart from popular national leagues, the UEFA competitions are consumed globally and African players who play in such competitions tend to grow in visibility and popularity across the world.

The entrance of China into the global football marketplace has created a new dispensation that widened the opportunities for African players. Whereas some Europe-based African players of advanced age seeking better contractual compensation look to try out the Chinese Super League, there are also young talented African players who see China as an opportunity to grow their reputation and their skills. The phenomenon of African football migration is therefore complex and influenced by multiple factors. The major driving force for player mobility is the economic disparity between African countries, and their football leagues, and other areas of the world. Many African countries face elevated levels of poverty and limited economic opportunities, making the pursuit of a professional football career abroad an attractive option for young players seeking financial security for themselves and their families. Foreign football clubs offer significantly higher salaries and better living standards compared to local clubs in Africa (Darby and Solberg 2017). One of the advantages of football is the simplicity and ease of learning the fundamentals of playing it. However, to develop talent to elite levels requires investment in financial, physical and personnel resources. African countries often lack the infrastructure and resources needed for youth development in football thereby predisposing talented youth to seek opportunities abroad. The scarcity of quality training facilities, coaching, and competition opportunities compels talented young players to seek opportunities abroad where they can receive better training and exposure to top-level training and competition infrastructure (Alegi and Bolsmann 2016). Sport today, especially football, is much more than raw talent, as the science of sports and talent management is much more sophisticated and methodical, and this is where Africa struggles.

The exposure of young African players at continental and FIFA's age-group competitions provides forums for international scouting and recruitment. Thus, the globalization of football has led to the increased scouting and recruitment of African talent by foreign clubs. Scouting networks extend into various African countries, identifying young prospects and offering them opportunities to join academies abroad. The global reach of football scouting contributes to the migration of African players (Maguire 2017). Although FIFA has tried to streamline the recruitment of young players, there are still a lot of hurdles that a player must navigate to earn an opportunity to play for a club abroad. It is noteworthy that African players often face challenges related to obtaining work permits and other visa restrictions when trying to move and play abroad (Darby et al. 2022). However, things have improved over the years with many countries liberalizing their policies. Stringent immigration policies can hinder the ability of players to move freely and may create barriers to their participation in foreign leagues. Apart from the legal barriers that prospective migrant players must navigate, there are also cultural and social factors that play a significant role in the choice of the team, league, country, and the process of transitioning in the new set-up. Many African players are inspired by the success stories of compatriots who have made it in foreign leagues, which has created a cultural narrative that emphasizes migration as a pathway to success (Akindes 2018). Widespread live coverage of foreign football competitions continues to inspire talented African youth to dream of moving abroad, joining professional ranks, and earning a decent living to support and sustain their families in Africa. Countries with a higher transnational community presence tend to be more appealing as such communities help in the acculturation process for new migrant players. For example, many Western African players migrate to France due to the shared language and proximity. Thus, the presence of established African diaspora communities abroad can provide a support network for African players. These communities can help with cultural adaptation, language barriers, and navigating the challenges of living abroad (Darby and Solberg 2017). Despite the cultural and other factors favoring migration as well as being heavily sought after by football scouts, African players often face racial discrimination in foreign countries. This racial and discriminatory aspect of the migration experience can influence players' decisions and experiences abroad (Newman et al. 2021).

Transnational African football mobility is shaped by a complex interplay of economic, infrastructural, cultural, legal, and social factors. These factors interact differently for each player, leading to diverse migration experiences and outcomes. Some of the experiences of a migrant player from Africa are shaped and informed by the historical context, the globalization of football, and the agency of the players themselves within the broader socio-economic and political landscape. Europe has the most successful and well-known clubs in the world and the best players are attracted to the European national leagues (KEA and CDES 2013). In the context of the world system theory, the world is divided into tri-modal system or Trinitarian structure consisting of the core, semi-periphery, and periphery (Aniche and Ukaegbu 2016; Darby 2002) with Europe being the core and Africa on the periphery. The argument put forward via world system theory is that the world system and not nation-states should be the primary, but not exclusive unit of social analysis, and it entails the inter-regional and transnational division of labor. Core countries focus on higher-skill, capital-intensive production and the rest of the world focuses on low-skill, labor-intensive production, and extraction of raw materials. This kind of arrangement reinforces the dominance of the core countries that continually mine the raw materials from the peripheral countries causing the latter to be dependent on the former. The only hope however lies in the fact that the system is dynamic as it can be influenced by technological changes leading to some countries either gaining or losing their status over time (Njororai 2022). This explains the emergence of new destinations for African players such as the Middle East and China.

Migration of African footballers to China, although not on the same scale as those moving to Europe, is interesting given that some were already established in European leagues. Some of these players went to CSL when they had already passed their peak, but their experience and name recognition were an asset for a league starved of top-level football talent normally associated with European leagues. Whereas many studies have explored the exodus of African male players to Europe, there is not as much literature pertaining to the African-Chinese connection to which I now turn.

Professional Football in China and the Entrance of African Players

Professional Chinese football evolved from the initial National League A and B to the present Chinese Super League and China League One. The evolution of the Chinese professional leagues was characterized by changing policies on the recruitment and utilization of foreign players. Since professionalization began in 1994 there have been foreign players coming to play in China (Delgado and Villar 2020; Yang and Wang 2022). From 1994 to 2000, each team could register and field three foreign players. In 2001, the number of foreign players allowed to register was relaxed. For a time, four foreign players were allowed to register at the same time in a season, while only three were fielded. With the arrival of the new Chinese Super League in 2004 regulations kept shifting, but eventually the participation of Chinese teams in the Asian Champions League led to an adjustment to the policy allowing foreign players as well as Asian ones (Yang and Wang 2022). Between 2009 and 2016, five foreign players were registered with four being non-Asian, while one had to be Asian. However, only three non-Asian players could be fielded. To give what is judged to be appropriate opportunity for young Chinese players, regulation of the number of permissible foreign players (including Asian ones) is constantly adjusted: A dozen times since 1994 (Yang and Wang 2022). The rules ensure that the number of registered foreign players in each season is limited according to the Football Association regulations, to ensure the league's competitiveness and developmental opportunities. The number of foreign players in the Chinese Super League fluctuated between 91 and 109 in each season from 2009 to 2017 (Zhao 2019). In the 2018 season it was 75, reflecting the reduction of the number of registered foreign players by the Football Association (Yang and Wang 2022). As Table 6.1 shows, more than 141 players from 28 different African countries have played in the Chinese Super League between 2006 and 2023 (excluding 2004, 2005 and 2008 where there were no accessible records available to the author).

Table 6.1 shows that the dominant source of African players for the Chinese Super League is the West African region, which supplied 84 (60 percent) of all the African players in the Chinese League between 2006 and 2023. The West African countries of Nigeria (25), Senegal (13), Ghana (12) and Côte d'Ivoire (10) had the highest representation. The West African region was followed by Central Africa, which had 27 (19 percent) players drawn from Cameroon (16), Democratic Republic of Congo (7), Gabon (2), Central African Republic (1) and Congo-Brazzaville (1). The Southern Africa region was represented by Zambia (7), Angola (4), Mozambique (2), Zimbabwe and South Africa with one player each. The Southern Africa region was closely followed by Northern Africa that was represented by Tunisia (4), Morocco (4), Egypt (3) and Algeria with one player. The East African region trails in last place with only three players, two of them from Kenya and one from Uganda. In terms of countries, the greatest number of migrant players come from Nigeria (25), Cameroon (16), Senegal (13), Ghana (12), Côte d'Ivoire (10), Democratic Republic of Congo (7) and Zambia (7). Since 2006, some African countries have consistently had a player in the CSL. Countries such as Nigeria, Cameroon, Zambia, Côte d'Ivoire, Senegal, Ghana, Democratic Republic of Congo, and Mali have in several seasons, had more than one player in the league. Out of these countries, Nigeria, Ghana, Côte d'Ivoire and Senegal are among the top 20 player-exporters in the world (Poli et al. 2023).

These countries and their regions also happen to dominate African football going by their consistent appearance at the African Cup of Nations and the FIFA World Cup, as well as producing champion teams both at national and club levels. It can be argued that the West, Central, North, and South African regions, have nurtured a football culture that encourages the pursuit of professional football careers abroad and the Chinese Super League is just one of the recipients of these talents. It is a question whether many players who end up in China do so as a stepping-stone to more competitive leagues, and the pursuit of high-status opportunities, in Europe. It is noticeable that many of the players in the Chinese

Table 6.1 Number and percentage of African players in the CSL (2006–2023)

Region	Country	Number per Country	Total Number	Percentage
Eastern Africa	Kenya	02	03	2.13
	Uganda	01		
Southern Africa	Zambia	07	15	10.64
	Angola	04		
	Mozambique	02		
	Zimbabwe	01		
	South Africa	01		
North Africa	Tunisia Morocco	04	12	8.51
	Egypt	04		
	Algeria	03		
		01		
Central Africa	Cameroon	16	27	19.15
	Congo (DRC)	07		
	Congo-			
	Brazzaville	01		
	Gabon	02		
	Central Africa	01		
West Africa	Nigeria	25	84	59.57
	Senegal	13		
	Côte d'Ivoire	10		
	Ghana	12		
	Mali	06		
	Sierra Leone	05		
	Togo	02		
	Gambia	04		
	Cabo Verde	01		
	Burkina	03		
	Faso Guinea	02		
	Guinea-Bissau	01		
	Niger			
Total	28 Countries	141	141	100

Source: Adapted from Transfermarkt. n.d. "Chinese Super League." Accessed January 30, 2024. https://www.transfermarkt.co/chinese-superleague/gastarbeiter/wettbewerb/CSL/saison_id/gesamt.

league are not heavily counted on by their national teams, which implies that they are either aging and in decline, or they have yet to reach a level of performance worthy of selection by their respective national teams. This challenges the notion advanced by Yang and Wang (2022) that players from different countries around the world go to the Chinese Super League to continue their careers as opposed to winding down. If the Chinese Super League were recruiting players at their peak, it would be evident on the rosters of African teams at the African Cup of Nations (AFCON) or FIFA World Cup. Recent AFCON tournaments have been characterized by many players drawn from foreign leagues. At the 2017 edition, of the 368 players involved, 64 percent played their club football in Europe, Africa (28 percent), Asia (6 percent) and the Americas (1 percent). At that tournament, only two players from the Chinese Super League were called up, by Gabon. It is evident that by 2017, most elite African players were still turning out for European sides (Cockayne et al. 2022). It is instructive that these two players spent a brief time in China as one moved back to Africa and the other one ended up in lower leagues in Portugal after spending only one season in China. Most of the Europe-based players played in France (57), followed by England (37), Portugal (19), and Spain and Turkey (each 18) (Njororai 2017).

At the 2019 AFCON tournament, 317 (57 percent) of 552 players were selected from European clubs, 202 (37 percent) from the CAF region, 28 (5 percent) from Asia and five (less than 1 percent) from the Confederation of North, Central America, and Caribbean Association Football (CONCACAF). Of the 28 from Asia, only 5 were drawn from the Chinese Super League as shown in Table 6.2. Similarly, at the 2021/22 AFCON tournament, 407 (62 percent) out of 652 players were from European clubs, 210 (32 percent) from CAF, 29 (4 percent) from Asia and six (less than 1 percent) from CONCACAF. Of the 29 players from Asian Clubs, four players were selected from the Chinese Super League Clubs to represent Ghana, Côte d'Ivoire, Sierra Leone and Cameroon. Table 6.2 shows the trend at the African Cup of Nations where countries have called up players based in China for this elite biennial tournament from 2004 to 2022.

As Table 6.2 shows, 12 different African countries selected players based in China for AFCON tournaments between 2004 and 2021/2022. It is apparent that the launch of the CSL in 2004 and the policy to recruit foreign players from Africa has continued to grow. In the last two AFCON tournaments, CSL was represented by nine players: Five in 2019 and four in 2022, which is a major change from 2004 and 2008 when there was no representation. This shows that the league's influence is gradually growing as African countries are now selecting players based in China for elite national tournaments. Even though the numbers

Table 6.2 African players from the CSL selected for AFCON tournaments (2017–2022)

AFCON Edition	Country	Player	Club	Number
2004	0	0	0	0
2006	Zimbabwe	Gilbert Mushangazhike	Jiangsu Suning	01
2008	0	0	0	0
2010	Burkina Faso	Abdoul-Aziz Nikiema	Qingdao Jonoon	02
	Zambia	James Chamanga	Dalian Shide	
2012	Ghana	Lee Addy	Dalian Aerbin	03
	Zambia	James Chamanga	Dalian Shide	
		Christopher Katongo	Henan Construction	
2013	Zambia	Isaac Chansa	Henan Jianye	04
		Christopher Katongo	Henan Jianye	
		James Chamanga	Liaoning Whowin Dalian Aerbin	
	Mali	Seydou Keita	Dalian Aerbin	
2015	Zambia	Stoppila Sunzu	Shanghai Greenland Shenhua	01
2017	Gabon	Malick Evouna	Tianjin Teda	02
	Gabon	Merlin Tandjigora	Meizhou Hakka	
2019	DR Congo	Cédric Bakambu	Beijing Sinobo Guoan	05
	Zimbabwe	Nyasha Mushekwi	Dalian Yifang	
	Nigeria	Odion Ighalo	Shanghai Shenhua	
	Cameroon	Christian Bassogog	Henan Jianye	
	Kenya	Ayub Masika	Beijing Renhe	
2021/22	Ghana	Mubarak Wakaso	Shenzhen FC	04
	Côte d'Ivoire	Jean Evrard Kouassi	Wuhan	
	Sierra Leone	Mohamed Buya Turay	Henan Songshan Longmen	
	Cameroon	Christian Bassogog	Shanghai Shenhua	
10 editions	12 countries	19 players		22

Source: Author's own compilation.

are still small, it offers a glimmer of hope for growth. One of the highlights of teams at the AFCON utilizing players from the CSL happened in 2013 when both Christopher Katongo of Zambia and Seydou Keita of Mali were designated team captains of their respective countries. Captaining a national team is a significant honor. To have two captains drawn from the CSL was a huge boost to the league's image in Africa. African players have also been recognized for their leadership by their Chinese clubs. Ghanaian player Frank Acheampong was named captain of Tianjin Teda in the CSL in 2020 (Africans on China 2020). Acheampong's elevation to the captaincy was a reward for his hard work, dedication, commitment, exceptional leadership skills, and his performance level (Africans on China 2020). The appointment of an African player reflects positively on the CSL and the place of merit in the appointment of football club leaders.

Despite the leadership roles for some of these players selected from the CSL, it is intriguing that players selected seem also to have very brief stints in China, except for Christian Bassogog who happens to have changed clubs within the same league and James Chamanga who represented Zambia in 2010, 2012 and 2013, while still in China. It is noticeable that many Africans, like other big-name foreign players from other regions, have short tenures in the CSL For example, Seydou Keita, formerly of Barcelona, lasted only a couple of seasons playing for Dalian Aerbin. Similarly, Nicolas Anelka and Didier Drogba had brief stints, despite initially committing to long-term deals (Kayode 2016). Kwame Ayew, who played in China for many years, is quoted by Kayode (2016) as saying that many players do not last long because Chinese clubs are quick to terminate contracts at the slightest drop in a player's form. There are also those who argue that the CSL does not help to improve the skills of the African players and the players who go there are motivated solely by financial reward (Kayode 2016). A study by Poli et al. (2023) shows that three leagues with the most experienced (i.e., oldest) footballers are in Asia (China, Japan, and Saudi Arabia), which suggests aging players winding down their careers in (often highly remunerative) new settings. The study also revealed that there were geographical specificities in the age of the players making up the club squads, with a much stronger focus on young players in Europe than elsewhere in the world. For example, Qingdao Hainiu's team roster averaged 31.5 years, followed by Chengdu Rongcheng which posed an average of 29.8 years. In contrast, Europe had clubs with the youngest squads, implying that players spent their prime in Europe and moved to places like China, Saudi Arabia, and Japan to wind down careers. It is therefore clear that although the CSL has provided an option for African players, it is not at a level to compete effectively with the European clubs that continue to be premium destinations for talented African players in their prime.

In terms of the recruitment trends of the African players, figure one shows that on average there have been over 13 players plying their trade in the Chinese Super League between 2006 and 2023 each year.

As Figure 6.1 shows, 2006 was the year with the lowest number of African players (3). However, the numbers picked up and in 2015 and 2017, and the number of African players peaked at 19 per year. The advent of new rules and COVID-19 saw the numbers decline to a low of 14 in 2021 and 2022, although the CSL continues to attract African players. Some African players moving from Europe to China speak of their adventurer's spirit as well as a strategic desire to maximize their earnings. For example, when Yakubu Aiyegbeni left Blackburn Rovers in the English Premier League to play in China, he argued that the motivation was not money (Sportsmail Reporter 2012). Instead, Aiyegbeni felt that after scoring 137 goals in nine years in England there was nothing left to prove. He continued to argue that money cannot buy happiness and that he had found great love, happiness, sincerity, and warmth among the Chinese fans. He felt that he needed to be a part of the new football program in China. This fits Maguire's (1999) argument about the unfolding of transnational cosmopolitan culture occurring within globalization processes. For a time, Chinese clubs were some of the highest bidders for playing talent in the global football transfer market, but as

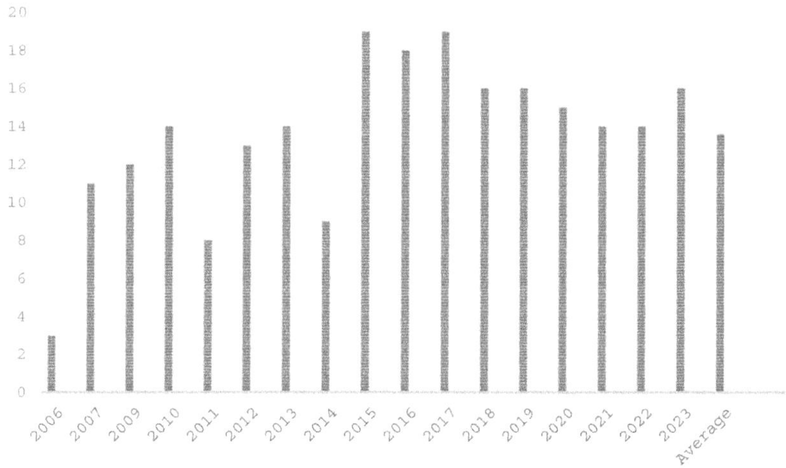

Figure 6.1 Number of African players in CSL between 2006 and 2023 per season
Source: Author's own compilation.

Aeyegbeni argued, the pull of China was also the novelty of the football initiative there and the pursuit of adventure and new challenges in a new setting.

Impact of African Players

The advantage that African players, and other migrants, bring to the CSL is competition for slots on the first team. According to Yang and Wang (2022), the presence of foreign players creates greater pressure for local players, which forces them to increase their effort and desire to excel. African players have made important contributions to clubs all over the world and their presence in the CSL affords them an opportunity to make a difference in an emerging league. For example, Kwame Ayew of Ghana was the top scorer in 2003 and during the inaugural CSL season in 2004. The tactical astuteness of African players such as Ghana's Acheampong, DRC's Cedric Bakambu, Cameroon's Christian Bassogog, and Sierra Leone's Buya Toure, has also been acknowledged, making these players the core of their respective teams (Yang and Wang 2022). Just as African players added an extra dimension to the European game, so they have started to enrich the Chinese League in significant ways. Indeed, the participation of African players has facilitated an expansion of tactical choices and game plans for teams, which has indirectly improved the competitive level of domestic players as well as the overall strength of teams (Li 2021; Yang and Wang 2022). According to Li, "African players are the hidden gems. Their reputation might not be as loud but they can quickly adapt to the CSL style" (2021, 51). African players frequently have attributes and performance levels equivalent to European and South American counterparts but are generally available for lower transfer fees and compensation packages (Li 2021).

The arrival of African players in the CSL has helped elevate global awareness of the league. The arrival of global superstars such as Didier Drogba, John Obi Mikel and Yaya Toure elicited plenty of media coverage that raised the profile of the CSL (Agbaje 2020). Some of the other top players that have boosted the image, attractiveness, and local support for the CSL include Cedric Bakambu from Congo, Benjamin Moukandjo from Cameroon, Richmond Boakye and Asamoah Gyan from Ghana, Gervinho, Demba Ba and Stephane Mbia from Côte d'Ivoire, Idion Ighalo, Aiyegbeni Yakubu and Obafemi Martins from Nigeria, Seydou Keita and Frederic Kanoute from Mali (Agbaje 2020). These African football stars who switched clubs from Europe to China made local and international headlines, boosting media coverage of the CSL and creating heightened interest in CSL matches. The unique presence and style of such star African players adds to the entertainment value of the league. According to Yang and Wang (2022), there are many factors influencing attendance of football matches in China, but there is no denying that Didier Drogba's star power was a key factor in the increase in attendance while he played for Shanghai Shenhua. Apart from increased stadium attendance, press coverage also increased especially in the foreign media (Yang and Wang 2022).

The presence of African players and their continued excellence on the field helps to create a positive view of China–Africa relations (Africans on China 2020). Apart from being football players, they also act as cultural ambassadors for their respective countries and the African continent. At the level of people-to-people exchange, African players interact with their Chinese teammates, fans and communities, thereby enhancing and sustaining cultural exchange and understanding. However, unlike the western countries, where many former African players comfortably settle and raise families, many Africans in China have described obstacles to settling down. A specialist in African communities in China, Castillo (2014) reports failing to find African residents who think of China as "home." This may also explain why many African players' presence in China has been relatively transient. Nonetheless, the presence of African players in China is helping to develop greater familiarity and affinity between the people of China and Africa, with the promise of lasting influences socially and culturally.

Conclusion

For many years African male football players have been in great demand from professional clubs in Europe and other contexts (Acheampong et al. 2019; Darby et al. 2022; Poli 2006a, 2006b, 2010). The popularity of the game driven by globalization processes and the interplay of economic, infrastructural, cultural, legal, and social factors all accentuated by changing technologies have opened new frontiers for talented players around the world. One emerging destination is China, with the CSL becoming a competitive option for African players (Delgado and Villar 2020; Yang and Wang 2022). China's sustained economic growth over the last two decades has contributed to an intense and multifaceted global engagement that includes the game of association football. This chapter has used various theoretical perspectives to explain African male football labor migration as well as highlighting some of the factors that underpin it. Globalization processes, which include the emergence of a globally connected economy, transnational cosmopolitan cultures, and a range of international social movements have made it easier for African players to move abroad where they are best rewarded for their athletic talent. Although the transnational mobility of African players is complex, Wallerstein's (1974) world system and associated dependency theories underscore the existing global inequalities that push players from Africa to other parts of the world. There are complex socio-economic, political, and cultural factors that drive the migration of players from Africa to established regions in Europe and North America and emerging ones in the Middle East and China. The transnational mobility of African male players is shaped by historical contexts, globalization of the game and the agency of the players themselves. Per the analysis set out in this chapter, the CSL is an example of Maguire's (1999) claim that modern sport is an example of cultural and geographical globalization as part of global homogenization processes. In substantive terms, the competitive emergence of the CSL has provided an alternative destination for African players who are less well compensated for their talents in Africa. It is evident that the CSL has appealed to African players of different abilities and experience. Some, not all, are aging stars exiting the European scene to explore new ventures and seek significant financial compensation. It is apparent that some African players, at different stages of their development, do not last long in the CSL. On a positive note, recent editions of AFCON show that there is consistent representation from the CSL at the tournament, testament to the increasing quality of players joining the league and its capacity to develop players to a high standard. A great diversity of African countries is represented in the CSL, which demonstrates the growing interest and recognition that the CSL enjoys among African players as a viable venue to develop as a professional. Some of these African players are also being called on to provide leadership roles for their clubs and their home countries. Thus, despite the transient nature of African players' presence, their impact is noticeable on the field of play as well as elevating the profile, standards, commercial value, and stadium attendance in the CSL.

References

Acheampong, Ernest Yeboah. 2019. "Giving Back to Society: Evidence from African Sports Migrants." *Sport in Society* 22 (12): 2045–2064.

Acheampong, Ernest Yeboah, Malek Bouhaouala, and Michel Raspaud. 2019. "Socioeconomic Analysis of African Footballers' Migration to Europe: Elements for Decision Making Based on the West African Case." In *Africa's Elite Football*, edited by Chuka Onwumechili, 58–73. Routledge.

Africans on China. 2020. "Ghanaian Player Makes History As First Captain Of A Chinese Topflight Side." Africans on China. Last modified August 24. https://africansonchina.com/ghanaian-player-makes-history-as-first-captain-of-a-chinese-topflight-side/.

Agbaje, Orire. 2020. "Are African Football Players Winning in the Chinese Super League?" Last modified December 9. https://africansonchina.com/are-african-football-players-winning-in-the-chinese-super-league/.

Akindes, Gerard A. 2013. "South Asia and South-East Asia: new paths of African Footballer Migration." *Soccer & Society* 14 (5): 684–701.

———. 2018. "Dream and Drudgery: Football and African Migrants in the European Union." In *The Palgrave International Handbook of Football and Politics*, edited by J. M. De Waela, S. Gibril, E. Gloriozova, and R. Spaaij, 345–362. Palgrave Macmillan.

Alegi, Peter. 2010. *African Soccerscapes: How a Continent Changed the World's Game*. Ohio University Press.

Alegi, Peter, and Chris Bolsmann. 2016. "Introduction: Africa and the Global Migration of Football Labor." *African Studies Review* 59 (3): 3–14.

Andreff, Wladimir. 2021. "Economic Globalization of the Sports Industry." In *The Palgrave Handbook of Globalization and Sport*, edited by Joseph Maguire, Katie Liston, and Mark Falcous, 271–295. Palgrave Macmillan.

Aniche, Ernest Toochi, and Victor Emeka Ukaegbu. 2016. "Structural Dependence, Vertical Integration and Regional Economic Cooperation in Africa: A Study of Southern African Development Community." *Africa Review* 8 (2): 108–119.

Castillo, Roberto. 2014. "Feeling at Home in the 'Chocolate City': An Exploration of Place-Making Practices and Structures of Belonging amongst Africans in Guangzhou." *Inter-Asia Cultural Studies* 15 (2): 235–257.

Cockayne, David, Simon Chadwick, and Jonathan Sullivan. 2022. "Chinese Football—from a State-Led Past to a Digital Future." *Journal of Global Sport Management* 7 (3): 345–354.

Darby, Paul. 2002. *Africa, Football and FIFA: Politics, Colonialism and Resistance*. Frank Cass.

Darby, Paul, James Esson, and Christian Ungruhe. 2022. *African Football Migration: Aspirations, Experiences and Trajectories African Football Migration*. Manchester University Press.

Darby, Paul, and Harry A. Solberg. 2017. "African Football Labour Migration to Europe: Player Motivations and the Socio-Political Implications in Sending and Receiving Nations." *Sport in Society* 20 (12): 1769–1785.

Delgado, Daniel, and Francisco Javier Villar. 2020. "It Is Not a Game: Soccer and China's Search for World Hegemony." *Soccer & Society* 21 (2): 225–238.

Engh, Mari Haugaa, and Sine Agergaard. 2015. "Producing Mobility through Locality and Visibility: Developing a Transnational Perspective on Sports Labour Migration." *International Review for the Sociology of Sport* 50 (8): 974–992.

Fottrell, Stephen. 2012. "African Football Stars' Exodus to China." BBC Sport. Last modified July 11. https://www.bbc.com/sport/football/18780903.

Frank, Andre Gunder. 1967. *Capitalism and Underdevelopment in Latin America*. Vol. 93. NYU Press.

Gratton, Chris, and Harry Arne Solberg. 2007. *The Economics of Sports Broadcasting*. Routledge.

Held, David, and Anthony McGrew. 2007. *Globalization/Anti-globalization: Beyond the Great Divide*. Polity.

Horowitz, Jonathan, and Stephen R McDaniel. 2015. "Investigating the Global Productivity Effects of Highly Skilled Labour Migration: How Immigrant Athletes Impact Olympic Medal Counts." *International Journal of Sport Policy and Politics* 7 (1): 19–42.

Kayode, Olukunle. 2016. "Chinese Leagues Promise African Footballers Big Money, but Is the Deal That Sweet?" True Africa. Last modified March 29. https://trueafrica.co/article/chinese-football-and-african-players/.

KEA, and CDES. 2013. *The Economic and Legal Aspects of Transfers of Players*. KEA European Affairs.

Li, Julian. 2021. "Impact of Foreign Players from Different Regions on Football Team Performance in the Chinese Super League." In *5th International Conference on Research in Humanities and Social Sciences*, Berlin, Germany. https://www.dpublication.com/wp-content/uploads/2021/12/8-1068.pdf.

Magee, Jonathan, and John Sugden. 2002. "'The World at Their Feet': Professional Football and International Labor Migration." *Journal of Sport and Social Issues* 26 (4): 421–437. https://doi.org/10.1177/0193732502238257.

Maguire, Joseph. 1999. *Global Sport: Identities-Societies-Civilizations*. Polity Press.

———. 2017. *The Global Football Industry: Marketing Perspectives*. Routledge.

Newman, Joshua I, Hanhan Xue, Ryan Chen, Yiming Chen, and Nicholas M Watanabe. 2021. "Football and Cultural Citizenship in China: A Study in Three Embodiments." *Sport in Society* 24 (12): 2222–2245.

Njororai, Wycliffe W. Simiyu. 2017. "African Footballers Face an Allegiance Problem: Country Versus Club." The Conversation. Last modified January 24. https://theconversation.com/african-footballers-face-an-allegiance-problem-country-versus-club-71634.

———. 2022. "The Origins, Status, Contributions and Contradictions of Association Football in Uganda." In *Football (Soccer) in Africa: Origins, Contributions, and Contradictions*, edited by Augustine E. Ayuk, 253–273. Springer.

Onwumechili, Chuka, and Unwana Akpan. 2020. "Nigeria: as Football Labour Scrambles, What About Family?" *Sport in Society* 23 (7): 1119–1135.

Poli, Raffaele. 2006a. "Africans' Status in the European Football Players' Labour Market." *Soccer & Society* 7 (2–3): 278–291. https://doi.org/10.1080/14660970600615369.

———. 2006b. "Migrations and trade of African Football Players: Historic, Geographical and Cultural Aspects." *Africa Spectrum* 41 (3): 393–414.

———. 2010. "Understanding Globalization through Football: The New International Division of Labour, Migratory Channels and Transnational Trade Circuits." *International Review for the Sociology of Sport* 45 (4): 491–506. https://doi.org/10.1177/1012690210370640.

Poli, Raffaele, Loïc Ravenel, and Roger Besson. 2023. *Team Demographics in 48 Leagues Worldwide*. CIES Football Observatory (Neuchâtel).

Rodney, Walter. 1972. *How Europe Underdeveloped Africa*. Bogle-L'Ouverture Publications.

Sportsmail Reporter. 2012. "It's Not the Money! Yakubu Claims He Signed Chinese Deal for 'Love'". Daily Mail Online. Last modified June 29. https://www.dailymail.co.uk/sport/football/article-2166325/Yakubu-signs-Chinese-Guangzhou-R-F.html.

Wallerstein, Immanuel. 1974. *The Modern World System*. Academic Press.

Yang, Kaijie, and Lianjin Wang. 2022. "Study on the Cooperative and Win-Win Relationship between the Introduction of African Football Players in Chinese Professional Football League." *Open Access Library Journal* 9 (7): 1–16.

Zhao, YC. 2019. *Research on the Current Situation and Countermeasures of Introducing Foreign Players into Chinese Super League from the Perspective of S-C-P*. Shanghai Normal University.

7

Chinese Football League Framing: Perception of Nigerian Football Fans and Football Labor Migration to China

Unwana Samuel Akpan,[1] Chuka Onwumechili,[2] and Kalema Elizabeth Meggs[3]

Background

Africa constitutes one of the largest populations of "football lovers" in the world (Akpan 2020; Poli 2010). Despite this, there is a paucity of academic research on the issues we address in this chapter, namely the attitudes of African fans toward African labor migration in football. While some related work has recorded the migration of African football talent to Asia and identified stops in Asia along the migration routes that take African players to clubs in Europe (e.g., Akindes 2013; Poli 2010), African football migration to China has received little attention outside the chapters in this book. This is an important lacuna given the significant number of African footballers, male and female, who have migrated to China to play professionally. Among the cohort of African players in China, West Africa is strongly represented, as noted in the previous chapter. This is unsurprising given the relative strength of West African football on the continent and is one reason

1 Unwana Samuel Akpan, Lecturer, University of Lagos, unwanaa@yahoo.co.uk.
2 Chuka Onwumechili, Professor, Howard University, conwumechili@howard.edu.
3 Kalema Meggs, Doctoral Student, Howard University, kalema.meggs@bison.howard.edu.

why we focus on the attitudes of fans in Nigeria, a West African nation with a rich football culture and long history of producing talented players.

Sporting migration from Africa to China cannot be separated from the general migration flows that follow similar routes and have been reported in the literature. Cissé (2021), for example, reports the impact of US$192 billion trade between China and Africa as the driving force in this migration. While the movement of labor has not been unidirectional, it is movement from Africa to China that is the interest of this paper since it is relevant to football labor. Cissé (2021) estimates that up to 500,000 Africans permanently or temporarily reside in China as part of economic, educational and people-to-people exchanges. China has become an attractive destination for African talent and labor in several sectors, not just professional football. Traditionally, African migrations tended to track colonial legacies, with migrants moving from former colonial territories to the home of erstwhile colonial powers. Aside from colonial linkages, many migrants moved between countries with shared languages, but that is obviously not the case with China. Neither has China traditionally stood out for the quality of its football. Indeed, at the time of writing, China was ranked 81st in the FIFA Men's rankings, behind 15 African national teams. So why do African footballers choose China as a destination? Reflecting on the migration of Africans to China, Adebayo suggests that some Africans find themselves in Chinese cities because they could not reach their planned country, an experience that positions China as "both a dreamland and an accidental destination" (2022, 887). The starting point for any discussion of African migration, must be the reality of many African countries' security, developmental and economic challenges, which have incentivized or compelled labor and other forms of outward migration. This flight is dispersed all over the globe to various European countries, the Americas, and to other African countries with safer or better economic conditions. In this context, Esson has emphasized the concept of social mobility to explain migration choices (2013, 2015, 2017), which we believe can also help explain why African footballers choose to play in China. Social mobility refers to the desire by individuals to climb the socio-economic ladder (Prais 1955) through which they accrue and utilize social, cultural and economic capital. Although the quest for social mobility acknowledges a complex array of variables, the most salient to explain footballer migration from Africa to China may be the simplest, namely income incentives and equality of opportunity (Brunetti and Fiaschi 2019, 3). Talented footballers of both sexes often face economic hardship playing in Africa, where salaries are low, and payments can delayed or not paid at all (Onwumechili 2024). Financial and professional betterment and the quest for individual and familial social mobility are an intuitive explanation for African players' migration choices. Our focus in this chapter is to assess how fans react to and perceive player motivations, contributions and prospects in light of their decision to move to a country strong on economic power but weak in football pedigree.

History of African Football Migration

Sport migration has become a prevalent process internationally. Young football players' migration from Africa has influenced perceptions of international mobility, creating an increased demand for the outward migration of football talent (Ungruhe and Schmidt 2020). African football migration to European and Asian countries is particularly relevant in Western Africa, where professional development opportunities in local leagues are incommensurate with the quantity and quality of talent produced in the region. In other African contexts, notably South Africa, where governments and economies are stable and domestic leagues better developed, more local talent "stays home" and clubs can attract foreign players from the broader region (Ungruhe and Schmidt 2020). However, the fact remains that many African footballers have historically aspired to play abroad, notably in Europe. Unstable or adverse social or economic conditions have driven many players to seek opportunities overseas, creating a talent drain from the continent. Migration not only provides financial relief to the players but also significantly enhances the quality of European leagues. The influx of African talent brings diversity, skill, and flair to the game, contributing to the overall appeal and competitiveness of European football. Early pioneers include Liberia's George Weah, Cameroon's Samuel Eto'o, and Ivorian Didier Drogba, who made significant impacts in European competition. These players not only showcased their exceptional skills but also paved the way for future generations of African footballers to pursue careers abroad.

Following the European experience, China has recognized the potential of foreign players to enrich their professional leagues. In a bid to increase levels of competitiveness and audience appeal, China has welcomed international talent, much of it from Africa. This openness to foreign talent elevates the quality of play, fosters cultural exchange and strengthens global football connections. The desire of African footballers to play abroad to escape economic hardship has benefited European leagues and the ripple effect has now extended to other regions like China and the Gulf, where embracing international talent has become a strategy to enhance competitiveness and entertainment value.

Nigeria-China Relations in Football

The CSL has made significant advances in terms of its professionalization, commercialization, organization, funding and quality of play. The rise of the CSL coincides with positive developments in China–Africa football relationships, as discussed in several chapters in this book. Nigerian football players represent the largest cohort of African players in the CSL (Liu 2019), with lucrative contracts offered to established European league players like John Obi Mikel, Odion Ighalo and Anthony Ujah. Numerous Nigerian football players have made substantial sporting contributions to their Chinese clubs, thereby raising the profile of Nigerian football in China. China has always shown readiness to invest in Nigerian football, illustrated by the Chinese Football Association signing a partnership agreement with the Nigerian Football Federation (NFF) in 2019 to develop grassroots football in Nigeria. The objective of the partnership was to provide technical support, training for coaches, and coaching exchange programs between the two nations.

In 2018, the Chinese government built, furnished, and donated a football stadium in Abuja, the federal capital territory (Chen 2019). Beijing's interest in developing the football relationship with Nigeria extends to the Nigerian and Chinese national teams playing each other in several international friendlies. These exhibition matches have deepened sporting ties and facilitated economic and people-to-people exchanges. They have also led to the expansion of Chinese scouting operations in Nigeria, increasing the prospect of a pipeline of Nigerian talent to the Chinese football leagues.

History of Notable Nigerian Footballers in China

Nigerian football players joining the Chinese football league can be traced back to the late 1990s and early 2000s. Christopher Ohenhen became the first well-known Nigerian football player to join a Chinese club, Bayi FC, in 1997 (Kobo 2018). He had a successful career in China which arguably created opportunities for other Nigerian players who would follow. While Ohenhen went to China at the tail end of his career and the move did not provide significant remuneration or attention among fans in Nigeria, it began a regular flow of Nigerian players to Chinese clubs. Most were not expensive or high profile, but that would change at the beginning of the 2010s, when more significant investment flowed into the CSL. Several established Nigerian talents followed. Yakubu Aiyegbeni, the renowned Nigerian striker and English Premier League stalwart, joined Guangzhou R&F in 2012 (Hao 2021). In 2016, Shanghai Shenhua signed Obafemi Martins, who enjoyed an impressive career with the club and left a lasting impact on the Chinese league (Cockayne et al. 2022; Yang and Wang 2022). In 2017, the highly respected midfielder John Obi Mikel joined Tianjin TEDA from Premier League club Chelsea. Another proven Premier League striker, Odion Ighalo, joined Changchun Yatai in 2017. His goalscoring record earned him a move to Shanghai Shenhua and subsequently Manchester United. In addition to these examples of established internationals playing for elite Chinese clubs, there have been many more Nigerians of less renown plying their trade in the CSL and lower leagues. Indicative of the incentive structure that pertains for established Nigerian players in China, the economic and sporting travails that hit the CSL during the COVID-19 pandemic and pursuant zero-COVID policies led to the rapid departure of many players. It appears that payment of wages by newly cash-strapped clubs was a significant contributor to some departures (McNicol and Raine 2023), although it is equally true that many less heralded players, possibly with fewer alternative opportunities, remained at their Chinese clubs during this difficult period.

In recent years a new type of Nigerian athlete has emerged onto the professional football scene in China: Mixed-race players born in China to Chinese and Nigerian parents who are exempt from CFA restrictions on foreign players and potentially eligible to represent Chinese national teams. Hao (2021) reports the case of Su Yuliang, a 16-year-old player of mixed Nigerian-Chinese parentage who joined the CSL club Guangzhou City FC from its academy squad. This history-making moment is unlikely to be the last such example, given the expansion of African communities in China seeking business and education opportunities. Many Africans are increasingly settling in China, particularly in Guangzhou and Zhejiang, where they actively participate in international trade (Muller and Rainer-Wehrhahn 2011). African expatriates run international businesses of various sizes, deepening economic connections between China and Nigeria. Many of these African businesspeople have grown up watching and playing football and are now enrolling their children in Chinese football academies. These children embody the expansion of Africa-China engagement in the realm of football and may mitigate the relatively limited consciousness of Chinese football in West Africa. The lack of a long-term footprint, not aided by the transient nature of top-level Nigerian footballers in China, has prevented the popularity of mediated Chinese league football in Nigeria. Despite Nigerian footballers' significant historical contribution to Chinese football, Nigerian media coverage has traditionally neglected these efforts, hindering the thickening of football connections between the two countries. It is to this issue that we now turn, seeking to explore the level of awareness of Chinese football among Nigerians.

Methodology

This study uses qualitative data gathered using a semi-structured interview instrument. The semi-structured interview is useful as it gives respondents flexibility to express complex ideas and perceptions (Kazi and Shidhore 2020). The study engaged 19 respondents using a purposive sampling method. The participants are self-described football fans above the age of 18. Selection was based on the six geopolitical zones in Nigeria (Northwest, Northeast, Southwest, Southeast, South-south, and North-central). The interviews explore participants' knowledge of Nigerian footballers playing in China, their feelings about Chinese football and their perceptions of the Chinese football league. Interviews were recorded, with permission, and transcribed. We analyzed the transcripts from the 19 respondent interviews using a thematic qualitative media analysis approach which helps probe broader cultural traits and perceptions. Nigerian football fans were interviewed face to face over a four-week period, using a 13-item semi-structured instrument conducted in English. Follow-up questions were asked where necessary to gain additional relevant information. The application of thematic analysis of the interview data was used to identify collective and common shared views.

Findings

From our in-depth interviews with 19 Nigerian football fans, several major themes emerged. We specify these themes below and illustrate them with representative contributions made by interview subjects reported pseudonymously.

Negative Perceptions of China

One of the dominant themes that emerged was the negative perception of Chinese football generated by broader economic perspectives, notably concerns about the quality of Chinese products. Emeka encapsulates the notion that China produces inferior products, which infuses his perception of Chinese football:

> I don't watch it [CSL] because everything about China is fake and adulterated. There is no serious football fan [who] would devote his precious time [to] watching let alone following the Chinese league. I don't know for others, but personally I don't watch it.

Dele expresses a similar view, while also alluding to the issue of corruption, which has plagued Chinese football since the inception of professionalization:

> I am very skeptical about anything to do with China, especially their products. I feel their football league could be a mirage. There might be tricks in their league. I don't think any serious player would want to play in China, because I believe that would be the end of his career.

Adamu added:

> I have never heard of any remarkable achievement from the Chinese league. Instead of watching the Chinese league, I [would] rather watch the Arab [sic] League. I strongly believe the Chinese league would be inferior. Even the football itself that they kick might be fake.

More than half of the interviewees expressed that the Chinese football league is inferior and considered African footballer migration to China in terms of "economic exploitation." These stringent views may reflect the deterioration of public opinion toward China observed in numerous African countries. This suspicion was borne out by the opinion of Osaze, who raised the seemingly unrelated issue of Chinese companies' treatment of African employees in Africa:

> Let me ask you, have you worked in a Chinese company before, or read in the newspaper the exploitative treatments Chinese companies mete out on their African employees? Please google them. The facts are there. Though they say China is the second largest economy in the world, but the way they mistreat their employees who are Africans on African soil is rather pathetic. Imagine, this is our own soil, you can imagine the kind of treatment that they would dish out to African footballers playing football in their own land. I can just imagine. I don't know what a Nigerian would be doing in such a situation when there is the European league.

Nevelyn expanded on this point:

> There's nothing exciting about the Chinese football league, because first, they have an image problem with Africans, especially Nigerians, in the way their

> companies hire, fire, and exploit Nigerians. Don't you think such treatment could be extended to Nigerians playing professional football in their country? I doubt if anyone in Nigeria here would say anything good about Chinese football, that is if at all they even know about it.

Absence of Entertainment Value and Media Coverage

While the trenchant views expressed above took us slightly by surprise, a further set of complaints was easier to anticipate. They relate to the relative lack of appeal that Chinese football has in sporting and entertainment terms, especially when, implicitly or explicitly, compared to European offerings like the English Premier League, as expressed by Dele:

> There's something you must understand, one of the things that big advertisers and football fans consider before placing in ad on any station, or any football fan staying glued to a league on TV is the audience base and the entertaining nature of how the play is embellished and reported, covered and analyzed in the media, and the Chinese Super League lacks this entertaining nature.

In the same vein, Umanah explained:

> If you watch the finesse, the razmataz and round-the-clock media coverage of the European leagues, COPA America or La Liga, you would realize that the Chinese football league does not even come close.

Shola explained that the CSL has failed to make itself into an attractive media product and has failed to generate the excitement that would appeal to African football fans like him:

> They might have what it takes for people to develop interest in their football league, but I can tell you that there's no media buzz about their league. For instance, look at the English Premier League, and how they draw so much attention by simply creating some buzz around it.

One respondent suggested that part of the problem may lie in the failure of Chinese media to fully leverage the internationalization of Chinese football. Despite the influx of foreign players of African and other origin, coverage of Chinese football remains parochial and subject to language and other accessibility barriers as expressed by Oke:

> I tried watching the Chinese league once, but I didn't enjoy their analysis because of the thick Chinese accent. Maybe it's deliberate to promote their language, but I believe if you brought Africans and other nationals to your country to play football, you should be able to engage English football commentators to do the commentaries, so it wouldn't be boring. This is what the Arabs [sic] are doing in their league. Another issue is their restrictions on internet activities. This way, we can't even follow the game on popular social media platforms such as Facebook, Twitter or Instagram.

The majority of respondents noted poor access to streamed games on major social platforms as an obstacle preventing Nigerians from developing an interest in Chinese football. This issue speaks to the limited internationalization experience of nascent football media operations in China, limited arrangements with international broadcasters to carry Chinese football and the issue of Chinese internet controls.

Migration of Football Labor to China

The respondents were asked to share their views on football migration and the specific issue of whether they would encourage Nigerian football players to migrate to China to play professional football. Consistent with popular narratives about the CSL, Alom explained:

> I have no doubt that any player, not just Nigerian football player moving to China is suicidal. I don't think any young man who wants to have a successful career in football can even contemplate moving to China to play professional football.

Such perspectives are frequently heard, not just in Africa, and are generally due to the perceived inferior quality of the sporting competition in China. However, Alom also raised a further issue that dovetails with opinions reported above on perceptions of labor conditions and fair treatment:

> Their dealings as a people are shrouded in secrecy, especially in business transactions. If they cannot be transparent in their business dealings, how then can they be fair with foreign players? Or are you not aware that they have integrity, credibility and image issues? I don't think any right thinking aspiring young Nigerian football player would even think of migrating there.

These negative stereotypes are clearly salient among the Nigerian fans we interviewed, as they surfaced time and again, coloring impressions about Chinese football by implication. Rufus provides an example of this thought process:

> I think the negative image that the Chinese people have due to them producing substandard products for Africans have some discouraging effects on Nigerian football players migrating to China. Who knows, their football league might be fake as well.

The impression of deficiency and artifice was recurrent, and we suspect that it reflects broader feelings about China and its engagement with Africa. Despite large numbers of Nigerian and other African nationals doing business in China and taking up educational opportunities, Hassan illustrates a pervasive impression:

> Instead of going to China to play football, why not Europe or Arab [sic]? There's something about China that is not real.

While a large majority of respondents do not support the idea of Nigerian footballers migrating to China for play in their professional leagues, there was no sense of blame attached to those who did so for economic motivations. The overriding feeling was one of perplexity that talented individuals should choose China as a host nation for football migration.

Conclusion

The study reported in this chapter found that the long and storied history of Nigerian participation in Chinese professional football has failed to generate a strong interest or attachment to Chinese football among the Nigerian fans we interviewed. This may be an artifact of our sample, or it could indicate a missed opportunity to use football as a vehicle to thicken the engagement between these two major powers and trade partners. At present, rather than an instrument of soft power that might bring the two sides together around a shared interest in sport, football, as expressed by our respondents, is a site where broader frustrations with China's engagement with Nigeria are articulated. However, in identifying several obstacles to the popularization of Chinese football in Nigeria, interviewees also pointed to ways in which China's football and media industries can do better. Chinese football needs to be more widely broadcast on both terrestrial TV and online via streaming platforms. Publicity and promotion of matches and coordinated efforts to generate interest and excitement are much needed. Here the CSL can learn from more developed football and media industry operations, such as those built around the English Premier League, which enjoys substantial popularity across West Africa. The continuing presence of African players in CSL, despite the pandemic-era departure of high-profile players, is one pole around which promotion might be built, since this appears to resonate with Nigerian fans. However, the broader perception of "quality" when it comes to Chinese products and brands, is something that is outside of the control of football operations. Yet, as Chinese brands, particularly in telecommunications, consumer technologies and electric vehicles, "go global" and move up the value chain, perceptions expressed by our interviewees may change. Perceptions around Chinese treatment of African workers also bleeds into attitudes toward Nigerian football player migration. This is an issue for Chinese companies and Chinese and African regulators to address, but in football, one way to promote positive exchanges is through the expansion of friendly matches, which interviewees endorse as a symbol of collaboration and mutual respect. Finally, and fundamentally, to improve the image of the CSL as a worthy recipient of Nigerian and African talent, the league must work to improve standards on the pitch and professionalize operations off it.

References

Adebayo, Kudus O. 2022. "'They did not allow me to enter the place I was heading to': being 'stuck-in-place'and transit emplacement in Nigerian migrations to China." *Mobilities* 17 (6): 885–898.

Akindes, Gerard A. 2013. "South Asia and South-East Asia: New Paths of African Footballer Migration." *Soccer & Society* 14 (5): 684–701.

Akpan, Unwana S. 2020. "Elite Local Leagues and Transnational Broadcast of European Football." In *Africa's Elite Football: Structure, Politics, and Everyday Challenges*, edited by Chuka Onwumechili, 34–44. Routledge.

Brunetti, Irene, and Davide Fiaschi. 2019. "Occupational Mobility: Theory and an Application in Italy." *The Journal of Economic Inequality* 9: 1–21.

Chen, W. F. 2019. "Research on the Feasibility of Naturalizing African Sports Talents in China." *Sports Excellence* (38): 86–88.

Cissé, Daouda. 2021. "As Migration and Trade Increase Between China and Africa, Traders at Both Ends Often Face Precarity." Migration Policy Institute. Last modified July 21. https://www.migrationpolicy.org/article/migration-trade-china-africa-traders-face-precarity.

Cockayne, David, Simon Chadwick, and Jonathan Sullivan. 2022. "Chinese Football—from a State-Led Past to a Digital Future." *Journal of Global Sport Management* 7 (3): 345–354.

Esson, James. 2013. "A Body and a Dream at Avital Conjuncture: Ghanaian Youth, Uncertainty and the Allure of Football." *Geoforum* 47: 84–92.

———. 2015. "Escape to Victory: Development, Youth Entrepreneurship and the Migration of Ghanaian Footballers." *Geoforum* 64: 47–55.

———. 2017. “A Social Negotiation of Hope: Male West African Youth, ‘Waithood’ and the Pursuit of Social Becoming Through Football.” *Boyhood Studies* 10: 22–43.

Hao, Tony. 2021. “16-Year-Old Nigerian-Chinee Player to Debut in China’s Pro Soccer League.” Radii. Last modified July 15. https://radii.co/article/su-yuliang.

Kazi, Mohammad M., and Asawari. A. Shidhore. 2020. “Google Classroom Sessions as a Modern E-Learning Tool for The Second-Year Undergraduate Dental Students—A Questionnaire Feedback Study.” *International Journal of Medical Science and Public Health* 9: 1–6.

Kobo, Kingsley. 2018. “Who Are the 12 Africans in the Chinese Super League?” ACL Sports, Last modified March 6. https://www.aclsports.com/10178-2/.

Liu, G. Y. 2019. “60-Year Historical Evolution and Modern Significance of China–Africa Sports Interaction.” *Journal of Wuhan Institute of Physical Education* 53: 19–24.

McNicol, Andrew and Andrew Raine. 2023. “Xi Jinping wanted China to be a global soccer power. What went wrong?” CNN, April 7, 2023. https://edition.cnn.com/2023/04/07/china/xi-jinping-china-football-dream-fail-intl-hnk-dst/index.html

Muller, Angelo, and Rainer K. Wehrhahn. 2011. “New Migration Processes.” *Geographische Zeitschrift* 99 (2–3): 104–122.

Onwumechili, Chuka. 2024. *Women's Football in Africa*. Abingdon: Taylor & Francis.

Poli, Raffaele. 2010. “African Migrants in Asian and European Football: Hopes and Realities.” *Soccer & Society* 13 (6): 1001–1011.

Prais, S. J. 1955. “The Formal Theory of Social Mobility.” *Population Studies* 9 (1): 72–81.

Ungruhe, Christian, and Mads B. Schmidt. 2020. “Why Are East African Players Absent in European Football? Localizing African Football Migration Along Structural Constraints, Colonial Legacies and Voluntary Immobility.” *Journal of Sport and Social Issues* 44 (5): 397–420.

Yang, Kajie, and Lianjin Wang. 2022. “Study on the Cooperative and Win-Win Relationship Between the Introduction of African Football Players in the Chinese Professional Football League.” *Open Access Library Journal* 9 (7): 1–16.

8

Leveraging African Talent to Achieve China's Football Dreams

Christopher Edyegu[1]

Since its formation in 2004, the Chinese Super League (CSL) has strived to become one of the world's better football leagues. To compete with globally dominant leagues such as the English Premier League, Spanish La Liga, French Ligue 1, Italian Serie A and German Bundesliga, the CSL sought to attract high-level talent from across the world, contracting football players from Europe, South America, and Africa. Some of Africa's biggest football stars migrated to the CSL, potentially broadening its appeal among football fans on the African continent. However, in recent years the CSL has fallen on hard times and its international appeal as a football destination for top players has diminished. Saudi Arabia has usurped China's position as the upstart challenger to Europe's "big 5" domestic leagues (Church 2023). The CSL no longer dominates the football transfer market as it did during the late 2010s, and the crop of African players in the Chinese league has dwindled in recent years. This chapter will therefore explore the motivations of various Chinese stakeholders that encouraged African footballers to migrate from Africa to China and how the Chinese government's policy on foreign players stymies the flow of foreign football players to CSL.

1 Christopher Edyegu, PhD Candidate, University of Cape Town, edychr001@myuct.ac.za.

Employing a political economy approach, this chapter demonstrates that in the interplay between the state and markets, the state is predominant and has the ultimate say in determining outcomes in China. The chapter will also argue that despite contributing to the rise of football in China and increasing the league's global appeal, the CSL's financial model was unsustainable in the long term, even without the intervention of the COVID-19 pandemic. Guided by the government's ambitious vision of boosting national soft power, galvanizing national pride and attaining sporting success on the global stage, CSL clubs spent unsustainable amounts of money on foreign player transfers, with some owners seeing it as a shortcut to accruing political capital (Ross et al. 2023). Therefore, while CSL clubs bear ultimate authority for their reckless and irresponsible spending, they were directly or indirectly guided by the government's grand vision for Chinese football. The state demonstrated its ability to regulate the market when it brought in strict limits on transfer fees and player quotas, which quickly drained the league's foreign talent pool. The exodus of foreign talent from the CSL over the past several years has been notable, with global stars moving to other leagues in pursuit of better money, football or conditions. Lastly, while the China–African football relationship is no longer a priority, it mirrors a drop in Chinese investment in Africa.

Political Economy: States versus Markets in the CSL

This chapter will use political economy theories to examine the movement of African players to the CSL and analyze relations between state and market forces that condition the Chinese professional league. Political economy is an umbrella term that does not focus on any singular perspective but encompasses a wide field of perspectives to understand the intertwined relations between economics and politics (Woods 2001, 244) that emerged as a sub-discipline of International Relations in the 1980s through the work of scholars like Robert Gilpin. Political economy draws on the three main traditions: liberalism (and its new variant, neoliberal institutionalism), economic nationalism (and variations of realism and mercantilism), and structuralist perspectives/radical theory (often under the Marxist umbrella) (Phillips 2023, 258).

Liberals endorse a limited role for the state in the operation of the economy, with it primarily playing a regulatory role and leaving the markets to self-regulate and decide political and social outcomes (Woods 2001, 249). Economic nationalism is a perspective of state building and emphasizes state dominance over the markets (Gilpin 1987, 26). Economic nationalists therefore argue that political interests should determine economic matters. Marxist approaches break with liberalism and classical economics in their understanding of how economics influences politics (Gilpin 1987, 26). While other perspectives of political economy have been developed, these three broad perspectives remain the starting point for most political economy analysis.

In the Chinese context, state decisions and regulation have had an undeniable impact on the trajectory of football development. China's self-defined political-economic model, that is, "market socialism with Chinese characteristics," suggests that the role of the state in the economy cannot be ignored. By selectively adopting some market characteristics, China implemented several resolutions that fast-tracked the economy's economic opening, giving private actors and the market more say in determining outcomes (Zajontz 2022, 278). But as will be demonstrated in this chapter, the state is still very active in the economy, and in football, where it directs the CSL through regulations that control its operations. Therefore, while the domestic football markets and CSL clubs compete freely with each other and largely determine their own business models, the state often intervenes to determine outcomes and influence how resources are distributed or managed. This dynamic will be explored further in this chapter.

Rise and Decline of the CSL

The CSL was established in 2004 from the ashes of the Chinese First Division or Jia-A League, launched in 1994. The first division came to an end on November 30 with 12 of its 16 top teams going on to compete in the new CSL competition (Li and Shao 2003). When the first division was established in 1994, it marked the professionalization of football in China. Despite attracting millions of fans, the league struggled under the weight of multiple match-fixing, gambling, and corruption controversies (Li and Shao 2003; Lynch 2021). 10 years of the first division went by without a sound and stable investment environment emerging. With a shortage of revenue and fan disillusionment, China's premier football markets of Jinan, Dalian, Chengdu, and Xi'an all shrank (Li and Shao 2003). Due to a lack of cohesion and ineffective regulation, the first division became a high-risk environment for investors. Long-term sponsor, Pepsi, withdrew early from its contract, and Chinese corporate sponsors like Wanda, Ping'an, Taida, Hongyuan, Quanxing and Songri drew down their support (Li and Shao 2003).

On top of these issues, the Chinese men's national team—a bell-weather for enthusiasm in Chinese football—suffered from a chronic shortage of international standard players. Fans questioned the credibility of the officiating and competitive intent, leading thousands to walk out of games in protest. There was a marked absence of commensurate improvements of either club administration or football skills on the pitch, and there was also a confusing mix of market and planned economy about the league's operation (Li and Shao 2003). After a decade of controversies, many fans, clubs, sponsors, and the wider football community looked forward to the demise of the first division. It was against this unpromising backdrop that the CSL was established, and few could have imagined the highs and lows that would come over the ensuing decade.

Encouraged by purportedly football-loving Chinese President Xi Jinping's vision for China to become a footballing power, CSL clubs invested heavily in foreign players (Reuters 2017). In the first hints of the CSL's growing power, numerous high-level African players moved to China as detailed in the previous two chapters, joined by other international talents like French striker Nicolas Anelka and Paraguayan forward Lucas Barrios (Lynch 2021). Several high-profile foreign coaches also joined the league, including Italian and Brazilian World Cup winners Marcello Lippi and Luiz Felipe Scolari. In 2013, David Beckham became the CSL's first global ambassador and Guangzhou Evergrande, after significant investment, became the first Chinese club to win the Asian Champions League, an achievement it would repeat in 2015 (Lynch 2021).

In the summer of 2017, the 16 CSL clubs spent a combined US$411 million during the Chinese transfer window (Reuters 2017). To emphasize just how far the CSL had grown, incomplete statistics show that Chinese first-division teams spent a cumulative CNY1.5 billion (about US$187.5 million) in the league's first 10 years (Li and Shao 2003). The CSL at its peak demonstrated that it was not simply a competitor in the transfer market but, for a time, was the pre-eminent spending force in world football (Church 2023). The 2017 CSL season kicked off with the arrival of several big stars, solidifying its stance as a challenger to the European leagues. These included Shanghai Shenhua's purchase of 32-year-old Argentina striker Carlos Tevez from Boca Juniors in December 2017 with a reported salary of US$753,000 per week (the world's highest-paid football player at the time) and Shanghai SIPG's acquisition of Brazilian midfielder Oscar from Chelsea for US$63 million (Church 2023). Such transfers garnered headlines internationally and confirmed the CSL and China's status as football's latest "El Dorado" (Church 2023). The investments by Chinese clubs highlighted the intent to be a major player in world football, yet several were owned by debt-fueled companies, which years later proved to be unsustainable.

In this period of rapid growth, the CSL saw viewership, broadcast reach and sponsorship grow along with its global ambitions. At various times, CSL has been broadcast to more than 100 countries and territories around the world (Siddiqui 2023). According to some reports, the CSL was the third most-watched league in the world after the EPL and La Liga, reaching around 700 million viewers during the 2019 season (Wright 2022). The average CSL stadium attendance of 24,107 was the highest in Asia and the league enjoyed a commensurate social media following, albeit mainly in China (Deloitte 2019; Siddiqui 2023). The rise in the league's global popularity has been credited to major investment by CSL clubs, lucrative sponsorship deals, the rise of social media and the influx of foreign football stars who helped raise its quality and attract more global attention (Siddiqui 2023).

2016 represented the peak of the CSL's rise, with many analysts predicting that the Chinese league could one day challenge for first place among global football leagues. While European clubs and agents saw the CSL as an easy option to raise millions for fringe or aging players, some also feared that the world's top talent would drain away from Europe (Fifield 2016). Revered Arsenal coach Arsene Wenger warned that the extremely high wages on offer in the CSL threatened to disrupt the previously unchallenged hegemony of European clubs over the world's top talent (Lynch 2021). Chelsea coach Antonio Conte agreed, averring in December 2016 that "the Chinese market is a danger for all. Not only for Chelsea, but all the teams in the world" (Fifield 2016). Leading sports marketer Andrew Georgiou, the chief executive of Lagardere Sports and Entertainment, said in March 2017 that "China has the financial capability to become the biggest league in the world [. . .] I think [the CSL] will overtake the Premier League at some point" (Reuters 2017). Other football industry insiders were less impressed, like Vancouver Whitecaps CEO Paul Barber, who described the CSL in February 2017 as "lightning in a bottle [. . .] bright, exciting, very contained and in danger of fizzling out" (Reuters 2017).

The COVID-19 pandemic hastened the decline of the CSL as a dominant spending force and destination for the world's top players (Lynch 2021). Three years of stringent lockdowns, fans absent from games, reduced sponsorship and broadcasting revenues and a domestic economic slowdown left many CSL clubs, many of which had spent heavily on top international players and coaches, struggling to remain solvent. Between 2020 and 2023, the CSL saw several teams collapse due to financial difficulties, corruption investigations among football executives and the exodus of many of the league's foreign assets (Associated Press 2023; SCMP 2023b). Liu Jun, the chairman of the CSL, was arrested by Chinese authorities on August 29, 2023, and put under disciplinary investigation on suspicion of severe violations of disciplines and laws (Global Times 2023; SCMP 2023b). According to the Beijing Youth Daily publication, Liu became the 14th significant figure in the Chinese football community to fall under graft investigations since November 2022 as part of an anti-corruption drive in sport. Weeks before Liu's arrest, Li Tie, head coach of the Chinese men's national football team, was arrested on allegations of corruption and bribery (Global Times 2023; SCMP 2023b).

The arrest of football officials indicates that there is constant precarity underpinning football in China due to political and economic headwinds. While the arrests could be interpreted as the state cracking down on mismanagement and corruption within the sport, it also raises concerns about the potential for political manipulation and influence in Chinese football. This can be contrasted with the situation in the English league, where reigning champions Manchester City were accused of breaching at least 100 financial regulations over a nine-year period, but no club officials have been arrested or face the possibility of arrest, even if the club is found guilty (Solhekol 2023). Furthermore, the English League's governing body operates independently of the state, which is not the case in China where the CFA must abide by state directives. While it is imperative to root out corruption in the CSL, political interference is a looming presence in Chinese football.

In addition to corruption scandals, several high-profile CSL and lower-league Chinese football teams collapsed under the weight of financial issues. On August 28, a day before Liu's arrest, CSL reigning champions Wuhan Three Towns, announced that one of its investors would no longer be funding the club from September 2023. The club promptly organized an emergency meeting where senior club management devised plans to ensure that payment commitments would be met until the end of the CSL season. Wuhan Three Towns and some other CSL clubs' financial struggles stem from China's economic slowdown following the pandemic, excessive spending and difficulties linked to the domestic property development sector (SCMP 2023b). Another major CSL club that faced serious financial challenges was Jiangsu Sunning which shut down in February 2021, three months after lifting the domestic title (SCMP 2023b). The club was forced to shut down after owners Suning Holding Group, which also purchased Italian Seria A giants FC Internazionale Milano in 2016, announced that they were withdrawing funding to focus on their hard-hit retail business. For the club, it was a stunning turn of fortunes as two summers prior in 2019 it had attempted to sign Welsh superstar Gareth Bale from Real Madrid (Lynch 2021). Sunning's title-winning team featured several foreign stars, such as Brazilian Alex Teixeira, who rejected an offer from Liverpool to make a €50 million (US$53.4 million) move to China in 2016. Additionally, Tianjin TEDA (now Tianjin Jinmen Tiger FC) almost collapsed in 2021 after its parent company, state-owned conglomerate Tianjin TEDA (Tianjin Economic-Technological Development Area) withdrew its funding and players went unpaid for 10 months. Rivals Tianjin Tianhai FC in May 2020 declared bankruptcy after being unable to recover from the imprisonment of owner Shu Yuhui. Chinese FA Cup winner Shandong Luneng was also expelled from the subsequent season's Asian Football Confederation (AFC) Champions League in February 2021 due to overdue payments (Lynch 2021).

Wuhan Yangtze closed down in January 2023 after being unable to meet salary commitments and in the process became the fourth CSL team to cease operations in four seasons (Church 2023). Additionally, Guangzhou, who were two-time Asian champions and winners of eight CSL titles in nine seasons to 2017, were relegated in 2022 due to the financial challenges faced by their owners Evergrande, which holds the dubious title of the world's most indebted developer. Guangzhou had previously led the CSL's spending spree in the years in which China had become a prime destination for top global players and coaches (SCMP 2023b). In March 2023, the Chinese Football Association (CFA) disqualified eight teams across China's top three tiers of football (including Guangzhou) from competition due to financial issues (Associated Press 2023). The combined weight of COVID-19, financial mismanagement and corruption effectively burst the CSL bubble.

Ultimately, the CSL's financial model of overspending had been unsustainable for many years and when the government implemented tighter new spending regulations in 2019 it signaled the end of China as a major spending force in global football. It was evident that the new rules signaled the government's disapproval of the exorbitant funds being spent by Chinese clubs. This was also one of the instances in which the state acted to influence markets, which is in line with economic nationalism thinking that politics should direct economic matters. However, while the CSL had been in decline since the financial regulations were implemented, the pandemic accelerated that process.

Chinese Stakeholders' Motivations behind the Recruitment of African Footballers

Sino-African engagement in football introduced a new dimension to a transcontinental relationship initially and still primarily based on economic and development-focused issues (Agbaje 2020). The presence of African stars in China also promoted cultural exchange and people-to-people bonds, potentially representing a conduit for future collaboration (Yang and Wang 2022).

Several reasons have been given for why various Chinese stakeholders sought to attract foreign football talent to play in the CSL. These include enhancing the Chinese league's competitiveness on the global stage, increasing the popularity of Chinese football in domestic and overseas markets, boosting the tactical and technical development of Chinese footballers and gaining access to new sponsorships and revenue streams (Agbaje 2020). In addition to their sporting excellence, African players have popularized leagues where they are significantly present, like the English Premier League, which has generated a substantial audience across Africa (Agbaje 2020). The presence of African stars, among them captains of the national teams of major African football powers like Ghana (Asamoah Gyan), Côte d'Ivoire (Yaya Toure) and Nigeria (John Obi Mikel) in the CSL was seen as a potential catalyst for popularizing the league on the continent (Agbaje 2020). As the previous chapter suggests, the reality was more complicated, and with the exodus of well-known African stars from the league following the pandemic, African interest in the CSL has waned further.

At its peak, the introduction of high-level African footballers was seen as necessary for the development of the CSL and the elevation of playing standards (Yang and Wang 2022). Often, though, it was driven by the parochial competitive needs of CSL clubs. For example, former Ivorian captain Didier Drogba was signed by Shanghai Shenhua in 2012 to help the team resurrect its fortunes and boost revenues (Daniels 2012). Despite being 34 years old and commanding a substantial salary, the struggling big club saw it as a worthwhile sporting risk. Owner Zhu Jun said "we feel that his experience and ability will be a very valuable asset to our squad," which was vindicated on the pitch (CNN 2012). John Obi Mikel, Drogba's former Chelsea teammate joined Tianjin TEDA in January 2017, and turned another struggling club's fortunes around (Soliman 2017). Yaya Toure, nearing the end of his career but with a CV full of top European clubs, signed for China League One side Qingdao Huanghai FC in 2019, and drove the club to promotion to the CSL. Two years later, the club dissolved. The prolific Ghanaian striker Asamoah Gyan was signed by SIPG (now Shanghai Port) in 2015, with the expectation of challenging for the CSL title (Oti Adjei 2017). As can happen in football, Gyan's time in the CSL was plagued by injuries and subsequent loss of form and a muted exit.

Various African players have had different motivations for migrating to play in the CSL. These motivations included generous financial incentives, the opportunity to improve standards of living, the appeal of the Chinese football market and new career opportunities (Africa News 2019). However, Africans playing in the CSL have faced numerous challenges. These include adapting to a new language and culture, racism, and career uncertainty from the collapse of clubs or sudden regulatory changes. Several African players found themselves unemployed due to their clubs collapsing, lack of payment or termination of contracts (Agbaje 2020). In 2013, even the superstar Didier Drogba terminated his contract with Shanghai Shenhua after just eight months due to a lack of wage payments (Agbaje 2020). An inconvenience for someone of Drogba's stature, such financial uncertainty can be ruinous for lesser-known African players.

Racism has also been a challenge for African players. For example, on July 28, 2023, Ghanaian and Shenzhen FC forward Frank Acheampong punched Henan's Gu Cao for allegedly racially abusing him during a league match (SCMP 2023a). Acheampong was fined CNY40,000 (US$5,580) and suspended for four games—it was his first red card in a professional career spanning more than 350 matches. Gu was fined CNY20,000 (US$ 2,743) and suspended for two matches "for provoking Acheampong with insults" (SCMP 2023a). Speaking on the incident, Acheampong expressed his love for China and the Chinese people but made clear that "it is unacceptable for any human to be subjected to racist insults let alone in the game of football" (Olander 2023). While the CSL has taken disciplinary action in cases of racial abuse, investment in awareness campaigns and promoting racial tolerance is minimal, and incommensurate with the league's ambitions for a global footprint.

China's Policies on Limiting Foreign Footballers in the CSL

At the height of the CSL's rise, the CFA came under pressure from the Chinese government to implement several changes that have had a major impact on attracting foreign players, international competitiveness and image. The recruitment plans of CSL teams were thrown into disarray on January 16, 2017, when the CFA suddenly announced that it had decided to limit the number of foreign players allowed to play in the 2017 season. Teams would be allowed to field only a maximum of three foreign players per match, inclusive of players from the AFC. Previously, CSL teams were permitted to field an AFC player in addition to three foreign players, however, that spot would henceforth have to be taken by a domestic player under the age of 23 (Church 2017). In its statement announcing the new regulations, the CFA said they were necessary to realize "the General Plan of Chinese Football Reform and Development and to benefit the overall development of Chinese football and Chinese local players, to enhance the quality of the national team and to keep the professional league on a healthy, stable and consistent track" (Church 2017). The governing body vowed that it would scrutinize the activities of CSL teams following a 12-month period in which they had broken the Asian transfer record five times. The federation enacted a further set of stringent regulations a few months later. On June 22, 2017, the CFA announced that all CSL clubs that were not making a profit (essentially all of them) would henceforth be face a 100 percent tax on foreign player transfers to be paid into a new Chinese Football Development Fund (Simpson 2017). Any Chinese club that paid more than CNY45 million (US$6.2 million) for a foreign player must pay an equivalent amount to a CFA youth development fund. Any transfer of Chinese players valued at over CNY20 million (US$2.7 million) would also face a 100 percent tax. Furthermore, for every foreign player on the pitch, all CSL teams were required to field an under-23 Chinese player. A CFA statement noted that the new rules were designed to reign in "irrational spending" and promote Chinese football development (Simpson 2017).

In addition to controlling spending on foreign players, the CFA announced a stringent salary cap ahead of the 2021 season (White 2020). Salaries of foreign players were capped at €3 million (US$3.26 million) under the new regulations, with those of Chinese players capped at CNY5 million (US$765,000) before tax. Furthermore, CSL clubs were not allowed to spend more than CNY600 million (US$91.74 million) on total salaries, with the salaries of foreign players limited to a cumulative €10 million (US$12.1 million) (Lynch 2021). In defense of the new salary regulations, CFA president Chen Xuyuan depicted an unsustainable bubble economy, with CSL club expenditures many times higher than comparators like South Korea's K-League and Japan's J-League (Lynch 2021). The new regulations to curb rampant spending and limit corporate influence effectively ended CSL's briefly held position at the top of the global transfer market.

Despite major criticism and resistance from Chinese fans and CSL clubs, the governing authorities had valid reasons for implementing the new policies. It was necessary to prevent bubbles and stem the flow of money used to acquire expensive foreign stars as it had become unsustainable, with clubs collapsing or on the brink due to shaky finances. Excessive transfer fees and wages were clearly a financial burden that some clubs could not sustain, with investments significantly outweighing "the economic value brought to the CSL through viewership, foreign investment and value" (Simpson 2017). Necessary and well-meaning, the regulations nevertheless had major consequences for both the CSL and African players in the league. For African players, the introduction of rules limiting clubs from fielding more than three in a game meant that there was increased competition for places and a reduction in playing time. Non-star African players, who in the past could expect to find a spot on the roster of a CSL team, suddenly found their opportunities curtailed. This influenced many to move on to other leagues for sporting reasons, and at one point only 12 African players remained in the CSL (Agbaje 2020).

Effects of the CSL's New Regulations

The new regulations implemented by the CSL to limit foreign players prompted reaction from different sides. Many former CSL players and managers expressed disappointment in the new regulations. The former Serbian defender and Guangzhou R&F player, Dusko Tosic, said in December 2020 that China's salary cap and stringent COVID-19 restrictions would prevent big-name international players from joining the CSL (White 2020). Despite admitting to enjoying his time in China, Tosic complained that he decided to leave the CSL because "the salary is reduced, then there are quarantines for the whole of next season and it is very hard" (White 2020). When Tosic made his comments, several of the CSL's big foreign players had decided to leave the league for similar reasons, leaving it with dwindling star power. They included SIPG's Brazilian forward Hulk (once Asia's record transfer signing), Guangzhou R&F coach Giovanni van Bronckhorst, and the 2019 CSL Golden Boot winner Eran Zahavi. With admirable understatement, the former Italian World Cup winning captain and Guangzhou and China national team coach Fabio Cannavaro said in October 2021 that the CSL "was seen as an attractive, quality league back in 2017–18 [...] but things changed" (White 2020). After giving up 15 months' worth of salary and bonuses worth up to US$27.9 million, in his "exit interview" Cannavaro emphasized the importance of foreign players for Chinese football development and the elevation of the CSL (White 2020). Cannavaro's assertion that the new rules would make the CSL less competitive in the global marketplace for players is borne out by Cristiano Ronaldo's move to the Saudi Pro League and Lionel Messi's switch to Major League Soccer. In years past, CSL clubs would have been in the mix to sign either or both of these GOATs (greatest of all time). It is ironic that Ronaldo was linked with a possible transfer to Tianjin Quanjian in 2018.

Five years later, with Ronaldo busy scoring goals in Riyadh, the Quanjian club was dissolved.

The Saudi Pro League has replaced CSL as a destination for high-level foreign talent, including African superstars like Riyad Mahrez, Sadio Mane, Edouard Mendy and Kalidou Koulibaly. Meanwhile, foreign football talent continues to drain away from CSL. The exodus includes the Nigerian Odion Ighalo and the Moroccan Abderrazak Hamdallah. Like China, Saudi Arabia, Qatar and the UAE all have ambitions to harness the power of football. Saudi Arabia is set to host the 2027 Asian Cup and the 2034 World Cup, which it was once thought China might host (Church 2023). While the Chinese state regulates activities in the CSL, Middle Eastern state involvement in football is even more pervasive, to the extent that the biggest spending Saudi Pro League clubs are directly owned by the state.

Conclusion: The Interplay of State and Market in the CSL

Applying a political economy lens to the CSL has provided valuable insight into the interplay between the Chinese state and market forces. Certain key observations have been set out in this chapter. While CSL clubs operate according to their own plans, the state, in line with mercantilist or economic nationalist perspectives, has maintained influence over the CSL and intervened several times to influence the outcomes or operations of clubs. The CFA, which is directly under the state's influence, regulates the domestic league in line with the government's regulations, which is at times at odds with market principles that guide club finances and player transfers. Some clubs are also owned by State-Owned Enterprises (SOE) or supported by state funds, which creates a direct connection between government interests and club policies, in many cases prioritizing political objectives over market principles. The Chinese central government has driven much of the CSL's development trajectory with the ambitious vision of boosting soft power, national pride, and attaining sporting success on the global stage. Therefore, while CSL clubs bear ultimate authority for their irresponsible spending, they were prompted by the government's own ambitious vision for Chinese football. The state demonstrated its ability to regulate the market when it imposed strict limits on transfer fees around player quotas. The new regulations were a clear indication of government disapproval of the clubs' reckless spending on transfers and wages. In a demonstration of the state's influence over the market, the Chinese entrepreneurs funding CSL clubs realized that spending huge money on the sport was no longer a shortcut to accruing political capital. That ultimately led to the swift decimation of the league's foreign talent pool. From a financial point of view, the CSL is arguably now back to where it was before the bubble era, with local firms supporting local clubs on modest budgets.

Despite significant state influence over the CSL, market forces are still in play in the Chinese league. Private companies invest in the league due to the potential branding and commercial opportunities. This brings market dynamics into the CSL, however, only within the key parameters set by the government. Additionally, while fan culture in the domestic league is still developing, CSL clubs are increasingly exploring commercial activities such as sponsorships. This is also an indication of market forces shaping club strategies, again guided by state regulation. Lastly, the inflow of foreign stars in the earlier years of the league, which aimed to strengthen the CSL and improve its technical level, was also a reflection of market forces influencing club objectives. However, CSL clubs distorted the global market by paying exorbitant prices for foreign players which led to crippling debt and, for some of them, to collapse. There is no question that the state is the ultimate authority over the league and has the ultimate say in its operations. It is also evident that there are no shortcuts to success in football, and while big money can attract the best global talents, that alone cannot develop a sustainable domestic league. That requires a flourishing local football culture to create the space for talent to grow organically.

References

Africa News. 2019. "Exodus of Top African Players to the Chinese League." *Africa News*, December 9, 2019. https://www.africanews.com/2017/02/28/exodus-of-top-african-players-to-the-chinese-league-football-planet//.

Agbaje, Orire. 2020. "Are African Football Players Winning in the Chinese Super League?" Last modified December 9. https://africansonchina.com/are-african-football-players-winning-in-the-chinese-super-league/.

Associated Press. 2023. "Chinese Football Fans Finally Back in Stadiums for New Super League Season After 3 Troubling Years." *South China Morning Post*, April 14, 2023. https://www.scmp.com/sport/football/article/3217006/chinese-football-fans-finally-back-stadiums-new-super-league-season-after-3-troubling-years.

Church, Michael. 2017. "Chinese FA Confirms Limit on Foreign Players for Super League Clubs." ESPN, January 16, 2017. https://www.espn.co.uk/football/story/_/id/37510603/chinese-fa-confirms-limit-foreign-players-super-league-clubs.

———. 2023. "Cristiano Ronaldo's Saudi Arabia Switch Another Symbol of Chinese Football's Decline." *South China Morning Post*, January 29, 2023. https://www.scmp.com/sport/football/article/3208342/cristiano-ronaldos-saudi-arabia-switch-another-symbol-chinese-footballs-decline.

CNN. 2012. "Drogba Seals Big-Money Move to Chinese Club Shanghai Shenhua." CNN, June 20, 2012. https://edition.cnn.com/2012/06/20/sport/football/drogba-shanghai-anelka-shenhua/index.html.

Daniels, Tim. 2012. "Chelsea Transfer News: Didier Drogba Joins Shanghai Shenhua." Bleacher Report, June 20, 2012. https://bleacherreport.com/articles/1228904-chelsea-transfer-news-didier-drogba-joins-shanghai-shenhua.

Deloitte. 2019. "Chinese Football Association Super League (CSL)—2019 Annual Review of Commercial Performance." Deloitte. https://www2.deloitte.com/cn/en/pages/technology-media-and-telecommunications/articles/chinese-football-association-super-league-200729.html.

Fifield, Dominic. 2016. "Chelsea's Antonio Conte: Chinese Super League Is a Danger to All Teams." *The Guardian*, December 16, 2016. https://www.theguardian.com/football/2016/dec/16/antonio-conte-chinese-super-league-danger-oscar-move-chelsea#:~:text="The%20Chinese%20market%20is%20a,is%20a%20really%20good%20player.

Gilpin, Robert G. 1987. *The Political Economy of International Relations*. Princeton University Press.

Global Times. 2023. "Chairman of the Chinese Super League Company Put Under Disciplinary Investigation." *Global Times*, August 31, 2023. https://www.globaltimes.cn/page/202308/1297299.shtml.

Li, Jingrong, and Da Shao. 2003. "China's Decade of Professional Soccer." China Org. Last modified December 16. http://www.china.org.cn/english/2003/Dec/82548.htm.

Lynch, Joey. 2021. "How the Chinese Super League Bubble Burst." *ESPN*, February 28, 2021. https://www.espn.com/soccer/story/_/id/37614644/how-chinese-super-league-bubble-burst.Olander, Eric. 2023. "Ghanaian Winger Frank Acheampong Slaps Opponent in Chinese Super League Match in Response to Alleged Racial Insults." China Global South Project. Last modified July 31. https://chinaglobalsouth.com/2023/07/31/ghanaian-winger-frank-acheampong-slaps-opponent-in-chinese-super-league-match-in-response-to-alleged-racial-insults/.

Oti Adjei, Michael. 2017. "Asamoah Gyan: I Work Hard for What I Earn." BBC, July 16, 2017. https://www.bbc.com/sport/football/33537887.

Phillips, Nicola. 2023. *Global Political Economy*. Oxford University Press.

Reuters. 2017. "Chinese Super League Could Challenge English Premier League for Domination." *South China Morning Post*, March 7, 2017. https://www.scmp.com/sport/china/article/2076571/china-could-challenge-english-premier-league-soccer-domination.

Ross, Tobias, Jonathan Sullivan, and Hongyi Lai. 2023. "Private Investment in Chinese Football Clubs: Political Capital and State–Business Exchanges." *Journal of Current Chinese Affairs* 52 (3): 518–541.

SCMP. 2023a. "Chinese Football: Video Shows Ghana Ace's Punch Flooring Opponent as Both Players Are Banned Amid Racism Claim." *South China Morning Post*, August 2, 2023a.

https://www.scmp.com/sport/football/article/3229736/chinese-football-video-shows-ghana-aces-punch-flooring-opponent-both-players-are-banned-amid-racism.

———. 2023b. "Chinese Super League Chairman Taken Away for Investigation, State Media Reports, as Football Crackdown Continues." *South China Morning Post*, August 29, 2023b. https://www.scmp.com/sport/china/article/3232718/chinese-super-league-chairman-taken-away-investigation-state-media-reports-football-crackdown.

Siddiqui, Sajid. 2023. "Top 10 Most Popular Football Leagues in the World 2023." September 19, 2023. https://thesportsmania.in/top-10-most-popular-football-leagues-in-the-world-2023/.

Simpson, Christopher. 2017. "Chinese FA Imposes 100% Tax on Super League Clubs Signing Foreign Players." *Bleacher Report*, May 25, 2017. https://bleacherreport.com/articles/2711721-chinese-fa-impose-100-tax-on-super-league-clubs-signing-foreign-players.

Solhekol, Kaveh. 2023. "Man City Premier League Charges Explained: What Are They? What Could Punishment Be? What's the Timescale?" Sky Sports, June 10, 2023. https://www.skysports.com/football/news/11679/12804623/man-city-premier-league-charges-explained-what-are-they-what-could-punishment-be-whats-the-timescale.

Soliman, Seif. 2017. "John Obi Mikel Joins Chinese Super League Side Tianjin TEDA." KingFut, January 6, 2017. https://www.kingfut.com/2017/01/06/john-obi-mikel-tianjin-teda/.

White, Jonathan. 2020. "No Big Names' in 2021 Chinese Super League Warns Dusko Tosic." *South China Morning Post*, December 21, 2020. https://www.scmp.com/sport/football/article/3114753/no-big-names-2021-chinese-super-league-warns-dusko-tosic.

Woods, Ngaire. 2001. "International Political Economy in an Age of Globalization." *The Globalization of World Politics* 4: 244–260.

Wright, Sean. 2022. "10 Most Watched Soccer League." Red Bull. Last modified October 31. https://www.redbull.com/us-en/most-watched-soccer-leagues.

Yang, Kaijie, and Lianjin Wang. 2022. "Study on the Cooperative and Win-Win Relationship between the Introduction of African Football Players in Chinese Professional Football League." *Open Access Library Journal* 9 (7): 1–16.

Zajontz, Tim. 2022. "The Chinese Infrastructural Fix in Africa: Lessons from the Sino-Zambian 'Road Bonanza.'" *Oxford Development Studies* 50 (1): 14–29.

9 StarTimes and Development Assistance: Perspectives from Ghana and Uganda

Angela Lewis[1]

Football has become a space and a vector for development assistance between China and Africa. This includes high-profile stadium construction in numerous African countries, as noted in Chapter 2, which has enabled the hosting of several recent editions of the African Cup of Nations (Cockayne et al. 2022). One less examined area of development assistance is football-related Chinese media, the focus of this chapter and the one that follows it. The expansion of Chinese media into African markets has been one of the notable manifestations of Chinese "soft power" efforts over the past decade and has generated extensive coverage in the academic literature (Madrid-Morales 2021; Umejei 2020; Wekesa 2023). The stimulus for this chapter is the involvement of a Chinese broadcaster in Africa's most popular sport. Chinese media involvement in broadcasting African football and other global leagues to African viewers has political roots. For one thing, the Chinese state, through state-owned or loosely affiliated media organizations, is keen to signal to developing countries that it is both a leader and an ally in economic progress (Pu 2019), presenting itself as a model and partner to other nations. China's engagement with Africa is diverse and multifaceted, including its media operations. Sport, especially football, is seen as a useful vehicle for

1 Angela Lewis, Assistant Professor, Xi'an Jiaotong-Liverpool University, Angela.Lewis@xjtlu.edu.cn.

China's ambitions to extend its media offering in Africa. China's engagement in Africa has been criticized for its instrumentality, but in China it is framed as a developmental partnership, and sport is cast as a vehicle for encouraging sustainable development (Charway et al. 2023, 6). The context for China's development assistance framework is the Forum on China–Africa Cooperation (FOCAC), which meets every three years to devise action plans for what the Chinese government likes to frame as "win-win cooperation." The "cooperation" premise—rather than OECD-type aid—means that development assistance is provided on a loan basis, with funds from Chinese state organs such as Exim Bank and China Development Bank to fund projects. Those projects are in turn operated by Chinese companies.

The FOCAC multilateral agreements of 2015, 2018 and 2022 all enshrine legitimacy for Chinese enterprises to be involved with development projects. For example, in the 2022 agreement, under the "Press and Media" section, China pledges to "support the capacity building of radio and television media in Africa, promote the integrated development of African media" (Ministry of Foreign Affairs China 2021). Those involved in supporting this capacity building are entities from China. For instance, in football broadcasting it is a private Chinese firm that is responsible for buying football broadcasting rights and overseeing related TV programming. Although ostensibly private, the firm is obliged to operate within China's state-directed development assistance agenda. The Chinese company is therefore in the position of following a profit-oriented model while also being a development actor answerable to the Chinese state.

The company in question is StarTimes, which operated in Africa in a private capacity from 2008–2015, when it entered a public-private-partnership (PPP) with the Chinese government (CHINAFRICA 2015). This lent it authority to expand its involvement in a variety of broadcasting-related initiatives, including TV channels and program production. StarTimes' funding comes from Exim Bank and China Development Bank to the tune of hundreds of millions of dollars (Wang and Yang 2014). Loans must be paid off via profits from advertising and TV subscriptions. Subscribers will only increase if StarTimes gives African viewers what they desire, and sport—especially football—is the bedrock of pay-TV in Africa as it is in many global markets.

StarTimes' investment in sport has coincided with a significant rise in the number of subscriptions. According to Digital TV Research, StarTimes/StarSat is forecast to have the second-highest number of pay-TV subscribers in Africa by 2028. Subscribers benefit from a considerable catalog of football programming. Available European football assets include Spain's La Liga, Germany's Bundesliga and Manchester United TV, as well as a plethora of other competitions from Portugal, Saudi Arabia and Brazil. It also shows the African Cup of Nations and has been the official broadcaster of African professional football leagues in Kenya and Zambia.

However, it is in Ghana and Uganda that StarTimes' involvement in football is the most extensive. It has owned the broadcasting rights to domestic leagues in Ghana and Uganda for several years, with the long-term goal of building commercially viable brands. In 2017, StarTimes signed a US$17,950,000 10-year deal for all media rights to the Ghana Premier League (GPL) and lower leagues, as well as the Ghana Women's Premier League (GWPL), in the hope that the deal would stimulate the development of Ghanaian football (Ghana Football Association 2017). In 2018, StarTimes secured broadcast and title rights from the Federation of Uganda Football Association (FUFA) and the Uganda Premier League (UPL) for US$7.24 million over 10 years (Nsimbe 2018). It was hoped that this "football marriage" would be a "turning point" for domestic football in Uganda (FUFA 2018).

The experience in Ghana and Uganda has been a steep learning curve for both StarTimes and its African partners, with many obstacles. This chapter documents the continuing struggles to upgrade domestic leagues and Chinese actors' engagement in this development journey, through interviews with football and media industry practitioners. In contrast to much scholarship on sport in African countries, which emphasizes high-level political and governmental contexts (e.g., Charway and Houlihan 2020), this chapter prioritizes a grounded approach that gives voice to practitioner perspectives. The chapter deliberately foregrounds grassroots understandings of the issues around sports and media in Ghana and Uganda. Journalists, public relations and club officials provide perspectives regarding the role of StarTimes in terms of broadcasting and funding, highlighting the barriers that hindered company efforts to improve conditions for clubs and transform domestic football into an attractive media product. While the long-term aim for StarTimes is to create intellectual property with high value, first at home and then in overseas markets, problems both inside and outside its control are impeding progress.

One issue which is explored in this chapter is the fact that while StarTimes has secured media rights, this does not include sponsorship funding. Sponsorship is necessary to finance leagues and clubs. While it is hoped that broadcasting rights would encourage sponsors, various organizational and other issues have deterred corporate involvement. In Ghana, for instance, the curtailment of the 2019–2020 season due to COVID-19 followed the disbanding of the Ghanaian

FA in June 2018 due to a high-profile corruption scandal. The StarTimes contract with the Ghanaian league, signed in 2017, was subsequently modified, but it did not break entirely. In contrast, StarTimes terminated a contract with the Football Kenya Federation Premier League in 2021, which was blamed on unfulfilled obligations (Sang 2021). Not all clubs in Kenya, it seems, were willing to hand over broadcasting rights to StarTimes (Pulse Sports 2023).

Through StarTimes China could become an influential actor in African football. However, in-depth perspectives from football experts in countries that have StarTimes football relations are rarely explored in academic work. Despite the fact that partnerships have been running for over five years in both Ghana and Uganda, contexts and outcomes have been under-explored. This chapter reveals how the commercial value of media rights is directly linked to development issues. Fanbase cultivation and financial limitations on facilities and equipment provision have an impact on brand strength. In addition, tensions remain between local actors' interests and StarTimes priorities when exercising its broadcasting options.

Method

This chapter is concerned with two overarching questions. First, it aims to identify the problems facing football leagues in Ghana and Uganda. Second, it seeks to elucidate the perceptions of StarTimes' operations among local football practitioners and stakeholders. To explore these issues, the chapter provides insights into how StarTimes' engagement with leagues in Ghana and Uganda is seen by those with in-depth knowledge into the impact of the company holding media rights. To generate these insights, I conducted semi-structured interviews with Ghanaian and Ugandan public relations officials, journalists and club management between July and September 2023. Purposive sampling was used to identify and select key informants with "the ability to explain and 'translate' social phenomena, cultural values, and behaviors" (O'Neill and Godin 2020, 1).

The respondents representing Ghana comprised seven public relations officers working for football clubs and three journalists who serve as football pundits. They are anonymized as PRO 1–7 or Journalist 1–3. Ugandan interviewees consisted of three senior football club management executives, six PROs and four journalists. Correspondingly, they are referred to as Uganda Executive 1–3, PRO 1–6 and Journalist 1–4. The data generated through these semi-structured interviews were transcribed and subject to thematic analysis. Employing a qualitative approach, themes were identified as they emerged inductively across the corpus of interview responses. The findings sections below deal first with Ghana and then Uganda, with similarities and differences in perspectives noted. It is notable that common themes are present in both contexts, but with considerable variance in the way that practitioners perceive and articulate them. This observation is a reminder of the variation in different African countries' engagement with Chinese actors.

Rebuilding Fan-Club Relationships in Ghana

When StarTimes signed a broadcasting rights deal with the Ghana Premier League (GPL) in 2017, the GPL had a track record of success. Ghana Journalist 3 and Ghana Club Manager 1 reminisce about the days of passionate fans and high stadium attendances. However, subsequent years brought difficulties that broke the relationship with fans. The relationship repair process will involve a combined effort of the GFA, clubs and StarTimes to make the Ghana Premier League an attractive fan experience once more.

Many interviewees believe the GPL is still attempting to recover from a 2018 documentary called *Number 12,* which exposed widespread corruption in the GFA governing body. The documentarian, Anas Aremeyaw Anas, was subsequently murdered. Attendance at games collapsed, and in 2018 the GFA was disbanded and the GPL canceled. The StarTimes deal was renegotiated in 2019, with a reduction in duration and financial commitment: Five million US dollars over six years. Relationships with fans diminished further when the GPL was once again canceled for the 2019–2020 season due to COVID-19. These setbacks mean that the once vibrant league that attracted StarTimes in the first place has been struggling. StarTimes may not have been the cause of the problems, but they must deal with them to turn a profit.

One issue that respondents want StarTimes to change is the dominant focus on the top teams Asante Kotoko and Hearts of Oak. These teams, housed in 40,000 capacity stadiums, have been dominant since the 1970s and their matches have been prioritized for broadcast. Several respondents called for the televising of all matches to give equal opportunities to clubs and viewers more choice. "Telecast the game to people who want to follow from their house, to nurture back their interest to follow the league," advised Ghana Journalist 3.

Another dimension to the broadcasting strategy is how much access StarTimes should provide to matches. The company is the sole rights holder, and according to Ghana Journalist 3, it is telecasting only one or two matches a week. That statement is contradicted by StarTimes Ghana General Manager Akorfa Banson who said StarTimes aired up to five games weekly, giving free-of-charge access to state broadcasters GTV, GTV Sports Plus and another eight free-to-air channels (Zurek 2023). As a pay-TV company, StarTimes seeks to capitalize on broadcasting rights to increase subscriptions, but some respondents view the lack of sharing of media rights with local stations as a hindrance to the fan cultivation that StarTimes ultimately needs.

Also hindering fan cultivation is competition from other leagues, many of which are also shown on StarTimes channels. Respondents claim that fans have been driven toward foreign football competition partly due to insufficient preparation, finances and player commitment during Ghana's qualification phrase for the 2018 World Cup in Russia. Consequently, fans supported African-descent players in foreign leagues when African teams departed the competition. Similarly, overseas clubs with African players attract television audiences. Ghana Club Manager 1 believes increased promotion of the GPL is necessary to drive support for homegrown clubs.

However, promotion of the GPL would only achieve results if and when standards improve. This includes credible refereeing, but also improved television production facilities, such as outside broadcast vans. It has been felt that pay-TV has upgraded television production quality, but more could be done in terms of camera work (Darko 2021). Ghana Journalist 3 wants the same number of camera angles in games as in European leagues to improve game analysis for journalists, "to determine if a player is offside or not. How journalists talk about the game [is] also promoting the league."

Most issues regarding raising standards are related to funding, but resources to meet objectives have been lacking (Charway et al. 2023). Funding impacts facility purchases, equipment and personnel expertise. Ghana Journalist 2 mentioned that "Even though the government has constructed over 100 astroturf pitches, most clubs have a problem with the availability and location of these pitches for training." The original StarTimes contract required it to build 10 pitches, but that was cut out of the re-written agreement. An argument against broadcasting games from certain football grounds was the quality of the pitches (Lewis 2023), but Ghana Club Manager 1 quipped, "If [broadcasting] is about pitches, they won't cover any matches at all, because we don't have quality pitches." Construction of pitches has been important for the female game, to fulfill the social dimension of the Sustainable Development Goals (SDGs). However, Ghana Club Manager 1 says poor quality artificial pitches in communities become heated when games are played between 2 p.m. and 3 p.m., bringing discomfort to players. "They feel the heat in their boots [and] get blisters on their feet. They are constructing more artificial pitches, so I don't think it is going to improve for the foreseeable future." Ghana Journalist 2 cites the absence of sport science expertise and quality gyms for muscle training and fitness as further limitations.

Broadcasting rights are insufficient to support the development changes needed. Ghana Journalist 3 explained that US$950,000 of StarTimes' money in the first rights-holding year was split among many parties, including the GPL which received US$700,000, US$150,000 for the FA Cup and US$100,000 allocated for both women's football and the Division One league. Thus, although broadcasting rights sales generate funds for clubs, it has been insufficient. Some clubs have disagreed with the GPL negotiating broadcasting rights on their behalf due to their level of popularity, but changing the system so clubs negotiated on their own behalf would widen financial disparities between them (Darko 2021). Sponsorship is needed to fill the gaps at the individual club and institutional levels. Zylophone became a GPL sponsor in 2018 but withdrew following the Anas scandal (Darko 2021). Access Bank became the Division One headline sponsor in 2022 to the tune of US$250,000, while Betway sponsored the Ghana Women's Premier League (GWPL) from the same year. It is hoped the visibility of StarTimes broadcasts can encourage more companies to support the re-emerging GPL.

The Ghana Women's Premier League: Promising Green Shoots

There has been research into female football players and fandoms in European countries (Pfister and Pope 2018), but very little country-specific research into African female football. Most research has revolved around sports medicine and strength conditioning (Okholm Kryger et al. 2022), while Africa-centered scholarship in particular has looked at injuries and illnesses faced by South African female footballers (Mkumbuzi et al. 2023) and experiences dealing the menstrual cycle (Mkumbuzi et al. 2022). The 2023 FIFA Women's World Cup, where more African teams progressed further than on previous occasions, provides evidence that African female football warrants deeper scrutiny.

Respondents had strong opinions on the female game. The general view is that while there have been steps forward, the female game across Africa faces immense barriers. In Ghana at the government level, community-based female participation has been promoted as part of fulfilling gender equality pledges (Charway and Strandbu 2023). However, government edicts regarding gender equality have yet to translate into meaningful change. According to Ndimande-Hlongwa (2016, 76), "Female representation in football is hard to find at all ranks in the sport's organizational structures and women's football is poorly resourced and generally given scant recognition."

In Ghana, part of the problem is visibility and monitoring of female participation in sport programs (Charway and Strandbu 2023). Ghana Club Manager 1, a licensed coach and a former general manager of a female football club, hoped the World Cup would help raise the awareness of the female game. He noted that most in the successful Nigerian team played outside the country: "The more exposed they are, the better they become. They play on better pitches, [and] they play against better players."

A worldwide problem is how to cultivate a fan base for the female game (Giachino et al. 2024), and Ghana is similar in that regard. "In women's football, even though no gate fee is charged, it is free, they are not able to fill the stadium," Ghana Club Manager 1 revealed. Most Ghanaians follow the male matches and the national side, so marketing at community level is necessary. "Education should be given to women on the benefits of football, which includes special privileges and scholarships to Ghanaian universities and to foreign universities," Ghana Journalist 2 suggested. "They have to build great relationships with schools [and] engage in community development programs. The Ghana FA needs to find a solution to the integration of high school women footballers into the regional teams by providing equipment and further training to high school instructors."

Promotional efforts must counteract negative perceptions of women in sport in general, which are rooted in cultural traditions (Charway and Strandbu 2023) and imperial constraints; Onwumechili (2011) pointed out that British colonial regulations in Nigeria prevented female football and thereby thwarted any attempts at development. Research after the African Women's Championships (AWC)—which followed the 2010 FIFA Men's World Cup in South Africa—found public opinions on women players were mixed. While some challenged stereotypes linking female sexuality to involvement in sport, negative attitudes were still widespread (Ogunniyi 2016). "Most believe women footballers look rigid and unattractive aesthetically," said Ghana Journalist 2, who added, "However, the society seems more educated in the last two decades and is gradually embracing women footballers."

Other development issues are linked to finances. In the 2023–2024 season, funding for GWPL Southern Zone teams rose 50 percent from 40,000 Ghanaian

Cedi (GH₵) to GH₵60,000, while clubs in the Northern Zone received a 44 percent increase in money to GH₵65,000, up from GH₵45,000 in 2022–2023. The players are mainly part-time and clubs are usually state-owned—e.g., Police Ladies, Prison Ladies, Immigration Ladies—which gives players a salary. "When it comes to funding, they seem better than most privately-owned teams and most women footballers will love to join these teams because of their end-of-service benefits and lucrative salaries," Ghana Journalist 2 revealed.

One positive development regarding sponsorship is Malta Guinness' support of the GWPL, renamed the Malta Guinness Women's Premier League in light of a three-year GH₵10 million sponsorship deal that began in the 2022–2023 season. In addition, the GFA supplies equipment to clubs such as balls and boots, with some teams also getting buses for the 2023–2024 season. However, Ghana Club Manager 1 complains that tournament prize money is not enough: "Money for two to three weeks—that it is how small it is." That said, on the training side there has been some essential financial assistance. The minimum license requirement to coach in women's football is a CAF License B for the Premier League and some women were given free training in order to tackle the shortfall in female representation within higher management positions.

GWPL matches are broadcast on a local free-to-air channel in Ghana called Max TV, which is on a StarTimes platform. The visibility offered by Max TV is crucial. Ghana Club Manager 1 says that it is a "refreshing" development, as three seasons earlier there was no TV coverage female matches; the hope is that television will encourage sponsorship. Up to three games a week are televised, but as with the male matches, there are complaints that the same clubs are featured in broadcasts repeatedly and that the number of broadcasts is insufficient. In addition, currently the matches are scheduled as to not compete with male team broadcasts, but daytime timeslots mean fewer viewers. However, Ghana Journalist 3 still hails the TV coverage achievement, saying clubs are using resources successfully, developing facilities and technical professionalism. Through Max TV being a StarTimes channel, it seems that indirectly, China is playing a vital role in the nurturing of African female football.

StarTimes and the Uganda Premier League: Change and Optimism

StarTimes was welcomed with great fanfare into Uganda in 2010 in the presence of state dignitaries, underlining the government validation of its presence

(Wekesa 2023). By 2012, the Chinese broadcaster had overtaken Multichoice in viewing figures. In 2022, according to the Uganda Communications Commission, it had 214,000 subscribers compared to 194,000 for Multichoice (Uganda Communications Commission 2022).

By the second half of 2023, the US$10 million StarTimes deal to hold broadcasting and title naming rights to the Ugandan Premier League (UPL) had reached the five-year, halfway point. This was a suitable stage at which to reflect on the partnership by gauging the views of Ugandans with professional perspectives. These included senior management for the UPL and StarTimes, as well as TV pundits, show hosts and public relations officers (PROs), who hold extensive authoritative knowledge of StarTimes operations in Uganda. While the multilateral FOCAC agreement represented the Africa-wide framework for Chinese development assistance, it is stakeholders at national, provincial and local levels who implement policies, so their viewpoints provide feedback on policy enactment at grassroots level.

Governance and ownership major stakeholders are the UPL, StarTimes and clubs. The UPL controls the match fixture schedule while StarTimes has the right to invite more partners in consultation with UPL. Most football clubs are institution-entities, while a minority are owned and funded by individuals, such as Vipers, Arua Hill, and Kampala Queens (2022/23 women's champions). These teams usually reside either at the top or bottom of the league, while the institution-owned teams tend to be mid-ranking.

Interviewees mention numerous ways that StarTimes broadcasts have raised interest in Ugandan football. This has been necessary to draw attention from European leagues, which have dominated airtime (Sekamate 2022). One-way has been by increased coverage; StarTimes live game broadcasts increased in the 2022–2023 season, accounting for 70 percent of games—135 live matches, up from 114 in the 2021–2022 season. Television commentary on games has expanded considerably, including on local channels Sanyuka Prime, FUFA TV and NBS Sport. Uganda Senior Executive 1 credits StarTimes with sensitizing audiences to Ugandan football, expanding viewing figures, UPL followers and reclaiming fans from the English Premier League. Respondents report that live TV game broadcasts for the 2022–2023 season led to significantly increased viewing figures. Rural football fans could watch teams from their localities and also follow the tight three-way title race between SC Villa, Vipers and KCCA. The higher league profile also improved stadium match attendances.

Another reported benefit of live broadcasts has been reduced referee corruption and match manipulation, while poorly programmed daytime games were re-scheduled. Floodlights for night matches were installed at St. Mary's Stadium Kitende and MTN Omondi Stadiums, a trend which is set to increase.

But the biggest advantage of TV exposure to clubs has been greater leverage. Clubs possess greater bargaining power when approaching potential sponsors, as TV coverage gives sponsors mileage. Greater attention from international football scouts and coaches has led to players being sold to bigger leagues not because of agents physically at games, but because they watched matches on the StarTimes ON App. In addition, the number of foreign, higher quality and returning players has risen. Uganda PRO 5 mentions that "Four years ago we did not have as many foreigners in the UPL as we have today. This coming season, KCCA has 4 Angolans, 2 Brazilians, 1 Congolese. At Vipers they have a Ghanaian, Ivorian, Mauritian, Nigerian, 2 Brazilians and more." At the grassroots level, more children are joining football academies. Uganda Senior Executive 1: "The impact has gone beyond the playing pitch; it is no longer perceived as a game for academic failures, thanks to TV."

Measures to Improve Promotion

On the wish list for the second half of the StarTimes partnership with the UPL most respondents identified capacity building. They called for enhancements in most areas: broadcasting content, promotion, collaborations, facilities, equipment, and funding. While dealing with most of these issues is outside StarTimes' jurisdiction, all pertain to improving the brand value, which would potentially increase subscriptions.

More within StarTimes' purview is media content. Respondents said promotional programming of the league was necessary through adverts on TV and the radio, and expanded content outside of live games through specialist shows, on both terrestrial and digital platforms. Uganda PRO 5 also called for improved broadcast quality footage, given the higher international profile: "The picture quality and camera angles need to massively improve. As the league grows, it attracts more attention."

There is a desire for more live games, with Uganda Journalist 4 believing that teams outside the central region were not receiving enough coverage. Video footage of footballers and coaches on social media was considered a way to generate fandom engagement. Clubs were encouraged to maintain good fan databases and media officers needed to provide regular updates of team news.

Interviewees also recommended building connections and partnerships. This would be with other leagues to improve standards and grassroots development to nurture the next generation of players. This is something that happened in Ghana, with Bundesliga players from Borussia Dortmund visiting the country in 2022. To support fandom development, interviewees want collaborations with cultural institutions and for institutional clubs KCCA, URA, Maroons, NEC, and UPDF to further popularize their clubs among their staff. They called for links with other television companies to increase coverage of matches, but the StarTimes relationship with stations in some countries such as Ghana has been complex, due to perceived government favoritism and a power imbalance (GBC Ghana Online 2018).

Respondents drew attention to the need for facilities improvements, both in quality and in quantity, such as restrooms and sheltered seating. Uganda PRO 1 lamented that there were insufficient good facilities in the West Nile region, which hindered the creation of teams and ability to host teams from other regions. Uganda Senior Executive 2 pointed the finger at the government's lack of investment in sport infrastructure such as stadiums, but this is contradicted by Uganda Journalist 3 who said there had been an improvement on facilities due to new club licensing guidelines, which specified training pitches must be different from matchday pitches. However, even he said more improvements—to deal with weather conditions, install floodlights for night games and provide media facilities—were all necessary.

Most of the problems above relate to the lack of financial resources. That said, not all clubs were in the same position as clubs with institutionalized funding like KCCA FC and URA FC having more financial stability. StarTimes money was praised for helping improve operations at well-funded clubs, and to pay staff at under-funded clubs. However, the fact that the UPL have only one broadcast partner and title rights holder in StarTimes means deficit budgets every football financial year. Broadcasting rights revenue is insufficient to sustain a club for a whole campaign.

Financial constraints have wider consequences. Remuneration to players and clubs and is inadequate, leading to low loyalty of good players. Because the game is growing, so are player monetary demands, claimed one respondent. Others cited deficiencies in procurement of different jerseys for home and away ties, the correct balls and training gear, claiming it is noticeable on television. Uganda Journalist 1 divulged problems clubs faced in procuring training equipment and jerseys for the new season.

Prize money for clubs is considered inadequate, which makes the need to attract sponsors a priority. It was felt that more games on TV would continue to generate interest in Ugandan football outside the country and attract more eligible sponsors. An example is the SC Villa US$750,000 sponsorship by Chinese company LingLong Tyres. To support NGOs and companies to become sponsors, an interviewee called for a tax reduction. Affordable season tickets and replica jerseys as fan merchandise were suggested as other income streams. More than one interviewee said StarTimes should increase club funding and pay directly, avoiding delayed disbursement to UPL.

Technical and Managerial Standards

The Chinese broadcaster was lauded for improved game management. "StarTimes requires a high standard of organization and management of games for them to be broadcast live on TV," Uganda PRO 6 commented. "Before teams would be very disorganized, especially in their dress code." With regards to technical personnel, others disclose that FUFA training is given to coaches, media officers, administrators, matchday stewards and sports medics, among others. However, individual clubs need to raise management standards, for instance, having qualified grounds men for pitch maintenance.

On the coaching front, one interviewee lamented that the low caliber of the talent within the league was due to a lack of effort clubs make to build great players. Some coaches were fully professionals, while others coached as a hobby. Uganda Senior Executive 1 mentions that the 2022–2023 season's top three teams (Vipers, KCCA FC, and Villa) all replaced local coaches with foreign counterparts. Uganda Journalist 3 summarizes reasons for diminished trust in local coaches: "After getting their coaching badges, they do not bother to update their tactics. They remain on the cards of less ambitious clubs. Most local coaches are school dropouts. They find huge problems grasping tactics being taught to them."

Female Football in Uganda

On the women's game side, StarTimes does not hold the broadcasting rights, so teams do not gain financially. However, women's football is on FUFA TV, which is a StarTimes channel and women's football benefits from dedicated sport shows and social media campaigns to raise awareness. Live broadcasts and the top-flight league games were shifted from 4 p.m. to 10 a.m. to shield them from competing for viewers with the male and international games, the downside being the working hour timeslot. Kampala Queens gained coverage for its dominance, but due to them being predictable title winners, there was increased attention on the relegation battle.

According to Uganda PRO 2 there are "very few technical personnel with specialization in the women's sector." Increased FUFA workshops to train more technical personnel with a bias toward the women's game was suggested, which is already underway with FUFA training more female coaches. While Uganda PRO 2 believes promotion and exposure of the female game is on the right path, increased games on TV and collaborations with men's sides to access resources was necessary. Uganda Journalist 3 believed the FUFA Women's Super League deserved StarTimes broadcasting rights support alongside the male league. To attract financial partners, he said a rebranding was paramount to deal with cultural barriers, the perception that football is a men's game.

Decision-Making Control: Exercising Agency

There are mixed feelings about whether clubs have a sufficient role in decision-making in the UPL-StarTimes partnership. There can be sensitivities regarding a power imbalance between foreign and domestic actors in partnerships, and in the past decade Chinese loans to Africa have been criticized as "debt-traps" (Brautigam 2020). However, it seems that the largest concern is around the governing body FUFA's relationship with individual clubs, as it holds full control in decision-making. The StarTimes-UPL deal was entirely negotiated and put in place by StarTimes and FUFA, which distributes it to clubs and the UPL Secretariat.

Uganda PRO 3 believes clubs lack free speech is due to this power hierarchy. "When club administrators talk about some things they think are not going well, they are replied to with threats, fines, bans, and more." Uganda Journalist 4 agrees that clubs do not have enough say, especially on financial matters. "Clubs need to get more money from the deal like in the neighboring leagues and the leagues we draw inspiration from. As the coverage of the games improves, the financial aspect of the deal needs to improve too!" Others counter that clubs do take part in decision-making. Uganda PRO 5 said that clubs are represented on the FUFA Executive and there are symposiums that FUFA and the UPL organize where club administrators are briefed on developments at the Federation and also asked for their opinions.

All stakeholders fundamentally are concerned with the right way to address the many deep-seated problems in top-tier Ugandan football. But in addition, grassroots need special attention; bodies that will supply the next generation for the UPL—female, youth and regional teams—all need upgrades in strategies and technical standards. It is FUFA that must deal with these issues step-by-step, and despite difficulties, there are always signs of light, such as the Kadiba facility and Lugazi Stadium. These progressions become opportunities that StarTimes can capitalize on.

Conclusion: Football and Media Development Assistance Lessons

This chapter discussed issues facing top-tier football leagues in Ghana and Uganda and perceptions of the role played by StarTimes. Similar issues need tackling in both countries. There is a need to build fandoms by drawing attention away from European leagues, and to enable that, respondents in both Uganda and Ghana want StarTimes to increase sharing media rights with free-to-air broadcasters. There are also calls for StarTimes to augment broadcasts of different teams in more remote regions, using increased cameras angles for a better audience experience and post-match analysis. Facilities and equipment shortfalls are due to a lack of funds that can only be remedied by attracting more sponsors, because broadcasting rights revenue and league winning prize money are insufficient. Social and cultural barriers against women playing football remain in both countries, but efforts are being made to change attitudes through televised games. In neither country did StarTimes directly broadcast female matches, with games on free-to-air channels carried by StarTimes. The priority seems to be improving personnel through training before the female leagues gain higher exposure.

This article also provides an illustration of China–Africa partnerships in practice. While development assistance policies are devised in Beijing and ratified through FOCAC, implementation is conducted by hybrid actors such as StarTimes, which in turn engage with local stakeholders. StarTimes must balance its development project remit with its own for-profit orientation. Through these types of public-private-partnerships, China is learning—project by project—how to engage and extend influence, and to test the realities of cooperation and assistance. The Ghana and Uganda football leagues are using broadcasting money to raise technical standards, improve media profiles and cultivate loyal fandoms, although progress is halting.

It is clear from interviewee comments that StarTimes involvement has brought more optimism to both countries, where the Chinese presence is viewed as bringing positive change. However, successful broadcasting rights outcomes have also brought higher expectations and increased demands. Most are far outside the StarTimes realm of control, such as poor facilities and the demands for management improvements at clubs and in football regulatory bodies. But there are requests for StarTimes to increase its development assistance in numerous directions. It is noticeable in Belt and Road publicity that football on StarTimes is included as a selling point for China's ambitions. But the Chinese government needs to listen to feedback from these stakeholders affected by political decisions made in Beijing. The more African football leagues are satisfied, the greater likelihood of profitable China–Africa football ties in the future.

References

Brautigam, Deborah. 2020. "A Critical Look at Chinese 'Debt-Trap Diplomacy': The Rise of a Meme." *Area Development and Policy* 5 (1): 1–14.

Charway, Derrick, Bright Baffour Antwi, Ørnulf Seippel, and Barrie Houlihan. 2023. "Sport and Sustainable Social Development in Ghana: Analysing the Policy-Implementation Gap." *Sport in Society* 26 (8): 1319–1339.

Charway, Derrick, and Barrie Houlihan. 2020. "Country Profile of Ghana: Sport, Politics and Nation-Building." *International Journal of Sport Policy and Politics* 12 (3): 497–512.

Charway, Derrick, and Åse Strandbu. 2023. "Participation of Girls and Women in Community Sport in Ghana: Cultural and Structural Barriers." *International Review for the Sociology of Sport*. https://doi.org/10.1177/10126902231214955.

CHINAFRICA. 2015. "Digital Dividend." *CHINAFRICA*, December 7, 2015. http://www.chinafrica.cn/Special_Report/txt/2015-12/03/content_709254.htm.

Cockayne, David, Simon Chadwick, and Jonathan Sullivan. 2022. "Chinese Football—from a State-Led Past to a Digital Future." *Journal of Global Sport Management* 7 (3): 345–354.

Darko, Sampong Ernest. 2021. *Television Rights and Its Effects on the Ghana Premier League. A Case Study of the Ghana Football Association*. Ghana Institute of Journalism.

FUFA. 2018. "StarTimes Take over Naming and Broadcasting Rights of the Uganda Premier League." Last modified August 9. https://www.fufa.co.ug/startimes-take-naming-broadcasting-rights-uganda-premier-league/.

GBC Ghana Online. 2018. "GIBA Kick Against Star Times TV Deal." Available at: https://www.gbcghanaonline.com/general/giba-kick-against-star-times-tv-deal/2018/ Accessed: September 20, 2024.

Ghana Football Association. 2017. "StarTimes Acquire Ghana Premier League Media Rights." Ghana Football Association. https://www.ghanafa.org/startimes-acquire-ghana-premier-league-media-rights#:~:text=StarTimes%20will%20pay%20%2417%2C950%2C000%20for,Ghana%20and%20other%20African%20countries.

Giachino, Chiara, Maurizio Valenti, Alessandro Bonadonna, and Luigi Bollani. 2024. "Women's Football: Don't Judge Me, Support Me! Evidence from Young Generations." *Soccer & Society* 25 (1): 45–61.

Lewis, Angela. 2023. *Chinese Television and Soft Power in Africa*. Taylor & Francis.

Madrid-Morales, Dani. 2021. "Sino-African Media Cooperation? An Overview of a Longstanding Asymmetric Relationship." In *It's about Their Story: How China, Turkey and Russia Try to Influence Media in Africa*, Johannesburg: Konrad-Adenauer-Stiftung, 9–70.

Ministry of Foreign Affairs China. 2021. *Forum on China-Africa Cooperation Dakar Action Plan (2022–2024)*. Ministry of Foreign Affairs of the People's Republic of China.

Mkumbuzi, Nonhlanhla S, Senanile B Dlamini, Fidelis Chibhabha, and Fredrick M Govere. 2023. "Injury, Illness, and Medication Use Surveillance during the 2020 COSAFA Women's Championship: A Prospective Cohort Study of Football Players from Southern Africa." *Science and Medicine in Football* 7 (1): 74–80.

Mkumbuzi, Nonhlanhla S, Senanile B Dlamini, Fidelis Chibhabha, Fredrick M Govere, and Lucinda Manda-Taylor. 2022. "The Menstrual Cycle and Football: The Experiences of African Women Football Players." *Science and Medicine in Football* 6 (5): 626–632.

Ndimande-Hlongwa, Nobuhle. 2016. "Gender Inequality and Discrimination in South African Football: Black Women Demand a Bigger Share of the Pie and the Limelight." *Agenda* 30 (1): 76–84.

Nsimbe, John Vianney. 2018. "What You Do Not Know About StarTimes-Fufa Sponsorship Deal." *The Observer*, August 31, 2018. https://observer.ug/sports/58556-what-you-do-not-know-about-startimes-fufa-sponsorship-deal.html.

O'Neill, Sarah, and Isabelle Godin. 2020. "Key Informants in Socio-Epidemiology: Advantages and Pitfalls." *Developmental Medicine & Child Neurology* 62 (12): 1346–1346.

Ogunniyi, Cassandra. 2016. "Perceptions of the African Women's Championships: Female Footballers as Anomalies." In *Women's Sport in Africa*, 89–101. Routledge.

Okholm Kryger, Katrine, Albert Wang, Ritan Mehta, Franco M Impellizzeri, Andrew Massey, and Alan McCall. 2022. "Research on Women's Football: A Scoping Review." *Science and Medicine in Football* 6 (5): 549–558.

Onwumechili, Chuka. 2011. "Urbanization and Female Football in Nigeria: History and Struggle in a 'Man's Game.'" *The International Journal of the History of Sport* 28 (15): 2206–2219.

Pfister, Gertrud, and Stacey Pope. 2018. *Female Football Players and Fans: Intruding into a Man's World*. Springer.

Pu, Xiaoyu. 2019. *Rebranding China: Contested Status Signaling in the Changing Global Order*. Stanford University Press.

Pulse Sports. 2023. "FKFPL: Macharia Goes to War with FKF over gung-ho Management Style." *Pulse Sports*, September 22, 2023. https://www.pulsesports.co.ke/football/story/macharia-goes-to-war-with-fkf-over-gung-ho-management-style-2023092208132845822.

Sang, Kiplagat. 2021. "StarTimes Reveals Reasons for Terminating FKF Premier League Sponsorship Deal." Last modified November 26. https://www.goal.com/en-ke/news/startimes-reveals-reasons-for-terminating-fkf-premier-league-sponsorship-deal/blt0b99a4bb8d89d211.

Sekamate, Naswiru. 2022. *European Football and Radio Contents Selection in Uganda: The Case of Radio Two*. Makerere University.

Uganda Communications Commission. 2022. *Market Performance Report 2Q22*. https://www.ucc.co.ug/wp-content/uploads/2022/11/UCC-2Q22_Final-Report_With-Response-to-ED-Comments-2-compressed.pdf.

Umejei, Emeka. 2020. *Chinese Media in Africa: Perception, Performance, and Paradox*. Lexington Books.

Wang, Sujuan, and Cheng Yang. 2014. "StarTimes Sees Huge Growth in Africa." *China Daily*, June 20, 2014. https://www.chinadaily.com.cn/kindle/2014-06/20/content_17604907.htm.

Wekesa, Bob. 2023. *China's Footprint in East Africa: Pessimism Versus Optimism*. Springer Nature.

Zurek, Kweku. 2023. "No Local Broadcaster Was Interested in the GPL When We Took up the Rights—Startimes." *Graphic Online*, July 10, 2023. https://www.graphic.com.gh/sports/sports-news/no-local-broadcaster-was-interested-in-the-gpl-when-we-took-up-the-rights-startimes.html.

10

China's Sport Diplomacy: StarTimes and Sport Broadcasting Rights in Africa

Tokunbo Ojo[1]

Sport diplomacy, which can be enacted and directed by the nation-state(s) and non-state actor(s), involves the enmeshing of sport, politics, socio-economic issues, public relations and diplomatic ambitions in international relations and global affairs. In tandem with other directed cultural and public diplomacy activities by nation-state agencies for the cultivation of positive public opinion in foreign countries, sport diplomacy provides alternate channels for international engagement beyond traditional modes of state-to-state diplomacy. It "transcends cultural differences, provides different avenues for increased dialogue and unites disparate peoples through a mutual affection for sport" (Murray and Pigman 2014, 1101). Due to its universal appeal, sport is a subtle foreign policy tool. Conceptually, sport diplomacy includes an array of diverse but interconnected activities such as sports exchanges, hosting international mega-events, financing stadium construction and renovation, public sport branding, and sponsorship of events and clubs. In this chapter, China's sport diplomacy is examined through the lens of the sport-media complex and the activities of StarTimes, a Chinese pay-TV company, in African media and cultural spaces.

1 Tokunbo Ojo, Associate Professor, York University, tojo@yorku.ca.

China and Sport Diplomacy in International Relations

Sport diplomacy has been a prominent and strategic element of China's foreign policy since the early days of the Cold War. Over the years, China has tactfully deployed sport in diverse ways to forge, repair, and strengthen its diplomatic relationships with countries in the global North and global South. During the Cold War era, China used the platforms that international sporting events and activities offer to both bond and establish diplomatic ties with several Asian and African countries. One of those countries was South Korea. For decades, China and South Korea were "born enemies of the Cold War's international structure," but South Korea's hosting of the 10th Asian Games and 1988 Olympic Games paved the way for both countries to engage in constructive diplomatic relationship-building (Zhang 2013, 221). Both mega-sporting events became a force multiplier for more amicable diplomatic dialogue between the two countries and in turn led to "a diffusion of reciprocity and mutual adjustment of public adversarial attitudes" (Zhang 2013, 223). The change of public attitudes had a ripple effect on people-to-people interactions and trade relationships, with rapid increases in tourist visits between the two countries and substantial increases in bilateral trade (Zhang 2013, 223).

China's strategic utilization of sport famously includes its use of table tennis to pave the way for amicable bilateral diplomatic relations with the US under the administration of President Richard Nixon. Equally, China leverages stadium diplomacy in its pursuit of geoeconomic and geopolitical capital in the Global South, particularly in Africa where stadiums hold political and cultural symbolism. As observed by Ojo (2022), stadium diplomacy is a means to an end for China in terms of facilitating both material and non-material opportunities for capital accumulation for Chinese state-owned and ostensibly private Chinese companies in developing countries. The findings reported by Dubinsky (2021) show that China often uses stadium diplomacy to obtain special political privileges and access to natural resources in many African nation-states. In general, China uses sport diplomacy for image projection, internal credibility, economic competitiveness, and geopolitical positioning in the world affairs (Dubinsky 2021; Ojo 2022; Will 2012).

Sport Sponsorship and Soft Power

Soft power, as Nye describes it (2011), is a nation-state's ability to wield influence through attraction rather than through coercion or military hard power.

A nation-state's soft power rests on three core resources, namely its culture, political values, and foreign policies. Culture, in this context, broadly encapsulates people, food, literature, music, sports and other socio-cultural activities that might orient a sense of imagined community. In addition to three core resources, positive economic activity is another viable resource for generating or enhancing a nation-state's soft power (Nye Jr 2011). Economic growth, competitiveness, and prosperity—whether in a state-directed market economy as in the case of China, or a neoliberal open market economy—produce an attraction in the comity of nations. Economically, when a country is considered a site for better quality of life for individuals, international trade with positive returns on investment and global equality outlook, there is an upward rise in the positive perception and global soft-power index of such a country (Anholt 2020).

Sport is one of the cultural resources that nation-states have mobilized in the pursuit of soft power. Strategically, China, Qatar, Russia, and several emerging states are "increasingly active in using sponsorship ventures in sports like football to gain influence and legitimacy among a global target audience of consumers, decision-makers, international institutions, and states" (Ahsan 2022, 374). International sport sponsorship involves a myriad of commercial and non-commercial events, activities, and programs, which accentuate commercial and political influence in the local and global contexts. These events range from hosting mega-events like the FIFA World Cup and Olympics, sponsorship of sport teams' uniforms and stadium naming rights, branding, and financing the construction of new stadiums or facilities.

Football attracts a substantial quantity of direct and indirect sponsorship agreements from both state-owned enterprises and corporate entities due to its global popularity, visibility and appeal. Moreover, football is a focal point of a globally hegemonic sports culture that induces broad cultural cosmopolitanism (Markovits and Rensmann 2010). In the 2019/2020 league season, the aggregate annual value of football shirt sponsorship deals alone across the English Premier League (EPL), Spanish La Liga, German Bundesliga and Italian Serie A was €867 million (Beek and Derom 2022). There were many other sponsorship deals involving these leagues, such as stadium branding and direct investment in club ownership, worth billions of US dollars, made by transnational corporate entities and state-owned companies from emerging nation-states and rentier states. In addition to the sponsorship of teams in football leagues, several of these entities, especially those under authoritarian regimes, are actively engaged in the sponsorship of major global sporting events such as the FIFA World Cup, and in a variety of other sporting activities. For example, FIFA sponsorship is now "increasingly dominated by China and Gulf region" (Kissin 2023). Prior to the 2006 FIFA World Cup in Germany, the sponsors of the world's biggest football event were "exclusively US, Japanese and Western European firms" (Kissin 2023).

Scholars have argued that investments in football and other sports by state agencies, state-owned companies and private firms are assets for a country's image and development of socio-cultural and economic relationship with foreign publics, due to the visibility and recognition that positive "corporate" brands bring to a country's international image (Ahsan 2022; Chadwick et al. 2022; Krzyzaniak 2018; White 2015). There is a correlation, to some extent, between the reputation of a corporate brand and the perception of a country's image in the minds of many global consumers, "since many companies remain associated with their countries of origin, the images of reputations of brands and states tend to merge in the minds of the global consumers" (Coaffee and Van Ham 2008, 194). In essence, sport sponsorship by state and non-state-owned corporate entities is partly a means to an end for their respective countries of origin in the pursuit of soft power. It aids countries' public diplomacy efforts.

Sport sponsorship in the context of soft power and international relations involves state and non-state actors including corporate entities, individuals, and civil society groups, but it does not occur in a social and political vacuum. Rather it is deeply "embedded in the structure and ongoing flows of relations of a nation which are always in flux" (Chadwick et al. 2022, 209). Sport sponsorship is thus inherently political. National politics, economic choices, and banal nationalism also drive impulses for sport sponsorship, and the hosting of regional and global sport events. As Chadwick writes, in reference to the rentier states in the Gulf region:

> Another illustration of the economic importance of sport as an economic choice is evident among rentier states, which generate rents externally by manipulating global political and/or economic environments. Saudi Arabia is an example of a rentier state (Baumann 2019). Its current sport investment programme is a conscious attempt to diversify its economy away from oil and gas dependence by incentivizing international sporting events to be staged in the kingdom. (2022, 296)

On one hand, there is an interlocking of mass corporatism, trade, and consumerism with the growing interdependence of sport, economics, and politics. On the other hand, there is the competitive geopolitical norm to build soft power, exert smart power, and in turn have a strategic advantage in agenda-setting in the new world order. Together, all these factors have accentuated the geostrategic importance of sport sponsorship as a foreign policy tool in the broader context of interpenetrated globalization processes and the global shifting order of power relations.

StarTimes

China's pursuit of soft power in Africa is real and evident in most spheres of socio-cultural, political and economic activity in many African countries. In the past decade, there has been a substantial influx of Chinese state and private investments into telecommunications, media, oil and gas, mining, construction, and textile industries in many African countries. It is estimated that there are over 10,000 Chinese firms currently operating across multiple sectors in Africa (Feng and Pilling 2019). StarTimes is among a cluster of Chinese media and telecommunication companies that have ventured into African media and communication industries since the China–Africa relationship was institutionalized in 2000 by the establishment of the Forum on China–Africa Cooperation (FOCAC). Established in 1988 as a Beijing-based privately-owned enterprise by Chinese businessman Pang Xinxing, StarTimes began its African operations in Rwanda in 2007. Currently available in 23 African countries, it has invested over US$400 million in infrastructure and content acquisition since 2007 (Shi 2015). Its content strategy is built largely around exclusive sports broadcasting rights, with a mixture of news and public affairs channels, local TV dramas and Chinese soap operas dubbed into African languages such as Swahili.

From the outset, StarTimes took aim at sports broadcasting rights to build a lineup of premium sports content, particularly football, for its subscribers. The sport content, in particular live telecasts, have been deemed as both "cash cow" and "subscription attractor" for pay-TV companies in cosmopolitan contexts. This is evident with the increasing centrality of sport and media globalization, which have fostered more cross-ownership of media companies and sports organizations in many parts of the world. The pay-TV Canal Plus partly owned Paris St-Germain in France from 1991 till 2006. MultiChoice, South Africa's leading pay-TV operator, owns one of the country's top football teams, Super Sports United. In Canada, the parent companies (Bell and Rogers) of the country's two main sports television outlets, TSN and Sportsnet, are partial joint owners of Maple Leaf Sports and Entertainment (MLSE), which has a football team and a hockey team in the Major League Soccer (MLS) and National Hockey League (NHL). The interlocking of sports and media economies has been vital in the globalization of Western media and communication companies, as ESPN exemplified. ESPN, which is one of the subsidiary companies of The Walt Disney Company, grew from a small-town American cable network to a US$50 billion global business enterprise based on a sports-media alliance (McGuire et al. 2015). Its 24-hour sport coverage and programs are an important source of sport content for many other television and media outlets across the world (McGuire et al. 2015). Rupert Murdoch's Sky Television is another example of a media company partly built on the sports-media economy.

Against this backdrop of interlocking relationships between sport and media economies, StarTimes invested heavily in exclusive sport broadcasting rights. It procured broadcasting rights for major European soccer leagues—German Bundesliga, Italian Serie A, and French Ligue 1. It secured five-year exclusive broadcasting rights (2015 to 2020) for German Bundesliga and sole rights to the Spanish La Liga to position itself as a viable competitor to MultiChoice, which has the exclusive broadcasting rights to the English Premier League in the Sub-Saharan African region. It has non-exclusive broadcasting rights for global football competitions such as the 2016 European Cup qualifying series, FIFA 2018 World Cup and UEFA Champions League. It has a broadcasting deal with the Chinese Super League (CSL) for the telecast of the Chinese league in Africa.

Within the continent, it secured a five-year media partnership deal with Kenya's Football Federation. The partnership, worth US$3 million, ensures that StarTimes has an exclusive broadcast right to all Kenyan national football teams' matches in the qualification series for African championships from 2015 to 2019. In 2020, it secured exclusive broadcast deal to telecast Kenyan premier league matches and national team matches live for seven years. The deal, which is estimated to worth about US$1.1 million per year to the Kenyan Football Federation, also includes live telecast of 30 matches of the second-tier league as well (Kwalimwa 2020). In 2016, it also acquired 10-year media rights for the Ghana Premier League, FA Cup, Women's League, and youth league. As part of the approximately US$18 million deal with Ghanaian Football Association (GFA), StarTimes would build 10 artificial football pitches in Ghana. The deal was, however, mutually terminated in December 2019. In January 2020, GFA and StarTimes signed a new broadcasting rights deal, which is worth US$5.25 million over a five-year period, for live coverage of Ghana Premier League and FA Cup matches (Ghanaian Football Association 2020).

The crucial importance of football to StarTimes' market consolidation is further underscored in its brand promotion, which is partially built around iconic African football stars and legends such as Nigerian Nwankwo Kanu, who played for Arsenal in the English Premier League from 1999 to 2004. StarTimes' use of iconic football stars for promotional campaigns capitalizes on the emotional attachment that sport fans and audiences have with these legendary African stars who are floating signifiers for the expansion of StarTimes' affective relationships with locals. These African sport icons' faces are not only on billboards, but they are also participants and facilitators in StarTimes-sponsored youth football camps in rural and urban areas. While their "iconic" and "celebrity" images are transformed to commercial spectacles in local contexts, their participation in local communities' activities disguise the global economic fetishism that underpins the production-consumption relations of sport culture and the pay-TV enterprises in this context.

StarTimes' first goal is market capitalization and business expansion across the continent. Whereas the StarTimes' first goal is market penetration and capitalization, its operation in connection with China's socio-cultural, economics and political interest on the continent cannot be overlooked. Like other private Chinese companies in Africa, StarTimes has received millions of dollars in the form of soft loans and grants from China's state-owned EXIM Bank and China Development Bank for its African business expansion and activities (Marsh 2019). It remains the only private Chinese company with the authorization license permit from China's Ministry of Commerce to operate abroad in radio and television industries (Marsh 2019). Under the broader framework of corporate social responsibility (CSR), it has partnered with governments in Nigeria, Kenya, and other African countries to connect thousands of rural villages to satellite TV through the provision of solar-powered digital boxes and television. It is also working, in partnership with some African governments to ensure the migration of the broadcasting system from analog to digital in a cross-section of African countries. These and other CSR activities parallel China's public diplomacy efforts on the continent. The Chinese government's public diplomacy efforts on the continent include the expansion of its media influence through the establishment of media outlets, financing digital technological infrastructure, cultural exchanges, and sponsored skills training for African journalists.

StarTimes amplifies China's public diplomacy efforts through its cultural capital investments in the sports sector. Apart from having a dedicated "Kung Fu" channel that promotes Chinese martial art via popular culture and its pay-TV content offerings in Africa, it regularly sponsors kung fu festivals and marital arts training programs for African publics to participate in. Kenya, Nigeria, and Côte d'Ivoire are among the countries where kung fu festivals have been held since 2018. The local participants demonstrate their marital arts skills in the presence of kung fu masters from China, who often serve as judges at these festivals. The chosen "winners" receive financial rewards and sometimes paid sponsored trips to "experience" China. StarTimes and its "deployment of kung fu as a tool of marketing and cultural diplomacy insists on the pleasure that African audiences experience in relation to this genre, thus making an attempt at connecting it to a specific Chinese brand and, more generally, to the perception of Chinese presence in Africa" (Jedlowski 2021, 244). In this regard, StarTimes complements the Confucius Institute's work and that of cultural affairs officials at Chinese embassies on the continent by connecting African publics to Chinese cultural values, norms, and ideals both through its sponsored kung fu festivals in African cities and its inclusion of the king fu channel in the basic pay-TV subscription package. Inevitably, through brand association and positive public participation in the festivals, the fans/audiences might be predisposed to having a favorable outlook toward China and its unique culture of marital arts.

Since President Xi Jinping revealed his vision for turning China into a powerful football nation by 2050, there has been a surge in the number of Chinese investors and businesses securing football properties abroad and getting involved in sponsoring regional and global football in diverse ways. Most notable examples include Wanda's FIFA World Cup sponsorship deal until 2030, while also buying Switzerland's Infront Sports and Media, which owned the media rights to the 2018 and 2022 World Cups. Wanda's international sports industry portfolio diversifies the company's investment in the sector, but it may also enable China "to exert political pressure on FIFA in respect of [future] World Cup hosting decisions" (Chadwick and Sullivan 2019, 533). In this vein, StarTimes' cultivated ties and "working" relationships with African football federations may be influential in canvasing support for China's hosting bid of the FIFA World Cup in the future.

Though soft power is neither absolute nor there is a guarantee that it can be secured by capital investment in sport itself, the attractiveness that StarTimes facilitates through its brand association with local and global football contributes to both its business visibility and China's soft-power resources on the streets in the football-loving continent of Africa. In a sense, by transmitting local football matches on TV, StarTimes provides visibility to the local leagues in the public consciousness. In so doing, it seemingly presents an opportunity for national football federations to strengthen local audiences/fans' affective engagement with the local football culture against a backdrop of the increasing popularity of European football on the electronic airwaves across the continent of Africa. On the other hand, in broad political economy terms, StarTimes' acquisition of broadcasting rights for local and global football leagues in African markets enhances its business profile and cultural capital, which are also linked to the politics of attraction and diplomacy.

Conclusion

Soft power and its relationship with sports has garnered considerable attention in the literature on international relations and the political economy of sports (Rofe 2022, 61). This is partly due to fact that sport sponsorship is one of the channels through which nation-states build up soft-power resources (Grix and Brannagan 2016; Krzyzaniak 2018; Ojo 2022), exercise soft power (Grix 2017; Rofe 2022) and extend their soft power around the world (Chadwick et al. 2022; Grix and Brannagan 2016). According to critical insights from the academic literature, nation-states, corporate entities, and political leaders continuously instrumentalize sports for a socio-political agenda, commerce, and international diplomacy. In the context of sport diplomacy and China's pursuit of soft power in Africa, this chapter examines the appropriation of sport sponsorship and broadcasting rights by StarTimes, a Chinese pay-TV company, in African media and cultural spaces. In assessing the social-cultural ramifications and political-economic dimensions that underpin the StarTimes' media-sports complex in African contexts, the chapter argues that StarTimes' acquisition of sport broadcasting rights and sponsorship of communal sport events are inextricably linked with China's broader pursuit of soft power on the continent. It points to the strategic importance of sport in China's foreign policy agenda. It concludes that StarTimes' sport engagement in Africa contributes to China's broader efforts to cement its global standing and extend its soft power around the world through sports.

References

Ahsan, Ali. 2022. "Just for Kicks: Football as a Potential Harmoniser in the China–Pakistan Economic Corridor." *Journal of Global Sport Management* 7 (3): 372–390.

Anholt, Simon. 2020. *The Good Country Equation: How We Can Repair the World in One Generation*. Berrett-Koehler Publishers.

Baumann, Hannes. 2019. "The Transformation of Saudi Arabia's Rentier State and 'the International.'" *Globalizations* 16 (7): 1165–1183.

Beek, Remco M, and Inge Derom. 2022. "Sponsorship Eras in the English Premier League: Changing Industries and Globalization between 1992 and 2021." *Soccer & Society* 23 (4–5): 349–366.

Chadwick, Simon. 2022. "From Utilitarianism and Neoclassical Sport Management to a New Geopolitical Economy of Sport." *European Sport Management Quarterly* 22 (5): 685–704.

Chadwick, Simon, and Jonathan Sullivan. 2019. "Football in China." In *Routledge Handbook of Football Business and Management*, edited by Simon Chadwick, Daniel Parnell, Paul Widdop, and Christos Anagnostopoulos. Routledge.

Chadwick, Simon, Paul Widdop, and Nicholas Burton. 2022. "Soft Power Sports Sponsorship—a Social Network Analysis of a New Sponsorship Form." *Journal of Political Marketing* 21 (2): 196–217.

Coaffee, Jon, and Peter Van Ham. 2008. "'Security Branding': The Role of Security in Marketing the City, Region or State." *Place Branding and Public Diplomacy* 4 (3): 191–195.

Dubinsky, Itamar. 2021. "China's Stadium Diplomacy in Africa." *Journal of Global Sport Management*: 1–19.

Feng, Emily, and David Pilling. 2019. "The Other Side of Chinese Investment in Africa." *Financial Times*, March 27, 2019. https://www.ft.com/content/9f5736d8-14e1-11e9-a581-4ff78404524e.

Ghanaian Football Association. January 8, 2020. "Press Release: StarTimes named as Television Rights Holder of the Ghana Premier League and the FA Cup." https://www.ghanafa.org/press-release-startimes-named-as-television-rights-holder-of-the-ghana-premier-league-and-the-fa-cup.

Grix, Jonathan. 2017. *Sport Politics: An Introduction*. Bloomsbury Publishing.

Grix, Jonathan, and Paul Michael Brannagan. 2016. "Of Mechanisms and Myths: Conceptualising States' 'Soft Power' Strategies through Sports Mega-Events." *Diplomacy & Statecraft* 27 (2): 251–272.

Jedlowski, Alessandro. 2021. "Chinese Television in Africa." *Theory, Culture & Society* 38 (7–8): 233–250.

Kissin, Ellesheva. 2023. "The Soccernomics of FIFA's Changing Sponsorship" *fDi Intelligence*, March 3, 2023. https://www.fdiintelligence.com/content/feature/the-soccernomics-of-fifas-changing-sponsorship-82005.

Krzyzaniak, John S. 2018. "The Soft Power Strategy of Soccer Sponsorships." *Soccer & Society* 19 (4): 498–515.

Kwalimwa, David. 2020. "Lights . . . Camera . . . Action . . . Mwendwa Announces Multi-Million Broadcast." September 29, 2020. https://nation.africa/kenya/sports/football/fkf-nick-mwendwa-announce-multi-million-startimes-broadcast-deal-2452376.

Markovits, Andrei S., and Lars Rensmann. 2010. *Gaming the World: How Sports Are Reshaping Global Politics and Culture*. Princeton University Press.

Marsh, Jenni. 2019. "How China Is Slowly Expanding Its Power in Africa, One TV Set at a Time." CNN Business News, 2019. https://www.cnn.com/2019/07/23/business/startimes-china-africa-kenya-intl/index.html.

McGuire, John, Greg G Armfield, and Adam C Earnheardt, eds. 2015. *The ESPN Effect: Exploring the Worldwide Leader in Sports*. Peter Lang.

Murray, Stuart, and Geoffrey Allen Pigman. 2014. "Mapping the Relationship between International Sport and Diplomacy." *Sport in Society* 17 (9): 1098–1118.

Nye Jr, Joseph S. 2011. *The Future of Power*. Public Affairs.

Ojo, Tokunbo. 2022. "Sino-African Sport Diplomacy? 'New' Wave of Chinese Stadiums in African Cities." In *China's International Communication and Relationship Building*, edited by Xiaoling Zhang and Corey Schultz, 216–232. Routledge.
Rofe, J. Simon. 2022. "Diplomacy, International Relations, Soft Power and the FIFA World Cup." In *The Business of the FIFA World Cup*, 61–72. Routledge.
Shi, Anbin. 2015. "Re-Orienting the 'Charm Offensive' to the 'Charm Defensive': A Critical Review of Chinese Media Development in Africa." *African Journalism Studies* 36 (1): 135–140.
White, Candace L. 2015. "Exploring the Role of Private-Sector Corporations in Public Diplomacy." *Public Relations Inquiry* 4 (3): 305–321.
Will, Rachel. 2012. "China's Stadium Diplomacy." *World Policy Journal* 29 (2): 36–44.
Zhang, Qingmin. 2013. "Sports Diplomacy: The Chinese Experience and Perspective." *The Hague Journal of Diplomacy* 8 (3–4): 211–233.

11

Dalian Shide FC's Lion Cub Program: Player Recruitment and Naturalization

Tobias Ross[1]

Between July and October 2001, Chinese professional football club Dalian Shide FC brought a total of 24 football players between the ages of 14 and 18 from Cameroon to the northeastern industrial city of Dalian (Sohu 2001b). Labeled the "Cameroon Lion Cub Program" (*Kamailong youshi jihua*) by Chinese media, the plan was to develop the teenagers into competitive talents, with the intention of eventually transferring them to other clubs for financial gain, and perhaps even represent China as naturalized players. At the time, such a concentration of foreign visitors was unusual beyond major metropolitan centers like Beijing, Shanghai and Shenzhen, and the notable concentration of African expatriates in Guangzhou (Bork-Hüffer and Yuan-Ihle 2014). As a result, the Cameroonian teenagers became a minor sensation in football-mad Dalian, and sparked curiosity among national sports writers. However, after several disruptions to the program, including a labor strike by some players, after less than a year 16 of the 24 players had been expelled (Titan Sports 2002). Although certain players had prior experience with Shide-affiliated clubs, none of these players contributed to the club's financial gains, nor did they meet the qualifications to represent the Chinese national team.

1 Tobias Ross, Researcher, University of Nottingham, tobias.ross@nottingham.ac.uk.

Despite generating local media coverage at the time, and recent interest rekindled by China's intensified naturalization initiatives prior to the Qatar World Cup qualifying campaign (Sullivan et al. 2023), the Lion Cub case remains largely unstudied. This knowledge gap impedes a more comprehensive grasp of the case itself and its broader implications for the examination of China–Africa relations in the context of one of China's most prominent professional clubs operating during the nascent stages of the industry's development. By using data from semi-structured interviews with experts on the program as well as Chinese-language media reports, the chapter closes this gap by analyzing the program's motivations, challenges, and outcomes from the perspective of both the club and the players. After reviewing the literature dealing with migration and athlete recruitment, the chapter provides a short introduction to the Chinese football industry at the turn of the century and Dalian Shide FC's role in it before setting out the case study methods and findings.

Migration and Athlete Recruitment

A substantial body of research concerning the athlete and football labor market grounds its analytical framework in the enhanced global interconnectedness within the realm of the football and adjacent commercial industries (Darby 2013b; Magee and Sugden 2002). This interconnectedness leads to an amplified interdependence observed within football (Giulianotti and Robertson 2012). Multiple studies have substantiated the observation that a growing number of players in Europe's top leagues were born in a different country (Giulianotti and Robertson 2009; Lanfranchi and Taylor 2001; Magee and Sugden 2002; Velema et al. 2020). For instance, from 2003 to 2011 approximately 40 percent of players in Europe's top-seven leagues held nationalities different from the country in which their league was based (Velema et al. 2020). Of this group, approximately 9 percent originated from African nations. Notably, the English Premier League boasted the highest percentage of non-native players, with a substantial 55 percent.

Various theoretical concepts have evolved to elucidate the growing internationalization of the football labor force within Europe's top leagues and elsewhere. One of the earliest theories tried to explain the increasing diversity of nationalities in Europe's top leagues with a combination of micro-level individual motivations among migrant football players and the broader macro-structural influences of political, economic, cultural, and social forces shaping migration patterns (Magee and Sugden 2002; Maguire and Pearton 2000; Maguire and Stead 1998). Researchers in this field have developed a framework to incorporate macro-structural factors at the national level when scrutinizing migration patterns, particularly focusing on cultural and linguistic similarities rooted in colonial legacies (Darby 2013a; Maguire and Pearton 2000). Nevertheless, more recent findings by Jansen and Engbersen (2017) indicate that, within the context of the Olympics, colonial connections have diminished in significance as explanatory factors for migration trends (as discussed in Chapter 6 of this book in the context of African football migration to China).

Some scholars argue that the economic disparities between players' home countries and the countries they migrate to, as well as between less developed and more advanced football leagues, serve as a driving force for player migration (Darby and Solberg 2013; Njororai 2010; Pedo Lopes et al. 2023). These studies, and several earlier chapters in this book, suggest that the migration of African football players is fundamentally influenced by a multifaceted interplay of socio-economic and political factors that both compel and attract them. The migration is propelled by "push factors," encompassing economic hardships, political instability, and career uncertainty in their home countries. Conversely, athletes are attracted by "pull factors," including the allure of better salaries, superior sporting infrastructure and competitions, and the prestige associated with foreign leagues and clubs (Darby and Solberg 2013). In this domain, some scholars contend that these dynamics contribute to a gradual erosion of sporting proficiency within the athletes' home nations, as discussed, for instance, by Thibault (2009). Additionally, these scholars argue that host nations often exploit the athletes' dependencies, a point further elaborated by studies such as Poli (2006) and Njororai (2012).

Other scholars have analyzed disparities at club-level and their link with athlete migration. They contend, for instance, that the expanding disparity in player salaries across clubs and leagues serves as a catalyst for player migration from economically disadvantaged to wealthier circumstances (Hoey et al. 2020; Poli 2006; Velema et al. 2020). According to Poli (2006), most African clubs are unable to match the salaries paid in more developed football leagues and thus are not able to prevent outward migration. Conversely, financially less robust European clubs strategically acquire young African footballers with the intent of reselling them to wealthier clubs at a profit. This speculative approach is driven by the widening gap that sets apart the affluent clubs in major leagues from the rest in descending order. African players are highly coveted in this context due to their reiterative commercial value (Poli 2006, 289).

Chinese Football at the Turn of the Century

The early 2000s in China were characterized by significant economic growth and an increasing focus on global integration. China's admission to the World Trade Organization at the end of 2001 marked a significant milestone, further facilitating its integration into the global economy. The country's economy was becoming more open to international trade and investment, leading to increased globalization of Chinese businesses after decades of isolation (Lai 2006). This shift in the economy was also felt in football. Founded in 1994, after decades of a state-controlled and state-funded sports system, the Jia-A league was China's first sports league allowing corporate owners and a commercial business model. The league garnered instant enthusiasm among fans, although this was somewhat dampened by the corruption scandals of the late 1990s and early 2000s. However, the excitement was reignited following the country's historic World Cup qualification in October 2001 (Chadwick and Sullivan 2019). Dalian Shide played a notable role in this development, with numerous players representing the national team and substantial financial impacts. In 1994, the Dalian football club long funded and managed by the municipal Sports Committee was bought by the private, and at the time still mostly local, real estate firm Wanda. It thereby became the first fully privately-owned club in China. Retaining a close working relationship with the local government, the club went on to win a record eight league titles between 1994 and 2005. The owners, Wang Jianlin (1994–2000) and Xu Ming (2000–2012), rose to national fame, which established them and their companies as major figures in Chinese football (Xue et al. 2020). After their takeover of the club from Wanda in 2000, the Dalian-based building material company Shide invested in several football projects. At one point in time, Shide had direct or indirect financial links to seven clubs in China's football pyramid (NetEase 2022). The company reportedly even intended to expand its club network globally (Epoch Times 2001; Sohu 2002). Known as the Shide system (*shide xi*), numerous players were transferred between these clubs, including several participants from the Lion Cub program. Shide's pioneering of the multi-club model later adopted by City Football Group and others, was hindered by match-fixing allegations, which formally required the firm to limit its investment to one club (NetEase 2022). In practice, however, the company sustained links to several clubs long after its official exit from them.

Despite the company's extensive football network, international player recruitment was underdeveloped, unsystematic and largely reliant on individual recommendations. Shortly after the inception of the professional league in the mid-1990s, foreign players assumed a pivotal role in the performance of numerous newly established clubs, even in the face of limitations such as a restriction of only three foreign outfield players per team and a later ban of foreign goalkeepers. For instance, in 1997, Paraguayan midfielder Jorge Campos won the league's Most Valuable Player award. Three years later, his fellow countryman Casiano Delvalle became the league's first foreign top-scorer (Sohu 2020). However, while Chinese clubs were increasingly keen to bolster their squads by bringing in foreign players, international networks and scouting operations for recruiting players were severely underdeveloped. The situation was further complicated by the lack of a standardized transfer system and club experience in handling the legal, managerial and logistical aspects associated with international player transfers. As a result, a significant number of the initial foreign transfers into China's professional leagues were perceived as overpriced, and were often accompanied by tales of concealed injuries and contractual breaches (Guangzhou Daily 1999).

Method

This chapter is concerned with the motivations, challenges, and outcomes of Dalian Shide's Lion Cub Program. Due to its age and limited publicly available information, many of the issues are only known to the people involved in the program. Thus, to generate needed insights, I conducted semi-structured interviews with two senior Chinese journalists, two players who participated in the program and the vice-chairman of the club at the time. The interviews were conducted in Chinese (journalists and club representative) and English (players) between October and November 2023. The interviews lasted between 25 and 75 minutes. Purposive sampling was used to identify and select these key informants (Barbour 2013, 64). It is worth noting that the entire sampling process posed challenges, primarily due to the program's long-standing history and the contentiousness (even rancor) surrounding the project. The interview data was transcribed and translated into English (if needed) and subject to back translation method following Brislin (1970). The study followed a narrative analysis approach in the sense of Almén (2003). Themes and meanings were identified as they emerged inductively across the corpus of interview responses. The findings section below deals first with the program and its outcomes, before discussing its motivations and, lastly, its challenges.

Program and Outcomes

In early 2001, a delegation of Dalian club officials traveled to Cameroon's economic capital of Douala. Among the delegation was vice-chairman Lin Lefeng and assistant coach Lin Jianwei, as well as a player agent from South Korea employed by the club (Football Weekly 2002). The scouting operation lasted one week and consisted of trials and training sessions. According to Lin Lefeng special attention was paid to players' physical fitness and technical skills (Lin 2023). Around two hundred teenagers from across the country participated in the trial sessions, with players recommended by the local Football Associations, clubs, and academies, including the renowned Ecole de Football Brasseries du Cameroun that had produced the continent's upcoming superstar, Samuel Eto'o (Njewel 2023).

A year earlier, in 2000, Cameroon had won their third African Cup of Nations title as well as the men's football tournament at the Sydney Olympics. The Olympic title in particular caught the attention of the global football community. Cameroon was the second African country in history to win the tournament, and the success was widely seen as testimony to the country's youth development system. Essentially an under-23 tournament with only three overage players allowed to participate, the team's average age was 21 years, with their youngest player aged 16 during the Games (ESPN 2020). According to Lin Lefeng, this strong sporting performance was an important factor in Xu Ming's decision to pick Cameroon as scouting location, alongside logistical and financial factors (Lin 2023). By 2000, Cameroonian players had an established history of playing professional football abroad. Of the Olympic gold medalists, 14 (of 18 players in the squad) plied their trade outside Cameroon, mostly in Europe. The transfer of Cameroonian players overseas, primarily to French clubs, was a long-standing practice (Berthoud and Frenkiel 2016). This established network likely facilitated the contracting of such a sizable group of players. Moreover, the Korean player agent affiliated with Dalian Shide had already forged connections with some of Cameroon's football institutions. Agents often engage in this "relational work," creating personal connections with prospective partners and clients to bridge physical gaps within networks (Darr and Mears 2017, 3). In the case of Shide's project, the agent was not only striking the link between the club and its Cameroonian counterparts, he was also handling the administration with the players and their parents, functioning as the intermediary between club and players (Bakalag 2023; Njewel 2023). Lastly, the transfer fees commanded by Cameroonian talents, especially in comparison to players from more developed football nations, were attractive for buying clubs (Poli 2006). The financial factor was confirmed by Lin Lefeng:

> Because [Xu Ming] knew that if we go to Cameroon to choose players it will be very cheap. Frankly speaking, he said he did not want to go to Europe to get players due to the very high prices. In Africa the market is very cheap, it is true, it does not cost much. (Lin 2023)

Such financial considerations are common in the modern football economy (Darr and Mears 2017; Velema 2021), especially among less wealthy leagues and clubs (Poli 2006, 2010). According to Poli (2010), in Europe's most prosperous football leagues, powerful clubs, scouts, and player agents collaborate to establish global value-added chains. These chains capitalize on the evolving international division of labor in football, where an increasing number of talented players originate from less developed leagues in the global South. European clubs occupy a top position within these speculative global value-added chains, aiming to maximize their profits in the labor market by acquiring cheap talent and subsequently reselling players for higher transfer fees to other European clubs (Poli 2010). Despite its relatively peripheral standing in the football world, Dalian Shide, supported by the affluent Xu Ming, pursued a similar strategy, capitalizing on the disparity between the football leagues in Cameroon and China.

Despite the program's lofty aspirations, not everything unfolded as intended. Shortly after the players arrival in July 2001, for reasons that remain unconfirmed (Epoch Times 2001; Football Weekly 2002), five of the initial 24 players were sent back to Cameroon, resulting in a total of 19 players remaining in Dalian for the first year of the program. The players were accommodated in dormitories at the club's training base in Dalian, had designated chefs, two French-language interpreters, and coaching staff, including the Frenchman Patrice Neveu, who had previously worked as the national team coach of Niger (Football Weekly 2002). According to Njewel, the majority of the teenagers spoke only their respective regional dialects, with some having proficiency in French (Njewel 2023). None of the players possessed proficiency in English or Chinese. Players were offered Chinese language and culture courses during their time at the academy. The teenagers were prohibited from leaving the training facility unless accompanied by club personnel. Per multiple media reports and my interviews, each player was reportedly compensated with RMB800 (ca. €100) per month, plus free accommodation and meals (Football Weekly 2002; Lin 2023; Njewel 2023). Initially the teenagers were intended to form an under-17 team and participate in the domestic Chinese youth league. However, the Dalian club did not receive approval from the CFA (Epoch Times 2001). As a result, the players were restricted to training within their group in Dalian and only occasionally participated in training games and youth tournaments with other teams (Bakalag 2023). This restricted the players' engagement in competitive football, impeding their overall sporting development.

Not long after their arrival, one of the players was sent to Shide's newly established farm team, Dalian Shidelong, for the remainder of the 2001 season. In early 2002, two additional players joined him at the team, which was also based in Dalian but competed in China's second division. Five other players regularly trained with Shide's second team and later the first team, but none of them were ever included in the squad (Titan Sports 2002). In July 2002, Ewana Ngassa and Guy Herve Ndem were loaned out for one season without a fee to Hong Kong first division club Double Flower, where they both made several appearances (Sohu 2002). After their spell with the club, both players left the program and continued their careers in Hong Kong and elsewhere. In 2003, the other five players (Njewel, Pouga, Baning, Simon, Bakalag) were sent to Shide's sister club Shidelong, which had been sold to Anping and was coached by Patrice Neveu. The team subsequently relocated to the southern city of Zhuhai and later Shanghai. After only one season the group was reduced to three players (Njewel, Pouga, Baning), of whom two quit the program and left China after the 2005 season. Only Didier Njewel remained in China. Aside from a short spell with South African Bidvest Wits FC in 2006, Njewel remained in China until the end of his career in 2012. The majority of Lion Cub players did not end up pursuing a professional football career in China or elsewhere. The ones that did mostly played in minor international leagues with mixed results. Several players received call-ups to represent Cameroon's youth national teams, with Albert Baning earning a spot in the under-23 squad that participated in the 2008 Beijing Olympics (Sohu 2023).

Commercial Motivations

Given the early stage of development in Chinese professional football and its relatively limited commercial revenue, Chinese clubs were seeking ways to bolster their income. The domestic player transfer market in China was still in its infancy, predominantly showcasing local talents. Simultaneously, Europe had a well-established track record of nurturing players and facilitating their transfers for financial gain (Szymanski and Smith 1997). This European model had gained global (and Chinese) recognition, due to high-profile transfers such as the Brazilian Ronaldo's €27 million move from FC Barcelona to Inter Milan in 1997, and other record-breaking transfer fees (Matheson 2017). In comparison, the record transfer in China that same year, Hao Haidong's move from Bayi to Dalian Wanda, was valued at RMB2.2 million (ca. €280,000) (Sohu 2005b). According to media reports at that time, the club scouted foreign players for commercial purposes, intending to train and develop them within the club network before reselling them in China or Europe. For the older players this process was supposed to take two to three years, before the club could gradually sell them on (Beijing Youth Daily 2002). To understand the potential economic returns, Lin Lefeng, in an interview in 2001, stated that the transfer of just one player could cover the costs of the entire program (Sohu 2001a). This plan did not work out, however. Even though some players were eventually transferred to other clubs, Lin stated that none of these transfers returned a profit for the club (Lin 2023). Additionally, Lin stressed the point that Chinese professional football in the early 2000s was still in its nascent stages, with the majority of clubs lacking global connections, primarily depending on a small group of player agents with international networks. He goes on to characterize the state of Chinese clubs in relation to foreign signings during that period as follows:

> [Chinese clubs] just rely on other people's recommendation [of foreign players], there are no trial trainings, a lot of them come and turn out to be not the real thing (*shuihuo*). As a result, the club spends a lot of money that should not be spent, and the club is back at the same place, again having to look for new players. (Lin 2023)

The issue of *shuihuo* is a recurring issue in Chinese football, especially in its earlier days. Originally an economic term denoting "parallel imports," within the context of football it describes a signing at a financial level that exceeds a player's actual sporting value. In numerous instances, the overpayment is exacerbated by challenges in adapting to the new football environment. This dependency on agents' recommendations was intensified by the limited telecommunications and scouting technologies available at the time (Guangzhou Daily 1999). In today's football environment, scouting is increasingly reliant on technology and data, generally reducing clubs' dependency on agents (Weinreich 2022). By retaining control over the recruitment of new players and the establishment of a club network infrastructure conducive to the gradual development of talent, Dalian Shide was a pioneer in China, adopting a practice that has since become commonplace among some of Europe's premier clubs, particularly within multi-club ownership networks (Egilsson 2018; Richardson 2023). In these setups, clubs own or cooperate with clubs and academies across the globe, thus enabling the provision of suitable training and competitive environments tailored to individual player skill levels. For big clubs it is often difficult for the first team to provide enough playing time for talents, but loaning out talents to smaller clubs allows players to gain the needed practical experience to eventually qualify for the primary team. Additionally, these clubs are not only capable of placing their players within these networks but also excel in scouting new talent through an expanded own scouting network (Egilsson 2018).

Naturalization

Naturalization has been a recurring topic surrounding the Lion Cub project. While several athletes born in China have chosen to become citizens of other countries, most prominently in the case of table tennis (Oonk and Oonk 2023), the concept of naturalizing athletes to represent China did not become a prominent concern until the 1990s. The growing focus on this matter was mainly triggered by Japan and South Korea's utilization of foreign players to establish themselves as dominant forces in Asian football (Manzenreiter and Horne 2007). Even though it suggests not being the club's primary motivation to introduce the teenagers from Cameroon, Dalian Shide did explore the possibility of player naturalization (Lin 2023). In an interview from August 2002, Shide's CEO, Xu Ming, confirmed the strategy and indicated clear interest from various players to naturalize (Beijing Youth Daily 2002). This interest was confirmed by Didier Njewel (Njewel 2023). Generally, athlete naturalization is influenced by two factors: the regulations of the local and international sport governing bodies as well as the nationality laws of the respective countries (Ross 2023). Before 2004, FIFA's regulations governing the change of a player's nationality were characterized by a higher degree of flexibility in comparison to the regulations subsequently introduced. Players had the opportunity to switch their national teams provided they satisfied specific criteria, which typically encompassed factors such as birthplace, parentage, or residency ties to the new country, contingent upon the approval of both relevant national associations (Hall 2012). Regarding the case of the players from Cameroon, FIFA regulations essentially allowed the players to represent China in international competitions.

Regarding the PRC's own nationality law, however, the situation was more difficult. According to the Chinese nationality law from 1980, Chinese nationality can only be acquired through birth, descent, marriage to a Chinese national, and naturalization, while the latter two are largely restrictive. In general, to obtain Chinese citizenship is particularly difficult. Applicants must satisfy one of three specific conditions: they should either be closely related to a Chinese national, have established a permanent residence in China, or possess other legitimate reasons (National People's Congress 2000). The third condition deliberately maintains a degree of ambiguity, resulting in its practical interpretation being grounded in utilitarian considerations. Dalian Shide encountered these restrictive policies, as the club engaged in conversations with both the Public Security Bureau and the Immigration Bureau (Lin 2023; Sohu 2005b). The former vice-chairman of the club describes the challenging situation as follows:

> At that time the [nationality] policy was really difficult to overcome. We tried to arrange things, see if these things can be done, see if they can apply for Chinese citizenship, this we all investigated. But there were a lot of obstacles at that time. After all, China was not very open at that time. So this path is very difficult, you cannot easily become Chinese citizen, you cannot join [Team] China. Whether it's the national team or youth team, you cannot get in, if you are not Chinese. (Lin 2023)

It is interesting to note that the Chinese Football Association (CFA) was largely absent from this process. Per Lin's account, the initiative for naturalization was exclusively driven by the club, which informed the national governing body but treated it as an internal club decision. He further characterizes the CFA's stance as "non-committal" and marked by a lack of clear positioning regarding the matter of naturalization (Lin 2023). This record reflects later observations by Sullivan et al. (2023) that the association refrained from any serious considerations to naturalize footballers until around 2015. Overall, with the exception of the isolated case involving the UK-born equestrian Alex Hua Tian in 2006, foreign athletes did not acquire Chinese nationality until the year 2019, a development coinciding with the lead-up to the 2022 Winter Olympics and the 2022 FIFA World Cup qualifiers, as noted by Ross (2023).

Challenges

Right from the start the program was plagued by several incidents. After the routine health inspection after arrival in China a group of five players was sent home for reasons not communicated to the remaining players (Njewel 2023).

While there were rumors about the health conditions of these players as well as the Cameroonian Football Association not allowing their participation in the program (Epoch Times 2001; Football Weekly 2002), the uncertainty reportedly caused fear among the remaining cohort. The fear of being excluded from the program and sent home was felt among many of the players, as captured by the statement of Didier Njewel:

> Then next time when we hear that we go to the hospital everybody was freezing. "Oh my God, why are we going to the hospital again?" [laughs] Everyone was afraid to go back home. (Njewel 2023)

The situation worsened in summer 2002 when the club requested the program's coach, Patrice Neveu, to provide an evaluation list assessing the players individually. Subsequently, all but eight players were sent back to Cameroon, a decision allegedly protested by some of the players (Titan Sports 2002). The intensification of competition was further compounded by CFA regulations limiting the number of foreign players eligible to play, exacerbating the regular intra-squad competition for playing time. These factors, combined with a determination to avoid the stigma of returning home unsuccessful, meant that players were compelled to navigate an increasingly competitive environment and the fear of being dismissed from the program. This heightened competition was palpable during the Chinese Super League (CSL) match between Dalian Shide and Shanghai Zhongbang in August 2005, a game that essentially involved two teams within the same Shide family. During this encounter, players Baning and Njewel from Shanghai Zhongbang engaged in repeated on-field altercations (Sohu 2005c). When questioned about the circumstances, Zhao Xuri, a midfielder for Shide, later characterized the two players as having been "abandoned" by Dalian and being in a position where they had to "demonstrate their abilities to match their peers," thereby explaining their fierce determination (Sohu 2005c).

Concerns and pressure to perform due to the possibility of athletes being expelled from their clubs have been recorded in various sports that recruit talent from less developed regions (Book Jr et al. 2021; Poli 2006). The athlete's reliance on the club in such instances has occasionally resulted in precarious situations marked by the exploitation of labor and discriminatory practices (Maguire and Stead 1998; Thibault 2009). In such situations athletes are often denied the rewards promised to them, like observed in the early 2000s among Cameroonian footballers in Switzerland (Poli 2006), in some cases even withholding athletes' passports (Njororai 2012). Regarding the Lion Cub program, both Njewel and

Bakalag have indicated that the group was initially assured higher payments than what they eventually received (Bakalag 2023; Njewel 2023). Instances of unpaid wages or incomplete compensation are frequently documented in Chinese football, including among foreign players (China Youth Daily 2004; Sina 2021). However, this case stands out because the players purportedly never received a copy of their contract, and their ability to comprehend the English-language contract was hampered by language barriers (Bakalag 2023; Njewel 2023). Although it is challenging to ascertain the precise details, the players' labor strike in May 2002 as well as the unclear contract situation surrounding some of the players' later transfers suggests that there were unresolved issues between the club and its players (Football Weekly 2002).

Besides these incidents, some of the players reportedly struggled with their new surroundings and situation in China. Reports of conspicuous consumption, poor discipline, challenging behaviors, homesickness, and the contraction of diseases were reported in Chinese media (Football Weekly 2002; Titan Sports 2002). Until about a decade ago, foreign immigrants were not a major focus of Chinese mainstream media, with the few exceptions framing foreigners as exotic, homogenous, and stereotypical (Gan 2023). Some of the reports concerning the Lion Cub program can be described as racist, linking certain characteristics and behavioral traits to the players' origin and skin color. Only in rare cases did media outlets include individual characteristics such as their tender age or recognize challenges stemming from the program and cultural differences, as factors contributing to the incidents. Many reports simply referred to the "black kids" (*hei haizi*) when reporting on the teenagers, sometimes portraying them as lacking respect and discipline, greedy, ungrateful, and extravagant (see, for instance, Titan Sports 2002). Interviewee Olivier Bakalag encountered a similar sentiment when, during a tournament in Guangzhou, a coach from a women's team kept him at a distance, fearing the transmission of diseases (Bakalag 2023). Overall, the program was often presented as a chance for the underprivileged teenagers to better their lives, and turbulence was framed as being caused by participants' greed and impatience. The labor strike in May 2002 received particular attention, characterized by one-sided coverage of the incident (see, for instance, Football Weekly 2002). The prevalence of biased reporting in this context presented a difficult challenge to exert influence, given the limited agency of the players and the club's assumed strategy to deflect blame for the program's shortcomings. Moreover, the players' constrained proficiency in both Chinese and English, with only Njewel and Baning reportedly having a sufficient command of Chinese to conduct interviews (Sohu 2005a), likely added to the challenge of reshaping the media narrative during an era where the public discourse about foreignness and race was very limited.

Conclusion

The Lion Cub program launched by Dalian Shide FC marked a pioneering venture at a pivotal juncture, when China's football industry was in its early stages of embracing external engagement and commercialization. Clubs, including the record-breaking Shide, were actively seeking supplementary revenue streams and strategies to navigate the challenges posed by their relatively insular and underdeveloped football business environment. Motivated by commercial interests and the prospect of player naturalization in response to restrictions on fielding foreign players, the program encountered challenges from its inception. By capitalizing on the economic disparity between Cameroon and China, including in the field of football, cultural and contractual misunderstandings led to the early dissolution of the project. Despite brief spells at some of Shide's affiliated clubs, no players produced any financial gains for the company, nor did they represent Chinese national teams at any level. Largely seen as a failure by both the club and the players, the program likely deterred other clubs from similar attempts in later years. Nonetheless, despite the personal experiences of the program's participants, China remains an attractive destination for players from Cameroon. Between 2004 and 2020, 17 players from Cameroon were plying their trade in the CSL, second only to Nigeria (28) among African countries (Yang and Wang 2022). Meanwhile, Dalian Shide FC ceased operations in 2012 due to a series of scandals involving their owner, Xu Ming, which ultimately led to his imprisonment in 2013.

References

Almén, Byron. 2003. "Narrative Archetypes: A Critique, Theory, and Method of Narrative Analysis." *Journal of Music Theory* 47 (1): 1–39.

Bakalag, Olivier. 2023. Online Video Interview: Player.

Barbour, Rosaline S. 2013. *Introducing Qualitative Research: A Student's Guide*: Sage.

Beijing Youth Daily. 2002. "Zhongguo zuqiu shi tunshi jinqian de heidong? Xu ming: Women jiu bu jiaoku" [Is Chinese Football a Black Hole That Swallows Money? Xu Ming: We Won't Complain]. Sohu. Last modified August 25. https://2014.sohu.com/69/27/sports_news164832769.shtml.

Berthoud, Jérôme, and Stanislas Frenkiel. 2016. "The African Turning Point in European Football: Immigration experiences of Cameroonian and Algerian footballers in France during the 1980's. In Vonnard Philippe, Quin Gregory and Bancel Nicolas (eds), *Building Europe With The Ball: Turning Points in the Europeanization of Football (1905-1995)*. Berne: Peter Lang, 201–22.
2016, pp. 201-222.

Bork-Hüffer, Tabea, and Yuan Yuan-Ihle. 2014. "The Management of Foreigners in China: Changes to the Migration Law and Regulations during the Late HuWen and early XiLi Eras and Their Potential Effects." *International Journal of China Studies* 5 (3): 571.

Brislin, Richard W. 1970. "Back-Translation for Cross-Cultural Research." *Journal of Cross-Cultural Psychology* 1 (3): 185–216.

Chadwick, Simon, and Jonathan Sullivan. 2019. "Football in China." In *Routledge Handbook of Football Business and Management*, edited by Simon Chadwick, Daniel Parnell, Paul Widdop, and Christos Anagnostopoulos. Routledge.

China Youth Daily. 2004. "Zhongguo zhiye hua zuqiu tuxian jingji wanji" [China's Professional Football Highlights Economic Problems]. China Youth Daily. Last modified September 07. https://zqb.cyol.com/content/2004-09/07/content_944612.htm.

Darby, Paul. 2013a. "African Football Labour Migration to Portugal: Colonial and Neo-Colonial Resource." In *Globalised Football*, 56–70. Routledge.

w 2013b. "Moving Players, Traversing Perspectives: Global Value Chains, Production Networks and Ghanaian Football Labour Migration." *Geoforum* 50: 43–53.

Darby, Paul, and Eirik Solberg. 2013. "Differing Trajectories: Football Development and Patterns of Player Migration in South Africa and Ghana." In *South Africa and the Global Game*, 118–130. Routledge.

Darr, Asaf, and Ashley Mears. 2017. "Locating Local Knowledge in Global Networks: Scouting in Fashion and Football." *Poetics* 62: 1–14. https://doi.org/https://doi.org/10.1016/j.poetic.2017.03.001.

Egilsson, Birnir. 2018. "Supply Chain Management in Professional Football." In *Routledge Handbook of Football Business and Management*, 319–333. Routledge.

Epoch Times. 2001. "Feizhou juntuan wu ren ruxian ka guo qing shide yaomai yidali julebu" [Five African Legion Players Selected for Cameroon National Youth Team Shide Wants to Buy Italian Club]. Last modified July 22. https://www.epochtimes.com/gb/1/7/22/n111822.htm.

ESPN. 2020. "Cameroon's Gold-Medal Winning Squad at the Sydney 2000 Olympics: Where Are They Now?" ESPN. Last modified September 29. https://www.espn.co.uk/football/story/_/id/37587794/where-now.

Football Weekly. 2002. "Shide kamailong tongzi jun shengcun baogao bei xingbing gaibian yanse de shaonian" [Shide Cameroon Boy Scout Survival Report: A Boy Whose Color Changed from a STD]. Sina. Last modified July 03. https://sports.sina.cn/sa/2002-07-03/detail-ikftssap9802324.d.html.

Gan, Chun. 2023. "Immigrants on Chinese Television and Limitations of China's Globalist Discourse." *Television & New Media* 24 (1): 54–70. https://doi.org/10.1177/15274764211061256.

Giulianotti, Richard, and Roland Robertson. 2009. *Globalization and Football*. Sage.

———. 2012. "Mapping the Global Football Field: A Sociological Model of Transnational Forces within the World Game." *The British Journal of Sociology* 63 (2): 216–240.

Guangzhou Daily. 1999. "Zhongguo zuqiu tuixing jingji ren zhidu da pilu" [Disclosure of Chinese Football's Agent System]. Last modified September 3. http://sports.2008.sina.com.cn/china/9909/033408.shtml.

Hall, Courtney D. 2012. "Fishing for All-Stars in a Time of Global Free Agency: Understanding FIFA Eligibility Rules and the Impact on the US Men's National Team." *Marquette Sports Law Review* 23: 191.

Hoey, Samuel, Thomas Peeters, and Francesco Principe. 2020. *Who Benefits from Transfers?* Tinbergen Institute Discussion Paper.

Jansen, Joost, and Godfried Engbersen. 2017. "Have the Olympic Games Become More Migratory? A Comparative Historical Perspective." *Comparative Migration Studies* 5: 1–15.

Lai, Hongyi. 2006. *Reform and the Non-State Economy in China: The Political Economy of Liberalization Strategies*. Palgrave Macmillan.

Lanfranchi, Pierre, and Matthew J. Taylor. 2001. "Moving with the Ball: The Migration of Professional Footballers."

Lin, Lefeng. 2023. Online audio interview: Vice-Chairman Dalian Shide.

Magee, Jonathan, and John Sugden. 2002. "'The World at Their Feet': Professional Football and International Labor Migration." *Journal of Sport and Social Issues* 26 (4): 421–437. https://doi.org/10.1177/0193732502238257.

Maguire, Joseph, and Robert Pearton. 2000. "Global Sport and the Migration Patterns of France '98 World Cup Finals Players: Some Preliminary Observations." *Soccer & Society* 1 (1): 175–189. https://doi.org/10.1080/14660970008721257.

Maguire, Joseph, and David Stead. 1998. "Border Crossings: Soccer Labour Migration and the European Union." *International Review for the Sociology of Sport* 33 (1): 59–73.

Manzenreiter, Wolfram, and John Horne. 2007. "Playing the Post-Fordist Game in/to the Far East: The Footballisation of China, Japan and South Korea." *Soccer & Society* 8 (4): 561–577.

Matheson, Victor A. 2017. "European Football (Soccer)." In Fizel, John (ed) *Handbook of Sports Economics Research*, Abingdon, Routledge.118–135.

National People's Congress. 2000. "Zhonghua renmin gongheguo guoji fa" [Nationality Law of the PRC]. National People's Congress. http://www.npc.gov.cn/wxzl/gongbao/2000-12/11/content_5004393.htm.

NetEase. 2022. "Zhongguo jiaqiu wo an: Xu ming yu 'shide xi', fei zhengchang siwang" [China's Match-Fixing Case: Xu Ming and the "Shide system", Abnormal Death]. *Netease*. Last modified October 7. https://www.163.com/dy/article/HBTJ5NOS0549RCZD.html.

Njewel, Didier. 2023. Online video interview: Player.

Njororai, Wycliffe W. Simiyu. 2010. "Global Inequality and Athlete Labour Migration from Kenya." *Leisure/Loisir* 34 (4): 443–461. https://doi.org/10.1080/14927713.2010.543502.

———. 2012. "Distance Running in Kenya: Athletics Labour Migration and Its Consequences." *Leisure/Loisir* 36 (2): 187–209. https://doi.org/10.1080/14927713.2012.729787.

Oonk, Gijsbert, and Alexander Oonk. 2023. "'This Is Not a Problem but an Issue': Chinese-Born Table Tennis Players Representing Another Country at the Olympics, 1988–2020." *The International Journal of the History of Sport* 40 (4): 350–369.

Pedo Lopes, Alexia, Khalid Ballouli, and Brian Mihalik. 2023. "Push–Pull Analysis of Motocross and Supercross Athletes' Migration to the United States." *Sport in Society* 27 (3): 438-458. https://doi.org/10.1080/17430437.2023.2279635.

Poli, Raffaele. 2006. "Africans' Status in the European Football Players' Labour Market." *Soccer & Society* 7 (2–3): 278–291. https://doi.org/10.1080/14660970600615369.

———. 2010. "Understanding Globalization through Football: The New International Division of Labour, Migratory Channels and Transnational Trade Circuits." *International Review for the Sociology of Sport* 45 (4): 491–506. https://doi.org/10.1177/1012690210370640.

Richardson, Christopher. 2023. "Taking on the World: The Internationalisation of City Football Group." *Review of International Business and Strategy* ahead-of-print (ahead-of-print). https://doi.org/10.1108/RIBS-06-2023-0047.

Ross, Tobias. 2023. "The Naturalization of Athletes in Mainland China." In *Routledge Handbook of Sport in China*, 322–328. Routledge.

Sina. 2021. "Qian xin 1 yi +yuexin 1 wan! Zhongguo zuqiu fengkuang qian xin cuo zai shei?" [100 Million Owed Salary + 10,000 Monthly Salary! Who Is at Fault for Crazy Wage Arrears in Chinese Football?]. Sina. Last modified November 05. https://sports.sina.cn/china/2021-11-05/detail-iktzscyy3784975.d.html.

Sohu. 2001a. "Kamailong tongzi jun lai la!—Shide bu gei tamen gaibian guoji" [The Cameroon Scouts Are Here!—Shide Will Not Allow Them to Change Their Nationality]. Sohu. Last modified July 17. https://sports.sohu.com/00/57/sports_news163345700.shtml.

———. 2001b. "Shide "tunji" 24 wei kamailong xiao qiuyuan jihua liang nian hou kaishi chushou" [Shide "Hoards" 24 Cameroon Young Players and Plans to Sell Them in Two Years]. Sohu. Last modified July 20. https://2014.sohu.com/04/01/sports_news163350104.shtml.

———. 2002. "Youyu ge zhong yuanyin xu ming jinjun aozhou he xianggang shichang jihua huanxing" [Xu Ming's Plans to Enter the Australian and Hong Kong Markets Have Been Postponed Due to Various Reasons]. Sohu. Last modified August 19. https://sports.sohu.com/69/48/sports_news164804869.shtml.

———. 2005a. "Guanzhu shanghai zhong bang waiyuan neng shuo liuli hanyu de "feizhou xiong shi" " [Pay Attention to the "African Lion" of Shanghai China Foreign Aid Who Can Speak Fluent Chinese]. Sohu. Last modified March 07. https://sports.sohu.com/20050307/n224570745.shtml.

———. 2005b. "Liansai shi da zui chenggong zhuan hui: Hai dong jiameng dalian 5 zhu qiu dui duoguan" [The Ten Most Successful Transfers in the League: Haidong Joins Dalian 5 to Help the Team Win the Championship]. Sohu. Last modified December 13. https://sports.sohu.com/20051213/n240958422.shtml.

———. 2005c. "Yang lin "zhugong" chengjiu shide qi lian sheng didier huo bing zhao xuri" [Yang Lin's "Assist" Achieves Shide's Seventh Consecutive Victory, Didier Becomes Popular with Zhao Xuri]. Sohu. Last modified August 22. https://sports.sohu.com/20050822/n226747496.shtml.

———. 2020. "Jia-A 10 da waiyuan! Ge ge shi qiu dui zhuli, 1 ren nianxin 6 qian meiyuan, 1 ren shengao 1 mi" [Jia-A Top 10 Foreign Players! All of Them Are the Main Players of the Team,

One Has an Annual Salary of 6,000 US Dollars, and One Is 1.64 Meters Tall]. Sohu. Last modified March 31. https://www.sohu.com/a/384607942_490674.

———. 2023. "Zhenjing zhongguozu tan de 'kamailong youshi jihua', guo zu gui hua qiuyuan de zuichu gouxiang" [The "Cameroon Lion Cub Project" that shocked Chinese football, the original idea of naturalized players for the national football team]. *Sohu*. Last modified March 4. https://www.sohu.com/a/649166713_121645023.

Sullivan, Jonathan, Tobias Ross, and Chaojin Wu. 2023. "Representing the Nation: Exploring Attitudes towards Naturalized Foreign Football Players in China." *Soccer & Society* 24 (5): 593–606.

Szymanski, Stefan, and Ron Smith. 1997. "The English Football Industry: Profit, Performance and Industrial Structure." *International Review of Applied Economics* 11 (1): 135–153. https://doi.org/10.1080/02692179700000008.

Thibault, Lucie. 2009. "Globalization of sport: An Inconvenient Truth." *Journal of Sport Management* 23 (1): 1–20.

Titan Sports. 2002. ""Hei haizi" hui jia yu xingbing wuguan juxi shi shide youshenglietai" [The Return of the "Black Children" Has Nothing to Do with STDs. It Is Reported That It Is Survival of the Fittest in Shide]. Sohu. Last modified July 12. https://2014.sohu.com/01/07/sports_news164600701.shtml.

Velema, Thijs A. 2021. "Globalization and Player Recruitment: How Teams from European Top Leagues Broker Migration Flows of Footballers in the Global Transfer Network." *International Review for the Sociology of Sport* 56 (4): 493–513. https://doi.org/10.1177/1012690220919676.

Velema, Thijs A, Han-Yu Wen, and Yu-Kai Zhou. 2020. "Global Value Added Chains and the Recruitment Activities of European Professional Football Teams." *International Review for the Sociology of Sport* 55 (2): 127–146. https://doi.org/10.1177/1012690218796771.

Weinreich, Philipp Andreas. 2022. "Data-Based Analysis in Football Transfer Decisions." MA, Universidade Nova de Lisboa. https://run.unl.pt/handle/10362/144804.

Xue, Hanhan, Nicholas M Watanabe, Ryan Chen, Joshua I Newman, and Grace Yan. 2020. "Football (as) Guanxi: A Relational Analysis of Actor Reciprocity, State Capitalism, and the Chinese Football Industry." *Sport in Society* 23 (12): 2005–2030.

Yang, Kaijie, and Lianjin Wang. 2022. "Study on the Cooperative and Win-Win Relationship between the Introduction of African Football Players in Chinese Professional Football League." *Open Access Library Journal* 9 (7): 1–16.

12

Building Socialist Cosmopolitanism: China's Stadium Diplomacy in Africa, 1970s–1980s

Charlie Qiuli Xue[1] and Guanghui Ding[2]

"Since the end of the civil war in 1949 and the creation of the People's Republic, it was unheard of for anyone from the Hong Kong government to visit China. China was a closed world" (Akers-Jones 2004, 76). On February 13, 1973, a delegation led by Sir David Akers-Jones, the then Secretary for the New Territories Hong Kong, flew from Paris to Cairo, then Rangoon, and on to Shanghai. The visit was undertaken under the aegis of the Hong Kong Football Association, where Sir Akers-Jones was the vice president. In its ice-breaking trip, the delegation visited Beijing, Nanjing, Wuxi, Suzhou, Hangzhou and Guangzhou. This movement signified a broader trend in the 1970s where sports emerged as a potent tool for facilitating social and political dialogue between the People's Republic of China (PRC) and capitalist nations. A pivotal event within this trend was the iconic "ping pong diplomacy" of 1971, which paved the way for the establishment of formal diplomatic relations between China and the United States (NMAD 2021).

1 Charlie Qiuli Xue, Professor, City University of Hong Kong, bscqx@cityu.edu.hk.
2 Guanghui Ding, Independent Researcher, tin_tin0504@hotmail.com.
This chapter is part of a study supported by the National Natural Science Foundation of China, Project No. 51878584.

The historical connection between sports and politics has deep roots (Gennaro and Aderinto 2019), yet this intricate interplay is particularly pronounced during periods of heightened geopolitical tension, notably during the Cold War. Regardless of whether China found itself in isolation or was more globally engaged, it has consistently harnessed sports as a distinctive tool for cultivating international relationships. One prominent aspect of China's involvement in sports is its employment of stadium diplomacy, as noted at various points in this book. By providing low-interest or interest-free loans, as well as generous grants, China played a substantial role in aiding developing nations to construct stadiums (Will 2012; Xue et al. 2019). This strategic approach emerged primarily from the agreement between donor and recipient countries, often driven by the latter's aspirations to host international sporting events or to enhance their domestic sports infrastructure. In tandem, China possessed the requisite expertise and capacity for designing, constructing, and managing stadiums after the country built a group of sport buildings in the 1950s. China has its own way of building technology and building technicians adapted to the conditions of the project site. This made it ready to extend technical and financial support to these projects.

The motivations behind China's stadium diplomacy are multifaceted. In the 1970s, the emphasis was on expressing political support and ideological solidarity, shifting to a focus on economic and technological cooperation in the 1980s, and then prioritizing market access in the first two decades of the twenty-first century. While the dominant intentions varied across each historical stage, stadium diplomacy represented a long-term strategy that integrated political, ideological, economic, social, material, cultural, aesthetic, and technological dimensions. Unlike construction firms from other countries seeking short-term returns in stadium construction, the Chinese government and state-owned enterprises were concerned with long-term interests and influence. This strategy of long-termism placed stadium diplomacy in a distinctive position among various forms of Chinese aid.

In contrast to many other building types, stadiums occupy a unique place within a country's urban landscape, encompassing a realm that intertwines sporting, political, and cultural events. As architect Sheard (2005) notes, "a stadium is able to put a community on the map, establishing an identity and providing a focal point in the landscape. Stadiums are the most 'viewed' building in history and have the power to change people's lives: they represent a nation's pride and aspirations." Following their completion, stadiums serve a multitude of purposes, ranging from hosting athletic competitions and musical/theatrical performances to facilitating civic and patriotic displays. This prominence allows stadiums to attract the attention of political leaders, local communities, and national media alike (Xue et al. 2019).

In recent years, China's stadium diplomacy has garnered increasing scholarly and journalistic attention. Researchers focus on not only its political and economic factors but also explore its implementation process and its societal and media impacts (Dubinsky 2021; Ojo 2022; Ross 2014; Vondracek 2019). However, scant attention has been paid to the origin and realization of this stadium diplomacy. This chapter undertakes a comprehensive examination of the political impetus, cultural interplay, potential socio-cultural ramifications, and technical mechanisms intertwined with China's stadium diplomacy. By reading China's stadium diplomacy through the lens of cosmopolitanism and situating its practice within the relevant historical context, the chapter scrutinizes how China engaged in transnational sports exchange by means of stadium construction.

It is paramount to underscore that the conjunction of stadiums and politics, particularly evident in the Chinese-funded projects across Africa, epitomizes the embodiment of socialist cosmopolitanism. The term "cosmopolitanism" is not often used in the Chinese-language context. Chinese government usually used a term "internationalism" to describe its foreign-aid activities. "Internationalism" concerns the moral standard and friendship, instead of mere economic consideration (Fangyi 2008). For example, Canadian doctor Norman Bethune, who served in the Chinese Communist Party's army during the Japanese invasion and passed away on the frontier, was extolled by Chairman Mao Zedong as an internationalist (Mao 1991). While cosmopolitanism entails diverse moral, political, institutional, and ideological facets, this chapter defines it as a mutual help between countries and a state in which Chinese governmental officials and construction experts displayed receptivity toward other cultures and manifested a disposition to honor differences across national boundaries (Ding and Xue 2022). In essence, cosmopolitanism captures how individuals or nations confront, interact with and exchange ideas with the world. African recipient nations exhibited their own form of cosmopolitanism, having engaged with colonial powers prior to gaining national independence and subsequently interacting with diverse donors from Europe, the Soviet Union, the United States, and China. However, this chapter specifically examines the Chinese approach to cosmopolitanism within the African context.

As articulated by Volland (2017), the manifestation of socialist cosmopolitanism in the PRC was evident in the active involvement of Chinese intellectuals and readers with world literature through translation, publication, reading, and other activities throughout the Mao era. Consequently, Chinese literature assumed a position within the broader context of world literature. Concerning China's provision of construction aid, socialist cosmopolitanism was characterized by state-led, ideology-oriented, top-down and elite-centric collective initiatives in transcultural engagement. This distinction is notable in contrast to the prevalent bottom-up and mass-oriented individual activities observed in a globally interconnected environment characterized by considerable mobility freedom.

The practice of stadium diplomacy exemplified this socialist cosmopolitanism in the way in which Chinese building professionals, appointed and deployed by state agencies to undertake the design and construction of stadiums abroad, demonstrated a propensity to actively engage with foreign cultures, collaborate with counterparts from other nations, and exhibit a respectful consideration for local conditions. Responding to the Chinese government's call, individuals engaged in stadium construction tended to set aside personal interests and considerations of gains and losses, dedicating themselves to the high-quality completion of tasks assigned by the nation, thereby bringing honor to the country. However, the process of constructing socialist cosmopolitanism was not without its challenges; it encompassed moments of excitement and anticipation, setbacks and discouragement, mutual assistance and inclusivity, as well as mutual understanding, along with instances of misunderstanding and cultural conflicts, as we can see in the following narratives.

China's Sport and Stadium Diplomacy

On June 10, 1952, Chairman Mao wrote the inscription "developing sports, enhancing the people's physique" (*fazhan tiyu yundong, zengqiang renmin tizhi*), which underlined the significance of sports for individuals and society as a collective unit (Xintiyu 1952). The construction of the Beijing Workers' Stadium in 1959 was a significant event that showcased support for sports from the Communist Party in China (Alekseyeva 2019). This stadium, which was part of the "Ten Grand Buildings" project to commemorate the ten-year anniversary of the People's Republic, was a comprehensive sports complex that included an 80,000-seat stadium, a 15,000-seat indoor gymnasium, and indoor and outdoor swimming pools. The stadium became the largest and most important sports venue in China at the time. It hosted the first National Games of China in 1959 and the 26th World Table Tennis Championships in 1961. These events brought national and international attention to the stadium and solidified its reputation as a top-tier sporting facility (Xue 2005). Architecturally, the Beijing Workers' Stadium was innovative and ahead of its time. The oval-shaped reinforced concrete stadium featured two levels of stands and cantilevered steel roofs that provided shelter for spectators. The circular gymnasium had an advanced suspension roof design that balanced functionality with aesthetics. The design of this sports complex was executed by a team of experienced architects and engineers from the Beijing Institute of Architectural Design (BIAD). Their expertise resulted in a model project that set a standard for future stadiums both within China and abroad (Jin et al. 2020).

While showcasing its achievement of socialist construction through sports and stadiums, the country also sought to enhance its international standing by sending sports teams abroad to compete and achieve glory for the nation. In the 1950s, China actively participated in international competition organized by the International Olympic Committee (IOC). However, tensions arose between China and the IOC over the issue of Taiwan's identity as the Republic of China. Due to disagreements regarding Taiwan, China decided to withdraw from the IOC as a form of resistance against the IOC's "two China policies." This withdrawal marked a period of strained relations between China and the IOC, and other international sport organizations (Fan and Xiong 2002). Additionally, the Sino-Soviet split in the early 1960s further reduced China's sports exchange with East European countries. In response to its political and cultural isolation, China began supporting developing nations to host international games. One notable example was the first Games of New Emerging Forces (GANEFO), which was established by Indonesia in 1963 as an alternative to the Olympic Games. China provided significant political, financial, and organizational support for GANEFO. China also played a crucial role in organizing the first Asian GANEFO held in Cambodia in 1966, in an effort to counterbalance the influence of the Soviet Union in Southeast Asia. Chinese builders were sent to complete the stadium designed by Cambodian architect Vann Molyvann, while referees were trained for the events. These efforts demonstrated China's commitment to supporting developing nations and fostering international interaction through sports and advancing its strategic interests in the region during the Vietnam War (Chang and Xue 2019).

China's sport diplomacy in the early 1960s was closely tied to its emerging foreign-aid initiatives in Asia and Africa. Despite facing its own domestic famine at the time, China extended support to developing countries that shared similar socialist ideologies and gradually to other countries. This support included countries like Mongolia, Vietnam, North Korea, Sri Lanka, Tanzania, and Guinea

(Ding and Xue 2015). The aid provided by China primarily consisted of industrial buildings and workers' dormitories, which aimed to assist recipient countries in developing their manufacturing capabilities and achieving self-reliance (Fangyi 2008). This shift from supporting industries like rubber and match factories to constructing sports facilities represented a significant leap. The decision to invest in sports infrastructure can be explained by several factors.

First, China's diplomatic work had a significant jump in the 1970s. From 1970 to 1976, China established diplomatic relations with 61 countries, and restored the relationship with six countries. The recipients of foreign aid expanded from 20 in 1970 to more than 60 in 1976 (Fangyi 2008). Because of the ceasefire in Vietnam War in 1973, China's military aid decreased sharply and the country had capacity to do more buildings in foreign aid. Second, the project of foreign aid was first proposed by recipient countries according to their needs, and then negotiated between donor and recipient. Some recipient countries visited construction projects of Chinese cities and proposed to build the projects they felt significant. From 1972 to 1976, China built a group of indoor and outdoor stadiums, and those projects impressed the Asian and African visitors (Zou 2001). When China received the request of building stadiums, it was able to do so technically.

The success of "ping pong diplomacy" in the early 1970s played a significant role in China's recognition of the power of sports in promoting international interactions. This diplomatic breakthrough, which involved the exchange of table tennis players between China and the United States, helped to thaw relations between the two countries and paved the way for further sports diplomacy efforts (Nixon 2001). China's experience in designing stadiums and organizing sports events in the 1950s and 1960s also contributed to its understanding of the potential of sports diplomacy. During this period, China built several stadiums and hosted a few international sporting events. These experiences provided valuable lessons on how sports can be used as a tool for fostering international cooperation and goodwill. Politically, the PRC's resumption of China's seat in the United Nations was supported by many developing nations. In return for this support, China was willing to offer material aid to these nations when requested. One common strategy employed by China as part of its foreign-aid efforts was building stadiums. For example, China helped Mongolia build a stadium in 1960, followed by assistance to Indonesia in 1963 and Cambodia in 1966. These early instances can be seen as evidence of China's stadium diplomacy, where it used sports infrastructure development as a means to strengthen diplomatic ties with other nations.

China's sport diplomacy is characterized by its willingness to engage with other countries, particularly those in the "Third World." This not only helped improve the infrastructure for sports in these nations but also created opportunities for Chinese building and sport professionals to interact with local people and culture. In Africa, these interactions went beyond just sports and encompassed various aspects of African culture, including arts, goods, languages, ideas, technology, foods, and lifestyles. This exchange of knowledge and experiences contributed to China's engagement with other nations, supporting their sports development, and respecting their political and cultural differences.

Meeting Africa

The visit of Chinese premier Zhou Enlai to Africa in 1963–1964 marked the beginning of the PRC's engagement with the continent. At that time, Chinese leaders recognized the importance of uniting non-aligned countries in the developing world and saw Africa as a potential ally (Song 2019). However, China had limited knowledge about Africa, and no senior leaders had visited the continent before. To facilitate Zhou's visit, a special airplane and crew were arranged from KLM Royal Dutch Airline since China's aviation was unable to fly across the continent. This gesture demonstrated China's commitment to establishing relationships with African countries (Song 2019). During his visit, Zhou visited 14 countries in Africa, Europe, and Asia. He aimed to consolidate relationships with countries that had shown support and hope for China. The reception Zhou received was positive, as some political leaders in newly independent African countries saw China as a potential role model for development.

One such leader was Julius Kambarage Nyerere, the first president of Tanzania. Nyerere visited China 13 times during his presidency and established a close relationship with Chinese leaders. During his first visit in February 1965, Nyerere met with Zhou Enlai and Liu Shaoqi, who promised material support for Tanzania. Before the famous Tanzania-Zambia railway project began, China built a stadium in Zanzibar in 1969. This stadium was the first Chinese-aided stadium in Africa and provided a venue for sports on the island. The stadium served as a symbol of China's growing presence and influence in Africa.

During Mauritanian President Moktar Ould Daddah's visits to China in 1967 and 1974, he met with Mao Zedong and other Chinese leaders. These visits created opportunities for African leaders to learn from China's revolutionary experiences and to strengthen ties between the two countries. The Peking

Review, an English publication of the Chinese Communist Party, highlighted the deep friendship between the people of China and Mauritania in their common struggle against imperialism, colonialism, and hegemonism (Peking Review 1974). This statement emphasized the shared goals of both countries in fighting against foreign domination. One notable member of the Mauritanian delegation was the Minister of Sport and Youth and the visit aimed to explore cooperation in various fields, including sports and youth development (Peking Review 1974). Deng Xiaoping greeted President Daddah and his delegation during their visits. Deng played a crucial role in leading China during the post-Mao period starting from 1977. As a result of these visits, a series of agreements were initiated and signed between China and Mauritania. These agreements likely covered areas such as trade, economic cooperation, cultural exchanges, and technical assistance. Deng also delivered promised gifts when he was in power. These gifts could have been symbolic gestures or tangible items meant to strengthen bilateral relations between the two countries.

Aside from the construction of factories, railway and stations, China's foreign aid to Africa was mainly embodied by national conference halls (named "Friendship" or "People's Palace" in some cases) in the 1970s. The most famous ones are the People's Palace in Guinea, 1967 and the Friendship Palace in Sudan, 1976 (Ding 2023; Gao et al. 2022). A series of agreements generated by the African visitors to China in the mid-1970s included stadiums. As mentioned above, stadiums are built to demonstrate the power and unity of nation and people. After political parties and governors come to power, they seek a symbolic venue to articulate the new conditions of the nation. Stadiums best serve this purpose. The first batch of formal stadiums donated and constructed by China appeared in the early 1980s. Up to 2020 around 70 stadiums had been built in Africa. Collecting data from open sources, we created an inventory of China's foreign-aid stadiums. The African part is shown in Figure 12.1, which includes 72 stadiums across 42 African countries. The statistics demonstrate that more intensive construction took place in the twenty-first century. Some countries including Kenya saw the largest stadium built in the region, while some countries received up to four stadiums from China. These stadiums are used mainly for training and games in local football leagues, matches in the African Cup of Nations (AFCON) as well as ceremonies. As the foreign aid of the 1970s–1980s embodied the Chinese government's cosmopolitanism view, we examine several typical examples from this period in the following sections.

Our selection of stadiums built in Benin, Mauritania and Kenya was guided by three primary considerations. Initially, these expansive and multifaceted

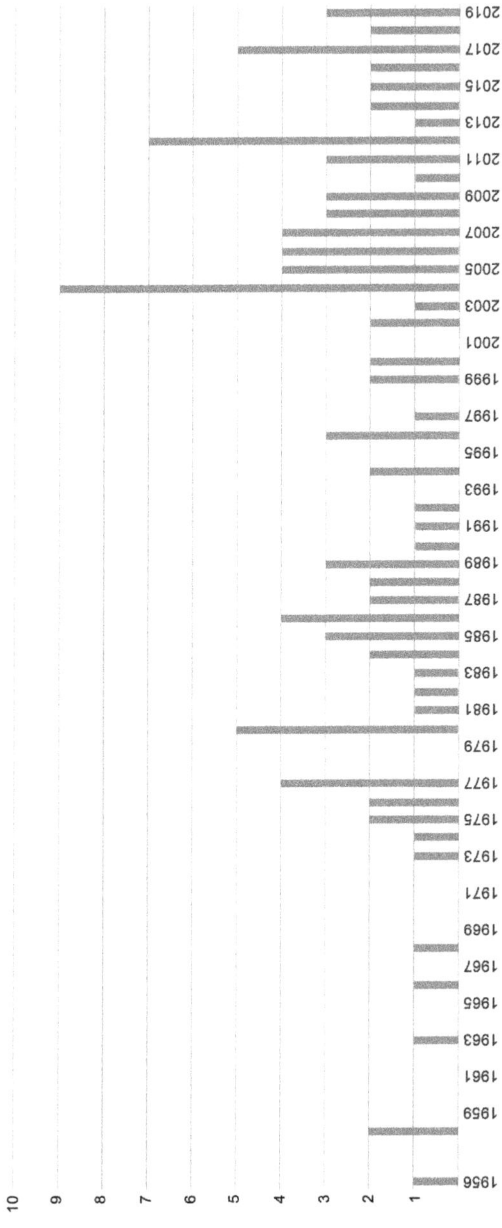

Figure 12.1 China-aided stadiums in Africa
Note: The year signifies the completion of the building
Source: Authors' own compilation.

sports facilities epitomized the pinnacle of design excellence and advanced technologies attained by China-sponsored stadiums during the 1980s. Secondly, in contrast to the ideology-centric, freely aided origins of the first two stadiums, the Moi stadium emerged as a product of market-driven economic and technological collaboration, jointly invested in by both participating entities. Thirdly, the examination of stadium diplomacy served as a nuanced illustration of the dynamics of socialist cosmopolitanism in the sense that socialist China engaged with the world in a way that emphasized a professional obligation to improve the built environment without asserting cultural superiority (Ding and Xue 2022).

Responding to Site and Climate: Stadiums in Benin and Mauritania (1982)

Benin established diplomatic relations with the PRC in 1964 before switching to Taiwan two years later. After a period of political instability General Mathieu Kerekou came to power through a military coup in 1972. General Kerekou resumed diplomatic relations with the PRC, adopted a Marxist–Leninist ideology, and renamed the country from the Republic of Dahomey to the People's Republic of Benin in 1975. The political and economic changes introduced by Kerekou's party were primarily motivated by practical concerns rather than radical leftist ideology, as these reforms helped to legitimize his regime (Allen 2015). The economic reforms centered on reducing dependence on France by diversifying trade and aid flows (Allen 2015).

In return for Benin's restoration of diplomatic relations with the PRC, the Chinese government donated a series of gifts to Benin, including a cigarette and match factory, a cotton mill, and other civilian projects. The Benin government, aspiring to underscore its "revolutionary power," envisioned the construction of a stadium in every province. Following official negotiations in 1974, China committed to contributing a sports complex in the port city of Cotonou. The stadium was financed by a 60-million-yuan interest-free loan from the Chinese government. In July 1976, Kerekou led a delegation to visit Beijing and received a warm welcome from Premier Hua Guofeng. In alignment with Mao Zedong's revolutionary diplomatic line, Hua asserted that "it is China's internationalist obligation to provide limited assistance to Benin and some other countries" (People's Daily 1976). During Kerekou's stay in China, People's Daily reported on various aspects of Benin's cultural, economic, geographical, social and political landscape, aiming to convey a positive image of Benin to Chinese citizens

(Xin 1976). Upon arriving in Cotonou one year later to work on the stadium project, Chinese crane operator Lu Gang personally experienced a country that was far more authentic than the descriptions in newspapers. He found himself grappling with the intense heat and humidity, battling malaria, yet also encountering the enthusiasm of the Beninese people. He was also pleasantly surprised by the abundance of seafood, meat and beer within the construction camp, in sharp contrast to food scarcity experienced in China (Lu 1987).

The design work was assigned to the Shanghai Institute of Industrial Building Design in 1974, with architects Ni Tianzeng, Qin Zhixin, Jin Kaiyu, and Xiang Zuquan leading the project, complemented by support from Fang Jianquan. A Tsinghua University graduate from 1962, Ni had accumulated overseas experience since the institute set up a design office responsible for foreign-aid projects in 1964 (East China Institute of Architectural Design 2016, 76–81). Noteworthy among Ni's prior experiences was his collaboration with Fang Jianquan in 1964, when they traveled to Tanzania to design a police training school in Moshi, a project suggesting the close relations between Nyerere's Tanzania and Mao's China (Bailey 1975). The stadium project in Benin offered Ni and his colleagues a crucial opportunity to demonstrate their professional creativity, amid the severe disruption caused by the Cultural Revolution.

The sports center in Cotonou, located on a 31-hectare site in the northwest suburb of the city, is a comprehensive facility that includes various sports amenities. The project encompasses a 30,000-seat open football field-track stadium, a 5,000-seat air-conditioned indoor gymnasium, as well as exercise grounds for field and track sports such as handball, volleyball, basketball, and tennis (Fang et al. 1982). Additionally, the complex includes a 1,500-seat competition swimming pool, a diving pool, and an exercise pool, a 100-bed hostel and provisions for 1,000 parking spaces. This type of sport complex required significant investment and was relatively uncommon in China at the time, aside from Worker's Stadium in Beijing. The architects strategically placed the indoor gymnasium at the terminus of the center, with the oval main stadium and circular swimming pools flanking this axis. The remaining portions of the site were allocated for training fields and parking. The main stadium and swimming pools delineated a distinct horizontal axis along with the training fields and hostel near the end of the site. The intersection of the central and horizontal axes forms a central square featuring a flagstaff and adjacent green lawns. This layout created a sense of hierarchy and monumentality, reminiscent of other sport buildings in Beijing and Shanghai. However, the compact and flexible site design demonstrated the architects' commitment to responding creatively and efficiently to the irregular shape of the site.

The vertical concrete *brise soleil* prominently featured on the facade of the main stadium and gymnasium stands as a pivotal element in the stadium design, devised to address Benin's hot and humid tropical climate. This design element helps to provide shade and reduce direct sunlight, keeping the interior spaces cooler. The *brise soleil* also adds a visually striking element to the building's exterior. In tandem with the *brise soleil*, the architects incorporated two narrow courtyards on the ground floor of the gymnasium. These courtyards serve multiple purposes—they enhance natural lighting by allowing sunlight to penetrate the interior spaces and facilitate natural ventilation by creating a pathway for air circulation. By maximizing natural lighting and ventilation, the architects aimed to reduce reliance on mechanical systems such as air conditioning, thus promoting energy efficiency and sustainability. This method was partly learned from African architecture and showed the technical exchange between China and Africa.

The construction of the sports complex in Benin was executed by a company from the state-owned Construction Engineering Bureau of Fujian Province in China. A collaborative effort involving about 300 Chinese technicians and more than 1,000 Beninese workers spanned a six-year period to complete the project (Fujian Provincial Chronicle Compilation Committee 1993). The official inauguration of the sport complex took place in November 1982. Prior to its full completion, the stadium hosted the first West African Nations Cup international competition, where Ghana emerged as champions. It was the first time Benin had hosted a sporting event on such a scale and enhanced the country's self and external image. In January 1983, French President Mitterrand visited Benin and delivered a speech at the stadium, further enhancing its significance. This visit marked a high point for the Kerekou regime's reputation and honor (Huang 2017, 152). However, after its completion, the stadium suffered from a lack of proper maintenance. This neglect exposed the harsh economic situation and governance challenges faced under Kerekou's rule. The inadequate maintenance of such an important infrastructure project reflected poorly on the government's ability to effectively manage resources.

During Kerekou's rule, the economy of Benin was stagnant (Seely 2009, 38). Only when Benin turned to multi-party democracy in 1991 did the country's economy start to grow. In the 1990s, the Chinese government sent a group of building and sports professionals to Cotonou to help maintain the stadium, operate lighting, broadcasting, media equipment and train local staff for both daily and event activities. Collaborating with local professionals, the Chinese technicians transformed the stadium into a versatile venue capable of hosting a variety of cultural and sports activities, including matches in the Benin, Nigeria, and

Togo football league. They only took half a year to effectively improve the utilization rate of the stadium and turn losses into profits (Yuan et al. 2016). Since its completion, the stadium has become the home of the Benin National Football Team, whose best achievement was reaching the quarter finals of the African Cup of Nations in 2019.

The case of Cotonou highlights the challenges faced by China's stadium diplomacy, particularly in economically underdeveloped and geographically small countries like Benin, Burkina Faso, and Liberia. These nations often lack the necessary expertise, financial resources, and organizational capabilities to effectively utilize and maintain the stadiums provided by China. In the context of Benin, the Friendship Stadium has posed a financial burden for local authorities, necessitating ongoing support from China for its maintenance. Since its completion, the stadium has undergone three rounds of restoration in 2004, 2012, and 2021 with assistance from China. The latest renovation was managed by the China Southwest Architecture Design Institute and involved various improvements such as replacing the natural turf on the football field, updating the sports field's plastic components and foundations, installing an LED display screen, enhancing sound reinforcement, and lighting, timing and scoring systems. Despite facing the challenges associated with the outbreak of COVID-19 in Benin in 2020, the project team persevered and completed the renovations on time. Some technicians even stayed on-site for three years without returning home. As a result of these efforts, the venue has been certified by the World Athletics Federation as a second-level venue.

During the late 1970s, while the Benin project was in design and construction, the Shanghai Institute of Industrial Building Design engaged in a number of foreign-aid projects across Africa, including several factories in Mauritania and Mali, and governmental headquarters in Zambia. Ni Tianzeng's colleague Cai Zhenyu was responsible for the design of a multi-purpose stadium in the center of Nouakchott, capital of Mauritania. Cai Zhenyu graduated from Nanjing Institute of Technology in 1956 and did his graduate studies in Moscow. The project includes a 10,000-seat stadium, practice fields for football, basketball and volleyball courts and an athletes' dormitory equipped with 100 beds, dining and reception halls. Spectator housing is concentrated in the east and west stands. Like the Benin stadium, a roof is cantilevered from the main building to partly protect audiences from strong sunshine and raining. The building is mainly constructed using reinforced concrete.

The opening of the stadium in 1980 marked a significant milestone for the country as it became the only international venue within its borders. It also became the home of the national football team, which reached the final week of the African Cup of Nations in 2019. In 2020, China played a key role in renovating the stadium, increasing its capacity to 20,000 seats. This renovation was made possible with China's assistance and highlighted a commitment to ongoing support for infrastructure development provided to other countries. The stadium is not only used for sporting events but also serves as a venue for music concerts.

Compared to the Benin stadium, the Mauritanian construction is smaller in scale and lacks certain facilities like a swimming pool. However, both projects share sensitivity toward the local hot and humid/dry climate, ensuring that they are suitable for their respective geographic locations. The territory of China mostly falls in cold, temperate and sub-tropical zones. Designing in a tropical zone was therefore a challenge for the Chinese technicians, and a reflection of their cosmopolitan view in the profession of architectural design. Knowledge of tropical architecture was acquired by Chinese architects visiting Africa and writing articles for the professional journals that were widely read by industry insiders during the 1960s and 1970s (Gao et al. 2022).

In the context of 1970s China, multi-purpose stadiums were still relatively rare. However, there was an increase in the construction of indoor sport gymnasiums in cities like Shanghai, Nanjing, and Hangzhou, presenting new design opportunities for Chinese architects after the circumscriptions of the Cultural Revolution period. However, the focus on international projects may have been to the detriment of domestic economic development. In the first five years of the 1970s, the demand for foreign aid surged, constituting 7 percent of China's national expenditure by 1973. Many factories prioritized the production of goods for foreign-aid projects, a coordination effort facilitated by the central government. On one hand, the government felt the heaviness of foreign-aid demands. On the other, top Chinese leaders were still willing to help their "poor" friends and fulfill their "international obligations," another reflection of Chinese socialist cosmopolitanism (Fangyi 2008).

Interpreting Local Tradition: Moi International Sports Centre in Kenya (1987)

While the Benin Stadium set a benchmark for China's stadium diplomacy due to its comprehensive programs and multi-purpose facilities, the China-aided stadium in Nairobi, Kenya expanded this technological sophistication and comprehension to a greater degree. The aid for constructing an Olympic-standard stadium in Kasarani, a suburb of Nairobi, was one of the "economic and technological cooperation" packages negotiated between China and Kenya during Kenya President Daniel Arap Moi's visit to Beijing in 1980. They included a variety of projects from technical support to two new universities, scholarships and military and cultural exchanges. The sports complex was intended to be completed in time for the 1987 fourth All-African Games in Nairobi. It would comprise a stadium with 60,000 seats, an indoor arena with 5,000 seats, a swimming complex with 2,000 seats, a diving pool, a recreational and children's pool, and an athletes' hostel with 108 rooms and auxiliary facilities. The entire site extended to 100 hectares.

The construction of the stadium in Nairobi reflected a shift in China's foreign-aid strategy, specifically in stadium diplomacy. The approach, shifting from Mao's ideological preoccupation to Deng's reform agenda, would now emphasize market mechanisms and economic collaboration. The project was a joint investment, with China and Kenya financing 52 percent and 48 percent respectively of the total cost of 930 million Kenya shillings (US$52 million). The stadium, which featured a fully covered stand, was considered the most advanced and largest sports facility aided by the Chinese government at the time.

In December 1980, Chief architect Xu Shangzhi of China Southwest Architecture Design Institute led a team comprising nine architects and engineers to Nairobi (Xu 2003). After visiting some Chinese-built stadiums in other countries and similar projects in Europe, Kenyan officials were initially skeptical about the ability of the Chinese designers and intended to commission their own trusted architects. Nevertheless, the Chinese authorities insisted on their own design team since the design rights were written into the 1980 contract between the two parties and the Chinese side of course hoped to use Chinese designs. Indeed, the design undertaking posed dual challenges for Chinese architects. On one hand they needed to showcase their creative prowess to their Kenyan counterparts, on the other, they needed to persuade Chinese officials overseeing foreign aid to accept their proposals.

Initially, certain Chinese officials and professionals were inclined to employ typical Chinese architectural forms and elements to represent such an engagement (Xu 2003). However, Xu was conscious of avoiding the kind of "great-power chauvinism" embodied by the Sino-Soviet Friendship Building constructed in Beijing in 1956. As an architect, Xu was reluctant to impose overtly Chinese architectural motifs on the sports complex. Xu had long maintained a design principle in relation to specific time, place and situation, arguing that "architectural style originates in the indigenous soil" (Xu 1981, 49). In his efforts to convince his colleagues, he drew upon the Sino-Soviet Friendship Building as a cautionary example of architectural aid, while simultaneously highlighting the Kenyatta International Convention Centre as a positive reference point. The latter, designed collaboratively by the Norwegian architect Karl Henrik Nøstvik and the Kenyan architect David Mutiso, and completed in 1973, stood as a testament to the close collaboration between the Kenyatta government and European partners. For Xu, the Kenyatta International Convention Centre represented a thoughtful combination of modernist architectural principles, the culture of Kenya's vernacular buildings and modern advanced technologies.

Xu garnered support for his design concepts, successfully persuading Chinese officials and his colleagues, including the Ambassador to Kenya Yang Keming, to endorse his vision (Xu 2003). Faced with considerable scrutiny, Xu and his team thoroughly investigated the local culture and architecture. Following seven months of rigorous on-site endeavors, their conceptual designs proved persuasive, securing the approval of the client. The main stadium, predominantly conceived by Xu's colleague, Li Tuofen, featured an oval shape. To address both climate features and functional requirements, the architects divided the stadium into 24 sections, assuming a petal shape supported by a cantilevered stand with tilted columns. The dynamic form of such a cantilevered stand was reminiscent of Li's prior project, the Chengdu Chengbei Gymnasium completed in 1979. According to the architects' description, the amalgamation of these 24 sections forms a blossoming flower, symbolizing the friendship between the Chinese and Kenyan people (Xu 2003). Enhancing the cultural resonance, above each entrance of the stadium, intricate mask relief sculptures portraying African features were incorporated.

The introduction of the all-round roof in the main stadium in Kenya represented a noteworthy technological advancement, particularly considering the limited utilization of large-scale roofing in domestic sports facilities at the time. This development necessitated substantial investment and the application of advanced technology. The deployment of this relatively novel and resource-intensive technology abroad reflected China's commitment to supporting its African counterparts. The primary purpose of the all-round roof is to provide comprehensive protection for the stadium and its spectators against adverse weather conditions. Beyond its functional benefits, the all-round roof has also had a positive impact on the stadium's overall aesthetic appeal. The design language employed in these stadiums is characterized by cantilevered and petal-shaped stands, contributing to a visually striking and cohesive look. While the structural framework of these stadiums remained rooted in reinforced concrete, a commonly used material in

China during the 1970s, there was a greater emphasis on incorporating cultural expressions into the design process. The designers were more conscious of creating spaces that reflect and celebrate local culture.

The athletes' hostel, designed by Li's classmate and colleague Sun Xianben, exemplified a more subtle approach to spatial composition. The hostel consisted of four separate two-story courtyard buildings that served as guest rooms, along with two single-story public buildings and a pyramid-shaped structure. These structures were all connected by corridors. The design incorporated open lounges and inner courtyards to create a transparent and lively atmosphere within the building. The utilization of exposed post and beam structures was symbolic of the Massai spirit of East Africa. For the past 35 years, the Moi Sport Centre has functioned as the home for the Kenya national football team, which has reached the final stages of the African Cup of Nations on six occasions. It is also utilized by Kenyan Premier League teams Mathare United and Tusker FC. The stadium is named "The Home of Heroes."

In the early 1980s, China had not played host to any major international sporting events for an extended period and had not constructed a facility of comparable scale for decades. The only project of analogous complexity at that time was the Beijing Workers' Stadium. Like the Beijing complex, the Moi Sport Center was conceived with a general layout centered around the outdoor stadium, eschewing grandiosity in favor of accentuating the harmonious integration of each architectural component. An additional pivotal element of the sport complex is the aquatic center. Owing to budget constraints, the completion of the aquatic center was delayed by several years later and the proposed man-made lake within the Moi Center remained unrealized. Initially conceived as an indoor stadium, the aquatic center ultimately took the form of an outdoor facility, featuring a standard pool, a diving pool, a warm-up pool and several affiliated structures used as restroom facilities, dressing rooms and management purposes. These buildings, characterized by expansive ground floors, inclined facades and dark brown outer walls, are reminiscent of the local cottages. These formal expressions of design language explicitly demonstrated Chinese architects' preoccupation with local expression of modern architecture.

The 1987 All-African Games, hosted in Kenya, attracted a significant number of athletes, officials, and delegates representing diverse countries. This event received extensive coverage in both national and international publications, contributing to Kenya's nation branding and soft power. *Jeux D'Afrique*, a renowned African sports magazine, dedicated two special editions to report on the games, providing detailed statistics and illustrations. The impact of the games extended beyond Africa and was featured in Chinese media. An article published in a Chinese magazine highlighted the successful organization of the games as a testament to the excellence of Chinese-built stadiums (Lu 1987). The stadiums, earning acclaim not only from Kenyan leaders but also from other African dignitaries, played a crucial role in dispelling contemporaneous doubts surrounding the quality of Chinese stadium construction. President Moi himself expressed profound satisfaction with the stadium, stating that he had seen many stadiums, but none rivaled its spectacular beauty. He even compared it to Wembley Stadium in England (Lu 1987).

Sport is an integral part of the process of modernization in Kenya (Gennaro and Aderinto 2019). Sports facilities such as the Moi Sports Center play a dual role in articulating Kenyan modernization. On the one hand, in terms of image projection and fostering national pride, the project stood as a distinctive symbol of Kenya on the global stage. On the other hand, concerning cohesion and participation, it is an accessible space for Kenyan publics to attend sports, cultural, social, and political events (Mählmann 1992). In 1993, the Central Bank of Kenya issued a 20-shilling banknote featuring the Moi International Stadium, disseminating the image of this state-sponsored project into the hands of citizens and promoting the Moi administration's legitimacy. The choice of stadium carried on the banknote, as a vehicle for constructing a sense of collective memory and nationalist culture, represented the Kenyan government's intention to shape "banal nationalism" through an iconic, visual strategy (Helleiner 1998).

Subsequent to the successful implementation of the Kenyan project, the team from China Southwest Design Institute extended its expertise to design sports buildings in Zaire, Ethiopia and Tunisia (Xu 2003), as China continued to provide its aid to friendly African countries. When, after decades of wear and tear in open air, these stadiums deteriorated, the Chinese government sent construction teams to rehabilitate them. The renovations included installing new turf, seats, and upgrading air conditioning, mechanical, electrical and electronic facilities.

During the 1970s and 1980s, China's stadium diplomacy exhibited a programmatic focus on the construction of multi-purpose comprehensive stadium designed to host international competitions. This diplomatic initiative was primarily, though not exclusively, directed toward African countries. The task of the stadium diplomacy was coordinated by the Foreign-Aid Office of the State Sports Commission in Beijing. Project designs were assigned to central and provincial state-owned design institutes and created by China's elite architects, many of whom were born in the 1930s and 1940s and graduated from architecture schools before the start of the Cultural Revolution in 1966. Having experienced the political turmoil of the Cultural Revolution, these architects cherished the rare design opportunity. They were dispatched to Africa for months-long research and design work, immersing themselves in the local cultural environment. In contrast to the contemporary aid work in the twenty-first century, the foreign-aid designs of the 1980s took longer time, and architects had sufficient time to elaborate on their designs. Consequently, these endeavors emerged as the architects' most distinguished and most representative works (Ding and Xue 2022).

Conclusion

No other nation has exhibited a commensurate level of dedication to the donation and construction of stadiums across Africa as China. This chapter has undertaken an exploration of the origin, progression, and ramifications of China's stadium diplomacy—a manifestation intricately linked to the principles of Chinese socialist cosmopolitanism. The insights derived from the experience of stadium diplomacy have significantly enriched our comprehension of the dynamics inherent in socialist cosmopolitanism, delineated in at least three discernible dimensions.

The initial insight gleaned from the experience of stadium diplomacy is the revelation that socialist cosmopolitanism was a state-led, ideology-oriented, top-down political initiative that embodied and extended Mao's "revolutionary diplomacy" (Armstrong 1977). This approach characterized the newly independent countries as comrades in a collective struggle against imperialists and colonialists (Fangyi 2008). China's construction of stadiums in Africa provided opportunities for Chinese building professionals—comprising architects, engineers, project managers, and builders—to engage with foreign cultures, encompassing both indigenous and colonial aspects. This engagement was particularly noteworthy during the late 1970s and early 1980s, a period when only a limited number of Chinese individuals had the privilege of international traveling. These China-aided stadiums emerged as venues for "cultural contact zones." However, it is essential to clarify that this term is employed here not in the post-colonial sense, where differing cultures blend, conflict, and contend with one another, marked by highly asymmetric power relations (Pratt 2012). Instead, these stadiums served as sites of cosmopolitan cultural interactions.

Furthermore, the experience of stadium diplomacy illustrated that Chinese socialist cosmopolitanism emphasized principles of racial equality, mutual respect, and consideration for local conditions. An exemplar of this approach transpired during the construction of the Benin stadium, where Chinese professionals collaborated closely with their Beninese counterparts, and eagerly learned the knowledge of tropical architecture. This collaborative partnership not only expedited the construction process but also fostered the exchange of cultures, ideas, knowledge, and expertise. Noteworthy is the case of Liu Gang, a Chinese crane operator, who dedicated four years to working in Benin. During this tenure, Liu not only shared his skills with local builders but also endeavored to acquire a basic proficiency in French for daily communication, thereby establishing a meaningful connection with his Beninese apprentices (Liu 2021). Chinese technicians living a similar lifestyle to their African colleagues presented a stark contrast to experts from Western countries, earning admiration from African leaders and the populace (Monson 2009). The commitment to equal living standards for Chinese and local experts, as articulated in Zhou Enlai's eight principles of foreign aid, is particularly significant in this context (Zhou 1990, 389). These cosmopolitan interactions find expression in both official declarations and personal accounts (Monson 2009). Importantly, during sporting events, these stadiums transform into platforms where athletes from diverse nations showcase their skills, passion, and dedication.

Moreover, the experience of stadium diplomacy underscores the inseparable connection between the practice of socialist cosmopolitanism and the dynamics of collaboration, understanding, tension, and contradiction. In pursuit of the task of stadium diplomacy with a focus on quality and efficiency, the Chinese government strategically appointed leading architects and engineers from prominent state-owned design institutes. Meanwhile, local building professionals in the recipient countries assumed a consulting role. Architects of note, such as Ni, Cai, and Xu, demonstrated concerted efforts to incorporate local cultural elements, even if, on occasion, such integration assumed a somewhat symbolic nature. Despite a willingness to collaborate within the confines of the design process, it is crucial to recognize that this Chinese-centric design approach could potentially engender disappointment among local architects and nationalists. The limited involvement of local designers was, in part, a consequence of the nature of these projects as gifts. In the context of most aid projects, recipient countries ardently sought timely realization to facilitate local economic improvement or enhance international standing. The Chinese donor, adopting a turnkey procurement model to ensure expeditious delivery, necessitated close coordination among Chinese manufacturers and constructors. Notably, the expeditious completion of projects was a distinctive feature of China's foreign-aid initiatives, differentiating it from other global donors. This efficiency was facilitated by the engagement of several Chinese state-owned companies from project inception to completion, proving both swifter and more cost-effective than involving numerous parties from different nations. Moreover, owing to constraints related to foreign currency availability, services encompassing design, site management, and associated aspects were often accounted for within the monetary framework.

The three outlined generalizations concerning the stadium diplomacy process prompt a critical examination of the insights these experiences can offer to the ongoing relevance of transnational stadium construction and the contemporary reformulations of socialist cosmopolitanism. The intricate process of stadium construction consistently confronted Chinese technicians with a myriad of divergent cultural concepts, management ethics, work methodologies, building codes, and even individual lifestyles. In her examination of Costa Rica's National Stadium, Verri (2020) posited that projects supported by China may have neglected crucial cultural exchanges, instead materializing as "products of specific transactions across the fields of politics, professional sport, the construction industry, architecture, and public administration in Costa Rica and China" (302). While this perspective may underestimate the intricate fabric of diverse, multi-level cultural exchanges extending beyond the domain of professional architects, it nonetheless sheds light on the complexities, mixed sentiments, and formidable challenges associated with stadium diplomacy. It is unsurprising that the interests and demands of various stakeholders are not always harmonious, at times conflicting with one another. This includes considerations such as the perspectives of officials, companies, and taxpayers in the donor country, as well as the ruling and opposition parties, local communities, contractors, and building professionals in the recipient nation. These stakeholders may either benefit from stadium construction or contend with issues of displacement and environmental justice.

The stadiums erected in Africa transcend a mere outcome of direct discourse between Chinese building professionals and their African counterparts. They defy categorization as straightforward transplants of pre-existing projects from China. Functioning as urban landmarks and integral elements of the urban landscape, these stadiums embody the collaborative endeavors of Chinese and African officials, professionals, and builders. The trajectory of stadium design, construction, and subsequent operation is the result of collective cross-cultural communications, collaborative efforts, negotiations, and even conflicts between the involved parties.

The manifestation of socialist cosmopolitanism within China's stadium diplomacy accentuated a tendency to recognize and appreciate local cultural, economic, and geographical distinctions. However, within the contemporary milieu, wherein the application of a cosmopolitan perspective encounters numerous challenges, it becomes imperative to contextualize stadium diplomacy within a global framework. This entails considering evolving local conditions, China's domestic landscape, and international evaluations. As an alternative to the prevailing "elite" cosmopolitanism and state-driven, urban-centric stadium construction, one inclusive strategy involves fostering transnational sport exchanges through community-based initiatives—small and beautiful—sports programs. This approach aims to provide marginalized communities with enhanced opportunities for sports participation, thereby effecting positive transformations in individual lives.

References

Akers-Jones, David. 2004. *Feeling the Stones: Reminiscences by David Akers-Jones*. Vol. 1. Hong Kong University Press.

Alekseyeva, Anna. 2019. *Everyday Soviet Utopias: Planning, Design and the Aesthetics of Developed Socialism*. Routledge.

Allen, Chris. 2015. "'Goodbye to All That': The Short and Sad Story of Socialism in Benin." In *Marxism's Retreat from Africa (RLE Marxism)*, 63–81. Routledge.

Armstrong, James David. 1977. *Revolutionary Diplomacy: Chinese Foreign Policy and the United Front Doctrine*. University of California Press.

Bailey, Martin. 1975. "Tanzania and China." *African Affairs* 74 (294): 39–50.

Chang, Wei, and Charlie Qiuli Xue. 2019. "Towards International: China-Aided Stadiums in the Developing World." *Frontiers of Architectural Research* 8 (4): 604–619.

Ding, Guanghui. 2023. "Constructing Geographical and Architectural Imaginations: the China-Aided Assembly Buildings in Africa, 1960s–1970s." *Journal of Chinese Architecture and Urbanism* 5 (1): 200.

Ding, Guanghui, and Charlie Qiuli Xue. 2015. "China's Architectural Aid: Exporting a Transformational Modernism." *Habitat International* 47: 136–147.

———. 2022. "Displaying Socialist Cosmopolitanism: China's Architectural Aid in the Global South, 1960s–1970s." *Architectural Theory Review* 26 (3): 547–577.

Dubinsky, Itamar. 2021. "China's Stadium Diplomacy in Africa." *Journal of Global Sport Management*: 1–19.

East China Institute of Architectural Design. 2016. *Youyuan de huisheng: hankou lu yibai wushi yihao*. Tongji University Press.

Fan, Hong, and Xiaozheng Xiong. 2002. "Communist China: Sport, Politics and Diplomacy." *The International Journal of the History of Sport* 19 (2–3): 319–342.

Fang, Jianquan, Tianzeng Ni, Zhixin Qin, and Kaiyu Jin. 1982. "Zuijin jiancheng de yuanwai gongcheng: beining youyi tiyuchang" [Recently Completed Foreign Aid Project: Benin Friendship Stadium]. *Jianzhu keji qingbao* 6: 6–10.

Fangyi. 2008. *Fang Yi zhuang* [*A Biography of Fang Yi*]. People's Press.

Fujian Provincial Chronicle Compilation Committee. 1993. *Zhonghua renmin gongheguo difang zhi fujian sheng zhi tiyu zhi* [*Local Chronicles of the People's Republic of China Fujian Provincial Chronicles Sports Chronicles*]. Fujian People's Publishing House.

Gao, Yizhuo, Charlie Qiuli Xue, Gangyi Tan, and Yingting Chen. 2022. "From South China to the Global South: Tropical Architecture in China during the Cold War." *The Journal of Architecture* 27 (7–8): 979–1011.

Gennaro, Michael J., and Saheed Aderinto. 2019. *Sports in African History, Politics, and Identity Formation*. Routledge.

Helleiner, Eric. 1998. "National Currencies and National Identities." *American Behavioral Scientist* 41 (10): 1409–1436.

Huang, Yushan. 2017. *Meihua xiangzi kuhan lai: yige daxue jiaoshou huiyilu* [*The Fragrance of Plum Blossoms Coming from the Bitter Experience: Memoirs of a University Professor*]. Tourism Education Press.

Jin, Lei, Chen Li, and Miao Miao. 2020. ""Collective History" of Foreign Aided Design of Beijing Institute of Architectural Design." *Hua Architecture* (1): 24–29.

Liu, Gang. 2021. "Feizhou sanji" [Chronicles of Africa]. Sisters of the Straits. https://m.fx361.com/news/2021/0623/11008236.html.

Lu, Ken. 1987. "Yici kongqian de chao fuhe jianyan" [An Unprecedented Overload Test]. *Guoji jingji hezuo* 12: 41–43.

Mählmann, Peter. 1992. "The Role of Sport in the Process of Modernisation: The Kenyan Case." *Journal of Eastern African Research & Developments* 22: 120–131.

Mao, Zedong. 1991. "Jinian bai qiuen" [In Memory of Bethune]. In *Mao Zedong xuanji*, 656–661. People's Publishing Press.

Monson, Jamie. 2009. *Africa's Freedom Railway: How a Chinese Development Project Changed Lives and Livelihoods in Tanzania*. Indiana University Press.

Nixon, Richard. 2001. *Memories of Richard Nixon*. World Knowledge Press.

NMAD. 2021. "Ping-pong Diplomacy: Artifacts from the Historic 1971 U.S. Table Tennis Trip to China." National Museum of American Diplomacy. https://diplomacy.state.gov/ping-pong-diplomacy-historic-1971–u-s-table-tennis-trip-to-china/.

Ojo, Tokunbo. 2022. "Sino-African Sport Diplomacy? 'New' Wave of Chinese Stadiums in African Cities." In *China's International Communication and Relationship Building*, edited by Xiaoling Zhang and Corey Schultz, 216–232. Routledge.

Peking Review. 1974. "President and Mme Ould Daddah Visit China." *Peking Review* 17 (38): 3–19. https://www.marxists.org/subject/china/peking-review/1974/PR1974–38.pdf.

People's Daily. 1976. "Zai keleiku zongtong juxing de yanhui shang hua guofeng zongli de jianghua" [Speech by Premier Hua Guofeng at the Banquet Held for President Kerekou]. *People's Daily*, July 21, 1976.

Pratt, Mary Louise. 2012. "Arts of the Contact Zone." In *Negotiating Academic Literacies*, 171–185. Routledge.

Ross, Elliot. 2014. "China's Stadium Diplomacy in Africa." Roads & Kingdoms. Last modified January 28. https://roadsandkingdoms.com/2014/chinas-stadium-diplomacy-in-africa/.

Seely, Jennifer. 2009. *The Legacies of Transition Governments in Africa: The Cases of Benin and Togo.* Springer.

Sheard, Rod. 2005. *The Stadium: Architecture for the New Global Culture.* Periplus Editions.

Song, Yimeng. 2019. Waijiao Fengyun [Diplomatic situation].

Verri, Valeria Guzman. 2020. "Gifting Architecture: China and the National Stadium in Costa Rica, 2007–2011." *Architectural History* 63: 283–311.

Volland, Nicolai. 2017. *Socialist Cosmopolitanism: The Chinese Literary Universe, 1945–1965.* Columbia University Press.

Vondracek, Hugh. 2019. "China's Stadium Diplomacy and Its Determinants: A Typological Investigation of Soft Power." *Journal of China and International Relations* 7 (1): 62–86.

Will, Rachel. 2012. "China's Stadium Diplomacy." *World Policy Journal* 29 (2): 36–44.

Xin, Bing. 1976. "Zhongbei renmin qingshen yichang" [Deep and Lasting Friendship between the Chinese and Beninese People]. *People's Daily*, July 17, 1976, 5.

Xintiyu. 1952. *Fazhan tiyu yundong, zengqiang renmin tizhi* [*Developing Sports, Enhancing People's Physique*]. China Youth Publishing House.

Xu, Shangzhi. 1981. "Jianzhu fengge laizi minjian: cong fengjingqu de lvyou jianzhu tanqi" [Architectural Style Derived from Folk Culture—Starting from Tourist Architecture in Scenic Areas]. *Jianzhu xuebao* 1 (49).

———. 2003. "Zai kenniya de riri yeye" [Days and Nights in Kenya]. In *Jianzhu baijia huiyilu xubian*, edited by Yongsheng Yang, 247–258. Zhongguo shuili shuidian chu ban she.

Xue, Charlie Qiuli. 2005. *Building a Revolution: Chinese Architecture Since 1980.* Vol. 1. Hong Kong University Press.

Xue, Charlie Qiuli, Guanghui Ding, Wei Chang, and Yan Wan. 2019. "Architecture of "Stadium Diplomacy"-China-Aid Sport Buildings in Africa." *Habitat International* 90: 101985.

Yuan, Lei, Yushuo Guo, and Dawei Yu. 2016. "Gaige kaifang yilai de zhongguo tiyu duiwai yuanzhu yanjiu" [Sports Foreign Aid in China since Reform and Opening up]. *Journal of Shenyang Sport University* 35 (4): 48–53.

Zhou, Enlai. 1990. *Zhou Enlai wai jiao wen xuan* [*Selected Works on Zhou Enlai's Diplomacy*]. 1st ed. Zhongyang wenxian chu ban she.

Zou, Denong. 2001. *Zhongguo xiandai jianzhu shi* [*Modern History of Chinese Architecture*]. Tianjin Science and Technology Press.

Notes on Contributors

Dr. Unwana Samuel Akpan is a multidisciplinary media scholar-practitioner with over two decades of broadcast experience. He has been a visiting scholar at the Department of Communication, Culture and Media Studies (CCMS), where he completed his Postdoctoral Studies in the School of Communication and Media Studies, Howard University, USA. He is the Editor of the University of Lagos Communication Review. He's presently a lecturer in the Department of Mass Communication, University of Lagos, Nigeria.

Dr. Mahfoud Amara is an Associate Professor in sport management and social sciences at Qatar University, Qatar. Dr. Amara's research focuses on sport, business, culture, and politics in the Middle East and North Africa. He explores issues of multiculturalism, intercultural dialogue, access to sports for ethnic minorities, and the relationship between Muslim communities and sports. He has authored and edited *Sport Politics and Society in the Arab World* (Macmillan, 2012), *Sport in Islam and in Muslim Communities* (Routledge, 2015), *Sport in the African World* (Routledge, 2018), and *The Olympic Movement and the Middle East and North Africa* (Routledge, 2018).

Dr. Youcef Bouandel is Professor of Politics at the Department of International Affairs, Qatar University, Qatar. He holds a License in Politics from the University of Algiers, Algeria, an MPhil and a PhD in Politics from the University of Glasgow, Scotland. He was Lecturer/Senior Lecturer in Politics at the University of Lincoln, England, and visiting professor in Bulgaria, Sweden, Latvia and the United States of America. He is the author of several articles and book chapters on the politics of Algeria and on sports and politics/ international relations.

Dr. Simon Chadwick is Professor of Sport and Geopolitical Economy formerly based at Skema Business School in Paris, France. His work examines the business and management implications of sport's geopolitical economy, with a particular focus on AfroEurasia. Chadwick has been researching and writing about sport in China for more than 20 years.

Dr. Guanghui Ding is an independent researcher, architectural historian, critic and designer. He worked as an Associate Professor of Architecture at Beijing University of Civil Engineering and Architecture, China. He is the author of *Constructing a Place of Critical Architecture in China: Intermediate Criticality in the Journal* Time + Architecture (Routledge, 2016) and, with Charlie Xue, co-author of *A History of Design Institutes in China: From Mao to Market* (Routledge, 2018) and co-editor of *Exporting Chinese Architecture: History, Issues and "One Belt One Road"* (Springer, 2022).

Christopher Edyegu is a PhD candidate at the University of Cape Town, South Africa. His research focuses on Africa and Global South relations. Currently, his primary focus is Africa-China relations. Christopher's PhD analyses Chinese investments in African manufacturing. Outside of academia, Christopher is an editor at the China Global South Project (CGSP) and a country risk analyst at Africa Risk Consulting (ARC), a UK-based business management and consulting company.

Dr. Peizi Han is a lecturer at the Management School of Beijing Sport University, China. He earned his doctoral degree in the sociology of sport from Loughborough University. His research focuses on sports, national identity, sport globalization, and migration. His work has been published in the International Review for the Sociology of Sport and National Identities.

Dr. Zhao Alexandre Huang is is an Associate Professor in Information and Communication Sciences at the Université Gustave Eiffel. He works at the DICEN-IDF laboratory. He studies institutional practices, political and public communication strategies, and the formation of strategic narratives in the practice of public diplomacy. His research interests include public diplomacy, strategic communication, public relations, social media, and China's propaganda and international communication.

Dr. Angela Lewis is an Assistant Professor in the Department of Media and Communication at Xi'an Jiaotong-Liverpool University in Suzhou, China. She specializes in China–Africa media relations.

Dr. Xiufang (Leah) Li currently works as a Senior Lecturer in the School of Media and Communication at RMIT University, Australia. She is an Australia-China scholar in communication with research, teaching and practice sitting at the nexus of public relations and digital communication. Her recent work can be found in *Public Relations Review*, *European Journal of Cultural Studies*, *Global Media and China*, and *Media International Australia*.

Kalema Elizabeth Meggs is a fourth-year doctoral student in the Department of Communication, Culture, and Media Studies at Howard University, USA. Her research focuses on sport communication with an emphasis on societal and cultural matters among African American/Black and Brown athletes, and how they are framed within traditional media and digital media platforms. As a former competitive figure skater, and current sport communication practitioner, Kalema is passionate in advocating for marginalized athletes through scholarship and collaborating with sport industry leaders.

Dr. Wycliffe W. Simiyu Njororai is a Professor and Chair in the department of Kinesiology and Health Science at Stephen F. Austin State University, Nacogdoches in Texas, USA. He has a PhD in Physical Education and Sport from Kenyatta University, Kenya. His research focuses on association football or soccer, track and field, and leadership in sport. He has taught at universities in Kenya (Egerton and Kenyatta University), Uganda (Kyambogo), and the USA (Wiley, University of Texas at Tyler, Stephen F. Austin State University). He frequently writes opinion pieces for The Conversation on various aspects of soccer and athletics in Africa.

Dr. Tokunbo Ojo is an Associate Professor in the Department of Communication & Media Studies, York University, Canada. His teaching and research interests are in global media studies, development communication, journalism studies, African media studies, geopolitics of international communication, and political economy of media industries.

Dr. Chuka Onwumechili is is Interim Dean of the School of Communications at Howard University in Washington, DC (USA). He is the author/co-author of more than 13 books focusing largely on several communication issues that pertain to Africa. These books touch on varied subjects including sports, telecommunications, culture, and development. His most recent books are Women's Football in Africa and Africa's Elite Football: Structure, Politics, and Everyday Challenges. He also serves as Editor-in-Chief of the Howard Journal of Communications and serves on the Editorial Board of the Communication & Sport journal.

Dr. Tobias Ross recently received his PhD in Political Science from the University of Nottingham, UK. His research interests include China's political economy, business-state relations and their impact on the local football industry, as well as athlete naturalization. Outside of academia, Tobias works in international football development and marketing.

Dr. Jonathan Sullivan is a China specialist and political scientist at the University of Nottingham in the UK. He is former Director of the China Policy Institute and Founding Director (with Prof. Simon Chadwick) of the China Soccer Observatory.

His research covers Chinese politics and foreign relations, Taiwanese politics, the Chinese internet and pop culture, and football. His latest book (with Lev Nachman), *Taiwan: A contested democracy under threat* (Agenda) came out in November 2023.

Dr. Charlie Qiuli Xue is a retired Professor of Architecture at City University of Hong Kong, where he held a tenured position 1995-2024. He has received awards for his writing and design works, including the International Committee of Architectural Critics (CICA) award in 2017 for his book on Hong Kong architecture. With 13 monograph books and 3 edited books to his credit, he has also published over 140 research papers in professional and international refereed journals, as well as 40 book chapters. Xue's research interests are focused on modern Chinese architecture, transnational design, and high-density environments.

No matter if political sciences, international relations, economics, or global studies, the subject of China–African relations has become an essential subject to properly understand the dynamics that shape our world. But until now, the role of sport in this connection was often merely a footnote. With this book, Jonathan Sullivan, Tobias Ross, and Angela Lewis have put together an excellent collection of case studies that puts the shared enthusiasm for football in the center of this politically, economically, and culturally loaded relationship. This makes not only for an enticing read but also for an outstanding and much-needed resource across many disciplines.

Dr. Tobias Zuser, Assistant Professor, Chinese University of Hong Kong

This book provides a comprehensive examination of the multifaceted interactions between China and Africa through football. Edited by Jonathan Sullivan, Tobias Ross and Angela Lewis, the book explores a wide range of topics, including stadium diplomacy, labor migration and sports diplomacy, and shows how football serves as an important conduit for political, economic and cultural exchange. The book offers a nuanced perspective on the intersection of sport, politics and international relations in the bilateral character of this engagement, moving beyond simplistic accounts to highlight the wider geopolitical and economic implications of China's presence in African football.

Dr. Ilker Gündoğan, Researcher, Ruhr University Bochum, Germany

Index

Sport in East and Southeast Asian Societies

Geopolitical, Political, Cultural and Social Perspectives

J.A. Mangan *Series Editor*

Modern sport is emotionally essential to billions worldwide providing ecstasy, escapism and excitement. It is simultaneously witness to a tectonic geopolitical, political, cultural and social shift in performance—West to East! It is experiencing a global transformation in the wake of contemporary East Asian confidence, self-belief and performance symbolised dramatically by Beijing 2008—a harbinger of shifting geopolitical 'plates'!

The editor of this new series from Peter Lang, Professor J.A. Mangan FRHS, FRAI, FRSA, D. LITT., welcomes and invites proposals for the series. Please send details to profmangan@gmail.com

To order other books in this series, please contact our Customer Service Department:

peterlang@presswarehouse.com (within the U.S.)
orders@peterlang.com (outside the U.S.)

Or browse online by series at:

www.peterlang.com

www.ingramcontent.com/pod-product-compliance
Ingram Content Group UK Ltd.
Pitfield, Milton Keynes, MK11 3LW, UK
UKHW020841290926
15470UKWH00004B/1473